THE DOG WHO COULD FLY

THE INCREDIBLE TRUE STORY OF A WWII AIRMAN AND THE FOUR-LEGGED HERO WHO FLEW AT HIS SIDE

DAMIEN LEWIS

THORNDIKE PRESS
A part of Gale, Cengage Learning

GALE
CENGAGE Learning·

Farmington Hills, Mich • San Francisco • New York • Waterville, Maine
Meriden, Conn • Mason, Ohio • Chicago

GALE
CENGAGE Learning·

LIBRARY OF CONGRESS CATALOGING-IN-PUBLICATION DATA

Lewis, Damien.
  The dog who could fly : the incredible true story of a WWII airman and the four-legged hero who flew at his side / by Damien Lewis. — Large print edition.
    pages cm. — (Thorndike Press large print nonfiction)
  Includes bibliographical references.
  ISBN 978-1-4104-7297-7 (hardcover) — ISBN 1-4104-7297-3 (hardcover)
  1. Bozdech, Václav R. (Václav Robert) 2. Antis (Dog) 3. World War, 1939–1945—Aerial operations, British. 4. Great Britain. Royal Air Force. Squadron, No. 311. 5. Airmen—Great Britain—Biography. 6. Airmen—Czechoslovakia—Biography. 7. German shepherd dog—War use—History—20th century. 8. Human-animal relationships—History—20th century. 9. Czechs—Great Britain—Biography. 10. Large type books. I. Title.
  D786.L486 2014b
  940.54'49410929—dc23   2014024198

Published in 2014 by arrangement with Atria Books, a division of Simon & Schuster, Inc.

"There is an old belief
That on some solemn shore,
Beyond the sphere of grief,
Dear friends shall meet once more."
— CHARLES HUBERT HASTINGS PARRY

"*Na množvstvi nehled'te;* never mind
their numbers."
— MOTTO OF 311 (CZECH) SQUADRON

For Robert, Pip, and Nina,
for allowing me to tell the story of
your father and his dog

PREFACE

In the early hours of a bitterly cold January day in 1940, a French Potez 63 fighter-bomber aircraft was shot down over the German front line. The French pilot and his Czech gunner survived the devastating crash landing, and in the epic escape bid that followed one of the most remarkable and enduring man–animal partnerships of the Second World War was forged.

I first heard about the relationship between the Royal Air Force's flying dog of war and Czech airman Robert Bozdech in a passing comment made by British soldier and bestselling author Captain David Blakeley (*Pathfinder* and *Maverick One*). Blakeley — a fellow dog lover — had read two of my previous books about extraordinary man–dog partnerships forged on the front line of war — *Sergeant Rex* and *It's All About Treo*, both of which were coauthored with the modern-day bomb-detection dog handlers whose stories they portrayed.

Blakeley's comment was: "If you want to read a truly amazing story of a man and dog at war, look up Ant and Robert Bozdech's story, from the Second World War. It'll blow you away."

My curiosity piqued, I went on to read as widely as I could about their story (see the references at the end of this book). But one thing struck me most powerfully: while the tale of the heroic man-and-dog duo who fought with Bomber Command during the Second World War had seemingly been told, it remained something of a riddle wrapped up inside a mystery in an enigma. Their story was supposedly related in the 1965 book *One Man and His Dog,* but Robert Bozdech was not the author of that book. It was written by the late author and journalist Anthony Richardson, and in its pages Robert Bozdech was strangely referred to as Jan Bozdech. Altogether, my reading of it seemed to raise as many questions as it answered.

The deeper I dug the more curious it all became. There was originally talk of a film to be made by 20th Century-Fox based upon the heroic duo's life story, but for reasons unexplained it had never gone into production. I wondered why. This of any story cried out to be turned into a dramatic and compelling movie. There was talk of Robert Bozdech's dissatisfaction with the book as it was published, but it remained unclear as to what exactly had troubled him. Did that perhaps explain why the book hadn't used his real name and why the film had never been made?

But most intriguing of all to an author such as myself, there was talk of an original manuscript written by Robert Bozdech, one telling the story of his airborne adventures with Ant, but one that had never seen the light of day. I wondered if such a manuscript had really ever existed, and if so what story it might reveal. Surely, it would tell the full and unexpurgated account of Robert and Ant's extraordinary adventures as written from the heart by the man who had lived it? If such a manuscript had been written it would have been penned sometime in the early sixties — over fifty years ago — which raised the question of whether a copy still existed today.

There was only one way to answer these many questions, and that was to make contact with the surviving members of the Bozdech family. After the war, Robert Bozdech had made Britain his permanent home — after a short sojourn in his native

Czechoslovakia — settling with his veteran war dog, taking British nationality, and raising a family. I found out that Robert's son, Robert Bozdech Jr., lived in a picturesque part of the west of England in what turned out to be the family home. I corresponded with Robert, we spoke on the phone, and in due course I traveled to south Devon to meet him, along with his two sisters, Pip and Nina. The rambling house seemed to have been shaped and formed by those who had lived there for so long, Mrs. Maureen Bozdech only recently having passed away. I was given a gracious welcome, and over tea and cake the questions to which I had for so long sought answers began to resolve themselves.

Robert Bozdech had helped with the writing of Richardson's *One Man and His Dog,* but the two men had not gotten on at all well. In fact, it seemed they had had some blazing arguments along the way. 20th Century–Fox had indeed resolved to make a film based upon that book, but for some reason it had fallen by the wayside. Most surprisingly of all, Robert Bozdech had not been able to reveal his true name — Václav Bozdech — or publish his own story in his own words, because of fears of reprisals against his family in his native Czechoslova-

12

kia. Shortly after the Communists took control in Czechoslovakia, Robert found himself a target of pogroms, intimidation, and threats, as did so many Czech airmen, sailors, and soldiers who had fought in the Allied cause. In a form of collateral damage resulting from the Cold War, any Czech with military links to "the West" was seen as being a potential enemy of Czechoslovakia, a state that then formed a part of the Soviet bloc. Hence it was that Robert's story had been effectively silenced by threats of violence, imprisonment, and worse emanating from the country of his birth.

It was then that I put the million-dollar question to the late Robert Bozdech's family: had their father actually written his own version of his and Ant's story in a book or a diary, one that had never seen the light of day?

"Oh, you mean Dad's original manuscript?" Robert Jr. replied. "Yes, of course. I'll just fetch a copy."

He wandered off into a back room, returning a few minutes later with an old-fashioned blue ring binder clutched in one hand. He rubbed it down, dust seeming to dance and sparkle in the sunbeams that streamed through the summer window.

He slid it across the table to me. "Here it

13

is. Dad called it *Antis VC.*" Robert paused, then laughed a little self-consciously. "It's far better than anything else that's ever been written."

"I'm sure it is . . ." I flipped open the file, and read the first line of a neatly typed manuscript: "The author, who served with distinction in the RAF during the last war, has lost touch with most of his old comrades. Perhaps this book may reach and reunite them . . ."

I glanced up from the page. "D'you mind if I borrow this for a proper read?"

Robert looked to his sisters, then back at me. I detected a twinkle in his kind and trusting eyes. "No, not at all. We've always wanted Dad's story to see the light of day. We'd be delighted if an author such as yourself might help tell it for us, and properly."

"So, how do you come to have a manuscript such as this . . . and yet it's never been published?" I asked.

"Well, you see, Dad wrote it out first by hand," Pip, Robert's older sister, explained. "For years we only had that handwritten version. Then, back in the time of typewriters — prior to computers — I offered to type it out. God knows what possessed me to do so, for it took forever," she joked.

"Anyhow, that's the version you're now holding. Dad included a lot of penciled notes in the margins, along with his original words, so I incorporated those as well."

I shook my head in amazement. "Well, all I can say is I'm glad you did and saved the story for posterity."

"Dad could never have had it published when the Communists were still in power," Nina, Robert's younger sister, added. "He had a wife and child that he was forced to leave in Czechoslovakia, plus all the rest of his family. The regime took horrible reprisals against those who'd fought with the Allies. He knew it would have to be published after his death or after the Communist regime had fallen, whichever came the sooner. Well, both things have come to pass now, of course, so . . ." She shrugged. "Dad would want you to read it, I'm sure."

I thanked the three of them, and as I left their home I felt as if I had a hidden gem clutched under my arm. I wondered if Robert Bozdech had written his manuscript in the very hope that one day it might be rediscovered. I could only imagine that was the case, for what other reason could he have had for doing so? On the drive home I was barely able to resist the temptation to pull into a rest stop so I could dive in. In

15

the peace and quiet of my study I was finally able to devour the story as told by Robert Bozdech, in his own words.

His manuscript told a tale of death-defying feats by brave Czech airmen driven to avenge their countrymen, and who refused to be cowed by the Nazi invaders of their country. It was a tale of bitter and bloody action above war-torn France, of a handful of airmen who battled overwhelming odds and far superior German warplanes as the defense of Europe crumbled under the Nazi blitzkrieg. It was a tale of an epic escape from occupied France, and of the remarkable bluff and chutzpah that got Robert Bozdech and his dog, Ant, safely into the UK, along with a handful of fellow Czech airmen. It became a story then of the most remarkable and renowned man-dog duo of the war — Ant becoming famed as the dog who flew countless death-defying sorties with the RAF over Europe.

I met several further times with Robert, Pip, and Nina, and they could not have been more gracious or generous in their support. In an effort to better reveal their father and his dog's incredible story, they dug out and dusted down suitcases full of their late father's personal effects — ones that had lain half forgotten in the attic of Pip's

Devon farmhouse. They contained dog-eared diary entries and flight logs, faded newspaper cuttings and scores of photographs, all from the time that their father and his dog flew with the RAF in the war-torn skies of Europe. There were postcards home and letters to family. There were scores of articles and short booklets written by Robert Bozdech immediately after the war, in his native Czech. There were even some ancient "four-inch" reel-to-reel tape recordings, ones that contained Robert's voice telling his and Ant's story in his own words — seemingly something to do with the widespread media coverage that he and his dog had enjoyed immediately after the war.

Remarkable.

What emerged from this plethora of material was above all else a story of the unshakable and unbreakable love between one man and his dog, a love that enabled the duo to survive numerous brushes with death in a way that seemed to defy comprehension. Ant (or Antis as he was subsequently re-named) was the only dog to fly and fight with the RAF's Bomber Command. He was repeatedly wounded on the ground and in the air, and shot down under fire. He had had his own doggie oxygen mask crafted for him by the Bomber Command technicians, and his ever more extreme brushes with death meant that he must have had many more than a cat's nine lives.

In short, the story as revealed in Robert Bozdech's original manuscript and the associated materials was a gripping account of the most celebrated partnership between man and dog of the Second World War, a tale that remains unparalleled to this day.

This, then, is their story, told as much as possible in Robert's own words.

Damien Lewis, Cork, Ireland, 2013

Robert Bozdech's flying dog of war, Ant, in suitably regal pose. He was a handsome devil of a dog, and his good looks got him and his master out of many a scrape.

All pictures courtesy of the Bozdech family unless otherwise stated.

ONE

A Potez 63 French warplane, of the type that Robert Bozdech was shot down in — leading to him finding a tiny German shepherd puppy in no-man's-land.

Aeronautics Aircraft Spotters' Handbook, *Ensign L. C. Guthman,*

1943

Robert Bozdech had a horrible, sinking feeling in the pit of his stomach as the twin-engine warplane began its shallow dive toward earth. But for once it wasn't fear of being pounced on by one of the enemy's deadly Messerschmitt 109s that so unsettled him. In the thick fog that had blown across the landscape, they were all but invisible to any marauding German fighters.

No. It was fear of the guns that lurked below that held him in its viselike grip.

"The fog is down so thick, Pierre!" he yelled across at his fellow airman. "It is foolhardy —"

"And if we return with no photos, we will be a laughingstock," Pierre Duval, the aircraft's French pilot, cut in. "Keep your eyes peeled!"

It had been a fine morning when the French Air Force's twin-engine Potez 63 fighter-bomber had taken to the dawn skies. Stationed at the aerodrome at Saint-Dizier, Pierre and Robert had been tasked with flying a reconnaissance mission over the German front, from where the massed ranks of enemy armor menaced the supposedly impregnable defenses of the French Maginot Line.

It was the winter of 1939–1940 and Germany and France were locked in the so-called phony war. But there was nothing very phony about it from Robert's perspective, when flying a French aircraft that was a hundred kilometers per hour slower than the nimble German fighters that stalked the skies above them. As he hunched over his twin machine guns in the rear gunner's seat, he couldn't help but notice how thick the fog had become. It was condensing in thick rivulets that cascaded down the Plexiglas turret.

Both a spirited maverick and a man of real principle, Robert had refused to bow to the jackboot of Nazi oppression as its forces had invaded his native Czechoslovakia several months before. He had escaped and made his way to France, and after a short stint in the French Foreign Legion had returned to what he had learned well in the Czech Air Force, serving as a turret gunner on a hunter-bomber aircraft. But what he hadn't quite bargained for was the difference in temperament between himself and some of the more flamboyant French aircrew.

Lacking little in terms of sheer guts and bravery, the Czech airmen tended to be a levelheaded and a solid bunch. By contrast, Pierre Duval, the aircraft's pilot and captain, had a tendency to be impetuous and unpredictable, as today's mission was about to prove. Sure, it was a brave move to dive headlong into the fog directly above the

German lines in the hope that Robert might be able to grab a few reconnaissance photos, but it was also a distinctly suicidal one.

No sooner had the aircraft begun to emerge from the lower reaches of the fog — its outer edges trailing tendrils of water vapor like wisps of smoke — than the air was rent by the pounding percussions of antiaircraft fire. The German gunners had heard them coming and were poised to strike. The aircraft was too low to be targeted by flak, but all around them the air was laced with the angry red trails of murderous tracer fire.

Their controlled descent through the mist was over in a matter of seconds. In spite of Pierre's desperate maneuvers, the German gunners quickly found their mark. Rounds ripped through the thin fuselage and shattered the Plexiglas cockpit. As smoke and fire bloomed from the port engine, Robert sensed that they were going down. They were barely two hundred feet above the snowbound earth when he saw the port propeller die completely and felt the enemy fire tearing into their starboard engine.

Robert braced himself for the impact of a crash landing or worse. The hard, frozen ground was rushing up to meet them, a wide expanse of glistening snow lit here and there a fiery red by the tracer fire. Barely minutes after they'd first been hit, the belly of the aircraft impacted with a terrible tearing of metal. The stricken warplane lifted once, settled again with an ear-piercing screech, and plowed toward a patch of dark woodland.

The doomed aircraft was thrown savagely around as its left flank caught on a thick trunk, and with a tearing of steel the wing was ripped clean away. By the time it came to a juddering halt, half buried in the snow and with its crumpled nose cone embedded in the thick foliage, Robert had lost consciousness.

He came to with little sense of where he was or how much time he might have lost. For an instant he mistook the thick wisps curling all around him for fog, and then the acrid smell of burning hit him. The very idea that their aircraft might burst into flames at any moment brought him back to reality with a savage jolt.

Choking from the acrid smoke, he reached down, groped for the release catch on his safety harness, flipped it free, and stretched up to clamber out onto the surviving wing. As he did so he felt a stabbing, burning pain shooting through his chest — no doubt the result of the safety harness biting into him upon the sudden impact of the crash landing.

Having dragged himself out of the shattered turret, Robert half tumbled the short distance to the ground and began to stumble away from the wreckage. After a few paces he collapsed into an exhausted heap on the snow, the shock and the trauma of being shot down overwhelming him. For a few seconds he lay there, struggling to regain his breath and fighting back the waves of nausea, before a thought struck him with the power of a speeding steam train: *Pierre! Where is Pierre?*

Robert searched with his eyes, scanning the wreckage and the tangled, splintered mass of bare winter branches all around him. The fog seemed almost to reach to the ground, mingling with the steam and smoke rising from the crumpled remains of the aircraft. It was an eerie, ghostly scene, one made all the worse by the fact that there was no sign of the French airman.

He risked a call: "Pierre! Pierre! Are you there?"

There wasn't the barest hint of a response. Apart from an angry hissing where the aircraft's hot engines met the snow, all was quiet. The Germans must have seen the fighter-bomber go down. From what Robert knew of how Pierre had thrown the aircraft around during their final few seconds, he figured they must have crash-landed somewhere in the no-man's-land between the French and German lines.

A flare of angry red in the aircraft's fuselage drew his eye. They'd been carrying over a thousand liters of fuel at takeoff, and barely a third of that had been used. Robert sensed what was about to happen and he knew exactly what he had to do. Pierre might well be dead. In fact, being in the front seat of the cockpit, he more than likely was. But that wasn't going to stop Robert from making an attempt to find him, no matter if the aircraft was about to burst into flames.

Scrambling back onto the wing, he yelled out the Frenchman's name, but there wasn't a word of reply. As he peered into the shattered cockpit he sensed the glowing licks of flame all around him — the fire beginning to take deadly hold. At the same moment he spotted a figure slumped over the aircraft's controls, his head twisted at an unnatural angle. It looked as if the silly bastard had broken his neck, but from this distance Robert couldn't be absolutely sure.

He reached forward and snatched at the remains of the cockpit hatch, dragging it open. As he did so he felt a stab of agony in his hand, from what had to be a broken or sprained finger. Ignoring the pain, and the frightening smell of aviation fuel that filled the air, Robert leaned in and felt for the pilot's release catch. He found it and pressed hard, but at the very moment that the metallic *thunk* signaled to him that Pierre was free, he heard a terrifying sound from below.

There was a hollow, evil crackling as fire rippled along the fuselage. Ignoring the flames at his feet, Robert pulled with all his might, his hands grasping Pierre's armpits as he fought to drag the deadweight up and out. He had Pierre's body halfway free when the pilot's harness caught on some obstruction — yet still Robert was determined not to leave him. They had flown together and fought together, and in spite of their differences they had bonded as brother warriors of the air.

In desperation Robert heaved for all he was worth. Not a moment too soon, the harness came free and Pierre with it, and Robert found himself falling backward. He landed in a snowdrift, the weight of the Frenchman driving him deeper into the cold whiteness. Above them the fuselage was awash with flame, and Robert knew it was only a matter of moments before one of the fuel tanks caught, rendering the wrecked aircraft a white-hot, seething fireball.

With his arms gripping Pierre's flight jacket, Robert struggled backward through the snow, dragging the Frenchman farther from the wreckage. He'd gone about thirty paces when there was a massive explosion as the aircraft's fuel tanks ignited. Robert felt himself thrown backward by the blast as a wave of heat and fire washed over him. Burrowing deeper into the snow, and forcing the Frenchman down alongside him, he did his best to shelter himself from the searing heat, and from what he knew was coming.

An instant later the aircraft's ammunition started to explode as it roasted in the inferno. The silence was torn apart by the terrifying snarl and roar of bullets ripping through the air. It would be just his luck, thought Robert, to have survived a suicidal French pilot and the German guns only to be killed by their own bullets exploding.

It was then that he remembered the full extent of their predicament: they were far from safely out of this one yet. They were well within sight of the ridge to their south, which marked the mighty trenches and bunkers of the Germans' Siegfried Line. If the enemy hadn't seen exactly where their aircraft had gone down, they were bound to know now — for a giant black fist of smoke had punched upward from the fiery inferno.

Just as he was wondering how they might make their getaway without being gunned down by the Germans, Robert heard a faint groan from the figure lying in the snow at his side. Moments later the French pilot had struggled into a sitting position, apparently oblivious to the bullets and shrapnel zipping past like a swarm of angry hornets.

"Bloody keep down!" Robert yelled at Pierre as he wrestled the wounded Frenchman back into the snow. "Keep down!"

"I've hurt my leg," Pierre groaned confusedly.

"Bugger your leg," Robert shot back at him. "If you don't keep down you'll lose your bloody head as well!"

Robert managed to keep the Frenchman still until the worst of the explosions had died away. The aircraft was still burning fiercely, but it seemed as if the ammunition had mostly spent itself. Robert felt a crushing, leaden fatigue, but he knew they were finished if they stayed where they were. Sooner or later a German search party would reach them and he knew well what that would mean. There was a price on Robert's head as a Czech fighting for the French. The Germans would send Pierre to a prisoner-of-war camp, but for him there would be only a bare post before a bullet-pocked wall and the firing squad.

"Wait here," he told Pierre, who seemed pretty much unable to move. "We've got to get a look at that leg of yours and I need to find us some cover."

Rising to a kneeling position, Robert spotted what looked like an old farmhouse a hundred yards or so to their north. He hadn't seen it during the crash landing, but as the smoke and heat from the burning aircraft drove off the mist more and more of their surroundings were becoming visible. Leaving the fiery remains of their aircraft to his rear, Robert began crawling through the trees toward that patch of cover. As he did so he realized that the woodland in which they had crash-landed was actually an orchard, one that backed onto farm buildings.

He stopped a good few yards from the farmhouse and studied it closely. He didn't think for one moment that it would be occupied, sandwiched as it was between the German and French lines, but you could never be too careful. He couldn't detect the barest trace of footsteps in the thick drift outside the door. The snow had lain on the ground for weeks now, and it looked as if the farmhouse must have been abandoned shortly after the Germans had started to shell the French lines.

Robert moved forward at a crouch, sticking to the cover of the trees to keep himself hidden from any watchful eyes. Skirting a rickety outhouse, he reached the back door, a wooden affair whose glass panes must have been blown out during the shelling. Robert reached through the broken glass, felt a key still in the lock, turned it, and with one hand eased open the door. With his other he drew his revolver, and with that thrust before him he moved into the dark interior.

A smell hit him immediately, one of a damp and airless neglect and of fireplaces long unlit. He didn't doubt for one moment that this place was deserted. He was in what was clearly the living room, with a long wooden dining table pushed against one wall and a stone fireplace opposite. He ran his free hand along the tabletop and brought it away coated in a thick film of dust. Plaster had fallen in chunks from the ceiling, a result of the repeated shelling.

He glanced at the grate and the ashes lying there were cold and black from where rain and snow had made their way down the unlit chimney. He crossed the room and turned left into what was obviously the kitchen. A wide fireplace was stacked high with thick oaken logs, piled up beside an iron stove. A blackened pot lay atop the stove, and Robert half expected it to be full of a moldering stew. It seemed that whoever had lived here had left the place in a terrible hurry.

Above him, the feeble winter light filtered in through a hole blasted clean through the roof, broken slates framing its jagged edges and scattered across the floor. For an instant Robert stood completely still and listened. As a boy growing up in his native Bohemia, he had spent many an hour tracking animals in the forests and mountains. He knew well the value of pausing to listen and to wait, just in case there was anything that chose to break cover and so disturb the silence. Thankfully, he could hear nothing but the beating of his own heart and the faint whistle of the wind through broken tiles.

He turned to leave, content that this was a safe enough place to hole up in while he tried to deal with Pierre's injuries. They were in dire need of shelter, for there would be no real movement possible until nightfall. The wide expanse of snow that lay between their position and the safety of the French lines was completely devoid of cover, and if they tried to cross it in daylight, he and Pierre would be done for.

As he reentered the living room Robert paused for a moment, tuning his ears to the sounds of the house above him, from what had to be the bedrooms. It was then that he froze. Faintly, almost imperceptibly, he'd caught the most unexpected and worrying of noises. For an instant he told himself that his ears had to be playing tricks on him, but as he strained to hear he caught the noise again.

From behind him came the distinct and eerie suggestion of snuffling. It was such an unexpected noise to have detected here, in this ghost house deep in no-man's-land, that it sent shivers up his spine. It sounded almost as if someone — some being — was back there in the kitchen and gently snoring. He turned soundlessly, and with his pistol thrust before him he retraced his steps, tracking the ghostly noise.

As far as he could tell it seemed to be coming from beneath an upturned chair set to one side of the kitchen stove, beside a pile of rubble. Robert cocked the pistol and fixed the sound with the cold steel of the barrel. Keeping his finger tight on the trigger, he took a step toward the chair. As he neared it the snuffling stopped completely, almost as if someone had woken up and was holding his or her breath so as not to be discovered.

"Get your hands up!" Robert growled. "Now! Or else! Show yourself! Come out from hiding!"

There wasn't the faintest suggestion of an answer or any response. As he swept the corner of the room with his weapon Robert detected the barest hint of a yawn, followed by the recommencement of the snuffling sound. There was no doubt about it: behind that upturned chair was a living presence, one that was failing to respond to his challenge.

Robert felt a rush of fear mixed with adrenaline, similar to what he had experienced as their stricken aircraft plummeted toward the snowbound earth. He didn't know enough German to cry out a challenge in the language of the enemy, but who else could have ignored his warnings issued in a rudimentary but workable French?

"Wake up, you bastard!" Robert snarled. "Get up and show yourself!"

Still there was no response, other than a momentary pause in the sleepy, snuffly intakes of breath. There was no other choice: he inched closer to the upturned chair, his finger bone-white on the trigger. He reached the back of it, but still he couldn't see anyone. *Confound the bloody enemy, where is he?*

Robert leaned forward and peered around the chair, sighting down the barrel of his gun. There before him lay the culprit. The instant Robert laid eyes on it, the sleeping figure seemed to wake. One moment there was a tiny ball of gray-brown fluff curled up beneath the chair, the next it had stumbled to its feet unsteadily and was peering up at him anxiously, growling out a throaty little challenge.

At the very sight of it, all of Robert's pumped-up aggression and killer instincts evaporated. He felt like a fool. He'd just spent a good few minutes stalking and yelling out dire threats at a tiny little puppy dog. Ignoring the bravest and most defiant of growls, he reached forward with his one free hand. For a moment the puppy tried to edge away, before its big, ungainly paws tripped over its own tail and it half fell back into the dust.

Before it could entangle itself still further, Robert whisked it up by the scruff of its neck — in exactly the same way its mother would have carried it in her jaws. As the puppy looked at him askance he clutched it to his chest, holstered his gun, and started to rub it fiercely around the back of the head. He worked his fingers deep into the thick folds of skin until he reached the special spot just behind the ears. In effect, he was giving the little guy a deep head massage, and within moments the puppy's fierce resistance had dissolved into surrender . . . and then sheer delight.

"So who left you here all alone and hungry?" Robert whispered as he held the puppy close. "And you bereft of any friends . . ."

In answer, a pair of big brown eyes gazed up at him and a little bare finger of a tail twitched happily to and fro.

A couple of minutes of such magical treatment and the puppy was totally smitten. It nestled closer to Robert's chest, its nose wrinkling contentedly and its eyes scrunched closed in delight. Robert had no idea where its mother might be, let alone its erstwhile human owners, but he sensed it had given up all thoughts of resistance — which was fortunate, for the last thing he and Pierre needed was a puppy causing a ruckus, with an enemy patrol likely to put in an appearance at any moment.

The house now secured, it was time to get

Pierre. The question was, what to do with his newfound friend? Robert could hardly deposit him behind the chair again, for knowing puppies as he did, this one would likely start whining just as soon as he had disappeared. It was crucial that he keep the little ball of fur happy and quiet, at least for now. He unzipped the front of his leather bomber jacket, slipped the puppy inside, and zipped it closed again.

Little did Robert know that this was the start of a lifelong friendship — one that would see him and the death-defying puppy take to the skies over war-torn Europe as they waged fierce battle against the enemy.

Two

Robert made his way back into the living room, only to discover that the wounded Pierre, despairing of a helping hand, had made his own way toward the house and was now clinging grimly to the doorway. His pale face betrayed the strain he had endured as he hauled himself across the icy earth, the blood from his injured leg forming a trail of spots and smears in the snow behind him.

He looked reproachfully at Robert. "You were so long I thought you had run into trouble."

Robert reached inside his jacket and presented the puppy. "Here's the trouble. I almost mistook him for the enemy and shot him!"

Pierre eyed the puppy suspiciously. "Looks like a German shepherd." He had stressed the word *German*. "But the house is deserted, yes? We're safe here?"

Robert nodded. "As safe as we'll ever be marooned in no-man's-land and with a burning aircraft nearby. We need to get a look at that leg of yours and get on the move."

Robert set the puppy down on the floor. Throwing an arm around Pierre's shoulder, he helped him across the living room to where they should be hidden from any passing patrols. He eased the wounded Frenchman to the floor. Dreading what he might find, he slit Pierre's pants with the pocketknife that he carried. Luckily, the wound was nowhere near as bad as he had feared. The bullet had passed clean through the calf muscle without so much as breaking a sliver of bone. In short it was a nasty flesh wound, but if he could stop the bleeding Pierre would live. Robert bathed the wound in a handkerchief dipped in some melted snow before binding it tight with a bandage.

Pierre leaned back against the wall, exhausted. "*Mon Dieu,* but it is good to be alive."

He had uttered not a single word of complaint as Robert had treated him, and there was no doubting the toughness or courage of the Frenchman.

Robert forced a smile. "Let's hope we stay that way. We're not out of this one yet. In fact, we've got one hell of a long way still to go . . ."

While Pierre had been captain in the air, Robert had far more battle experience on the ground, and he sensed it was up to him to take command now and come up with a plan to save both their skins. He spread out a map on the table and frowned: there was no easy way out of here, that was for sure. As he studied the details of their surroundings, he felt a warm wetness nuzzling into his hand. Almost without thinking he reached down and lifted the puppy by his belly and sat him on his lap.

With Robert busying himself over the map, Pierre fished around in his pants pocket and pulled out a bar of flying-ration chocolate. His hands shaking visibly, he fed a fistful into his mouth, then broke off a sliver to offer to the puppy.

"Poor devil," Pierre muttered. "Even though he is a *German* shepherd he was living in a *French* house, so perhaps we should show some solidarity . . . He looks half starved."

Pierre held the morsel closer to the puppy's mouth. He was expecting a grateful lick, but all he got for his trouble was a baring of needle-sharp fangs and as menacing a growl as a four-week-old puppy could muster in the face of a mean-looking predator many times his size.

Pierre tossed down the chocolate in disgust. "*Mon Dieu!* That's not a dog. That's a bloody wolf in disguise!"

Robert smiled inwardly. It was as if the tiny ball of fluff had expressed his own feelings toward the Frenchman, whose impulsive, some might argue reckless flying had landed them in their present, desperate predicament.

Robert pored over every minute detail of the map, picturing the terrain in his mind's eye and scrutinizing it for whatever hazards it might present. Even as he balked at the prospect of the perilous journey that lay ahead, he felt heartened by the way the little dog flattened his ears but made no attempt to resist his caresses.

"So, my friend, what is the plan?" Pierre ventured.

The Frenchman sounded about as finished as he looked. Robert knew full well that having the injured pilot with him limited his escape options considerably, but come what may, he was determined that the two of them would make it out of there.

"It's over one hundred kilometers to the nearest airfield at Nancy," Robert explained, "but first we've got to get out of this damned valley. As we crossed the Rhine I noticed a wood over on the west side where our boys are."

"Yes, but the Boche have their machine guns on the ridge overlooking the entire valley."

Robert hardly needed reminding. They were smack in the middle of a two-mile gap between the Maginot and Siegfried lines. The holes blasted in the farmhouse bore witness to the ferocity of the fighting between the two opposing sides here. There was no safe place in this entire expanse of terrain, not even in the spot where they had sought temporary shelter.

"How's the leg?" Robert asked.

"Aching like hell."

"The wood's about a mile away, practically due west. Do you think you can make it?"

Pierre raised his head defiantly. "When do we start?"

Robert considered the question. A light breeze had lifted the mist from the valley, leaving little more than vapor trails across the snow. If they tried to make a move they'd be seen, shot or captured. The only option was to wait until darkness, giving them the cover they needed to move unseen by the German gunners. Robert told Pierre they'd set out at last light, three hours from now. He watched anxiously as the wounded Frenchman limped to a nearby chair, settled himself into it, and closed his eyes. In an instant he was sleeping like a baby.

How different the two of them were, Robert reflected as he drew the puppy closer to him. Both were twenty-six years old and fighting for the same cause, but there the similarity pretty much ended. Pierre was short, stocky, and swarthy — a muscular little powerhouse of a man. His French Air Force comrades seemed to love his wild, carefree humor, while his dark eyes and delight in the pleasures of life had thrilled many a woman.

Robert, on the other hand, was a rangy six-footer whose air of driven intensity had settled upon him the day he had been forced into exile by the enemy. His iron will had spurred him to escape from the Nazis, transforming him into a war machine with a single purpose: to hit back hard and hammer those who had overrun his native Czechoslovakia and despoiled his country. He burned to be in action, taking the fight to the enemy, and that meant getting out of here intact and alive.

Something instinctive drew his attention back to the puppy, and his mood softened.

The animal was standing in his lap now, unsteady on his little legs, but studying Robert warily. The tiny dog glanced briefly at the sleeping Pierre and seemed to shudder visibly before turning his gaze back to Robert. He sensed that the four-week-old animal had made up his mind about the two strangers who had broken into his home — about who was his potential protector and who might do him harm.

Robert spoke softly and fondled the sleek black head. It was so tiny he could enclose it in the palm of his hand. A quiver of pleasure ran through the puppy's taut little body and he rewarded Robert with a nuzzle. The little dog would have bitten the hand that fed him if it belonged to Pierre, but Robert seemed to have earned his trust completely.

German shepherds were hugely popular in Robert's native Czechoslovakia, and he knew the breed well. Running his fingers along the brown back, he brushed away a thin layer of plaster dust to reveal a narrow black streak that ran the length of the dog's spine. Robert recognized this thin black line as signifying a thoroughbred, an aristocrat of the breed. No wonder the puppy had shown such pluck when he first laid eyes on these two intruders.

The puppy's body was so emaciated that the ears and legs seemed almost comically large, yet Robert detected a dignity in the animal that was striking. He had barely the strength to stand, yet he had guarded the miserable heap of straw and rags that had been his bed with the courage of a lion. The pitifully neglected puppy of today would surely grow up to be the most spirited and dependable of dogs if ever he survived the war.

As Robert worked his fingers deeper into the animal's coat, his mind drifted to a memory from childhood. He was ten years old and enchanted by everything the wild countryside of his homeland had to offer him and his gang of friends. One day they had penetrated deeper than normal into the remote mountains and woodlands. They'd come across a cave where, huddled together at the back, they had found three small wolf cubs.

Terrified by the thought that the mother might return, Robert and his friends had run from the scene as fast as their legs would carry them, fearing they would be savaged at any moment. Through such experiences Robert had learned to fear, love, and respect nature, and he had developed a close affinity with animals of all kinds. The physical resemblance between those wolf cubs and this German shepherd puppy was remarkable, doubtless explaining why the little pup had conjured up fond memories of far more innocent times.

Robert pictured his mother, whom he had left behind in Czechoslovakia, and wondered if he would ever see her again. His parents had doted on their only son, giving a warm welcome to all his friends in the Czech Air Force. But when the Nazis had rolled into Robert's homeland in 1938, the family had been torn apart. Relatives had been shot and tortured for daring to resist their Nazi "masters." Making a break for it alone, Robert had sneaked across the border to Poland, knowing that at any moment he might take a bullet from a German patrol.

From Poland he had enlisted in the French Foreign Legion with the aim of transferring swiftly to the French Air Force. There had been rough times with the Legion in North Africa, before the Air Force finally accepted him — at which stage he'd achieved what he hungered for most, which was to fight the Boche. But now disaster had struck and if he didn't make it out of here he was as good as dead, which would mean his battle against the invaders was over.

Thank God for an abandoned puppy with attitude, Robert told himself. Their companionship lightened his mood and put added steel in his soul. He heard a whimper from the little fellow. He was gazing up at Robert with dewy eyes, pleading for something.

"What is it this time?" Robert murmured. "What d'you want?"

He guessed the animal had to be hungry. Groping in his pocket, he found some chocolate and a few cookies. He offered a piece of each and the pup sniffed delicately, but would take neither. Suddenly Robert understood why: the poor wretch had very likely never been weaned. He held a piece of chocolate over a lighted hurricane lantern — one that he'd scavenged among the wreckage of the farmhouse — and rubbed the melt along his forefinger. This time the pup could not resist. After a few cautious sniffs and a tentative lick, he suckled Robert's finger hungrily until no trace of chocolate remained.

Robert repeated the process over and over again, and he was filled with affection for his new charge. He felt almost ridiculous entertaining the thought — especially in their present predicament — but in his heart he felt the two of them had a lot in common: they were both bereft of family, they were both fighting to exist, and they were both in deep trouble . . . but neither had given up the struggle.

"All right, boy, let's see what you make of something more solid."

Robert warmed some more chocolate, but this time he offered the hungry puppy a half-melted piece. The tiny tilted head and the confused gaze revealed the puppy's puzzlement. He didn't know what to make of the strange, sweet-smelling solid he was being offered. But finally his pink tongue flicked out and covered it in puppy drool, and seconds later tiny jaws closed over the morsel and it was gone.

The only problem now was that there was nothing with which to wash down the meal. Robert crossed the room, moving toward the doorway, watched at every step by a pair of tiny, shining eyes — as if the puppy feared being deserted again. After a few seconds he reappeared carrying a battered frying pan filled with snow. He warmed it over the lamp, after which he dipped his finger in the meltwater for the puppy to lick. Soon the tiny dog was lapping happily from the pan, having the first real drink of his short life.

"God only knows what we're going to do with you," Robert muttered.

Even as he said it, he could not escape the thought that there was something terrible he might have to do before they left — the kindest yet the most dreadful thing possible. Already he was wondering if he would have the heart for the job.

At six o'clock he woke Pierre. "Ready?" he whispered. "It's time."

Pierre spent a second or two rubbing the sleep from his eyes. He looked reasonably well rested — which was a bonus, thought Robert. Pierre glanced around him, realized where he was, and a focus and determination came into his gaze.

The Frenchman gestured at his bloodied and bandaged leg. "As ready as I'll ever be." He glanced over at the puppy. He was curled up and sleeping soundly after his meal. "What are we going to do with him? We can't exactly take him with us and if we leave him behind he'll starve."

Robert shrugged. "I've taught him to eat and drink. We can't do more than that. We'll leave him asleep and close and lock the door so that he can't follow. We'll give him some of our rations and a pan of water. He'll have to take his chances along with the rest of us. Now, d'you think you can make it to the woods?"

While Pierre readied himself Robert stared out of the doorway, trying to fix in his mind some landmarks to aim for along their route. He prayed for an overcast night, one bereft of moon or stars, to light their way. It would make navigation more difficult, but at least it would render them invisible to the enemy on the ridge. The faintest illumination might prove fatal, leaving the two men silhouetted against the white of the snowfields.

Before setting out Robert filled the frying pan with melted snow, heaping up a pile of broken cookies beside it. He opened the door, helped Pierre outside, then softly closed and bolted it. With a last look at the darkened room and a silent and regretful farewell to the slumbering puppy, they began the trek to what Robert hoped would be freedom and safety.

They had barely left the farmhouse when a series of vivid orange flashes tore through the night sky from the direction of the German lines. They were followed immediately by a barrage of equal intensity from the French lines to the west. The evening ritual of battery duels had begun. To make matters worse the heavy gunfire was accompanied by flares, which were fired high into the sky to be left hanging beneath mini-parachutes as they drifted lazily earthward. Each side was using them in an effort to reveal the location of any night patrols that might have been sent out by the enemy, so they could be picked off by snipers.

Pierre and Robert took cover in the outskirts of the orchard. The hot glare of the burning magnesium flares cast a skeletal pattern of black and white across the snow to either side of them. The entire area the airmen had to cross before they reached the sanctuary of the distant woodland was bathed in blinding light — the very thing that Robert had prayed they might avoid.

Pierre uttered a string of muffled curses. "*Mon Dieu,* but we'll never get through that lot!"

"We'll make it," Robert replied firmly. "The snow's deep and we can find some cover in the shadows of the steeper slopes."

There was no question anymore of Pierre being able to hobble with the aid of Robert's supporting arm. The only way to continue their desperate journey would be to crawl. They slithered forward on hands and knees, working their way slowly and painfully over the frozen snow.

Just as they reached the ditch that marked the boundary of the farm a flare burst directly overhead, blinding them. Both men lay flat on their faces in the cover of the snow-filled depression, sweating fear and mouthing silent prayers. The flashes of the German big guns intensified as they hurled their high-explosive shells at the French lines, and their rumbling shook the ground.

The flare went out like a snuffed candle, and in the momentary darkness that followed the big guns seemed to fall silent. Robert was just about to signal to Pierre that the time had come to move again, when a new sound filled the air. It was one that Robert had been dreading. The long-drawn-out howl of a puppy rent the night — a puppy who had just discovered that his new-found source of food, water, warmth, and love had deserted him, just as his mother had.

There was a second howl even more anguished than the first. It was as if the puppy understood that his chances of survival were diminishing with each step that his protector took away from him. He seemed determined not to be left to his fate, as if somehow he knew that his cries for help would force Robert to turn back.

Robert glanced at Pierre. "Wait there," he whispered. "I'll be back in a minute."

Pierre sensed the grim resolve in Robert's words. "I am sorry, my friend," he muttered, "but you know we have no choice."

Robert began to crawl back the way he had come. He was under no illusions as to what he must do, and he cursed himself for having been so soft. He felt for the knife he carried on his belt. To use a revolver would be easier, but far too dangerous now that the hour had come for night patrols to leave their posts and lie out listening in the snow — which was what the Germans did every evening as they tried to catch the French off guard.

As he neared the house Robert felt queasy, the nausea rising from the pit of his stomach. Pierre was right, of course — they simply had no choice — but Robert was unsure whether he could summon the courage to do what he had to do, even if their lives depended upon it.

He heard excited yapping as the puppy sensed his approach. He emerged into the open space between the orchard and the house, rising to his feet and blundering forward. He had to silence that dog, or it would bring every German patrol down on their heads. Another flare burst overhead. He threw himself down in the snow barely feet from the doorway, wondering if the howls and yaps had been heard.

The desperate yelping was replaced by a

new sound now — that of a dull thudding as a tiny body hurled itself against the door. Small and starved though he was, the puppy was trying again and again to batter down the door so he could be reunited with his erstwhile protector. For a split second Robert glimpsed a pointed nose pitching upward as the puppy tried to leap through one of the broken door panels, only to disappear again. The puppy was fighting as if for his very life, and if there was one thing that Robert admired it was a fighter.

Berating himself for his crazy sentimentality, Robert began to search for a log or a rock. Butchering the pup with his knife would feel far too much like savagery and murder. A sharp crack to the skull would spell instant oblivion, and was the most humane way. But as he felt around under the thick snow nothing came to hand.

Robert was growing desperate. Pierre lay injured in a ditch on the far side of the orchard, totally dependent upon him. He had to get this done before the puppy started to howl again. But how could he kill the little guy with his knife, especially when he had taught him to eat and to drink at his own hand?

Robert paused to consider his options. He had been in a few tight corners in the past couple of years, and he had never once given up the fight. The puppy was so close to death but still he was battling all the way. Robert recognized in him the pugnacious spirit he saw in himself. Hearing a desperate, pleading whine from the other side of the door, Robert felt his heart melt. He knew from this distance the puppy would be able to smell him — and Robert's was the smell he now recognized as that of his savior. Behind him the flare that had been hanging stubbornly in the night sky finally hit earth and fizzled out.

Robert rose to his feet in the darkness, scuttled forward, unbolted the door, and reached inside.

THREE

The puppy must have fallen after making an extra-determined charge at the door. He was lying on his side making feeble running motions with his paws as if willing himself to make one last go at it. Seeing the door open, he rose unsteadily to his feet, whimpering like a tired child desperate to be picked up by his father.

Robert grabbed the puppy and drew it toward him, two little orbs of glittering light meeting his gaze. The little dog gazed up at him in wide-eyed amazement, as if stunned that he had actually succeeded in summoning the stranger with the chocolate fingers.

Robert felt his resolution falter. "Looking for someone?" he whispered.

Hearing the familiar voice, the puppy tried to nuzzle into Robert's neck.

He pulled him closer. "All right, boy. It's all right. You're coming too."

Robert felt a pink tongue on his face, as if

the dog understood the momentous decision that had just been made. Unbuttoning his flying jacket, Robert placed the puppy snugly against his chest and turned back to the world outside.

A pale crescent moon had risen above the ridgeline. It played strange tricks with the light and shadows, hindering his and the puppy's progress back through the orchard. The stumps of blasted trees cast ghostly forms, ones that looked like half-hidden enemy soldiers waiting for a chance to strike.

Robert rejoined Pierre, slipping silently into the ditch. To his amazement the Frenchman had little to say when the puppy poked his head out of his flying jacket and gave a mean little growl. In truth Pierre disliked the animal only because it had so endangered their escape, and he understood his friend's inability to wield the knife. He had strained his ears for a squeal that would herald the coup de grâce, all the time suspecting that it would never come.

"I thought when you set off that I was glad it was you and not me," Pierre remarked quietly.

As the guns roared to left and right the men edged forward on their bellies, shredding the skin of their hands and knees where exploding shells had churned the ground into razor-sharp ridges of frozen rock and snow. Sensing danger, the puppy stayed perfectly still, insulated from the jarring percussions by the thickness of the fleece and comforted by Robert's murmurs of re-assurance.

But minute by minute Pierre was becoming more and more distressed. Each time he slipped, his face was scraped raw on the jagged crust of ice that had formed over the snow. The guns ceased firing as suddenly as they had started, but it didn't make the friends feel any less vulnerable. The only sound now was the crunching of frozen snow beneath their limbs, which in the silence sounded deafening. The noise of their passing rang out across the valley, as if signaling to the German patrols: *here we are; come and get us.*

Sporadic volleys from machine guns cut through the darkness. It was those weapons that the two men feared most, for if they were spotted the Germans were bound to try to rake them with fire. In their exhausted, disoriented state the pair couldn't seem to judge the distance of the guns or their targets. They had no option but to keep crawling. Each yard seemed longer than the last and the outline of the woodland they so longed to reach appeared to be coming no closer.

Time and again they lay half buried in the snow, braced for the challenge they were sure would ring out — one that would lead to imprisonment for Pierre and the firing squad for Robert. There were moments when Robert was so sure they had been seen that he hoped to be shot on the spot, rather than await his fate at the hands of the avenging Gestapo. But each of those moments seemed to pass, and he would chide himself for his cowardice and lack of fortitude, and urge Pierre forward.

They had been crawling uphill for a full hour when the moment of greatest danger seemed upon them. A pair of flares burst directly overhead and drifted toward the wreckage of the aircraft, which lay some four hundred yards behind them. Then came the staccato *rat-tat-tat* as the first machine gun opened up, followed by several more. This time there was no doubt about their target: the terrain all around the smoking wreckage of the French fighter-bomber was being raked by murderous fire.

Long bursts swept farther and farther out from the aircraft. Soon bullets were hammering into the snow within spitting distance of the two men, throwing chunks of snow and ice into their faces. As they tried to dig deeper with their frozen fingers they felt sure they had been seen, and they braced themselves for the searing penetration of flesh by hot metal. Robert felt the faint squirming of the puppy pinned beneath his ribs and imagined it would be his last sensation on this earth.

Then, as abruptly as it had begun, the firing ceased. Hardly daring to breathe, Robert lifted his head an inch or so and gazed around, scanning the slope for the enemy patrol that would surely be approaching. The flares illuminated an eerie scene. Ghostly figures surrounded the wreckage of the aircraft. A shrill cry rang out, triggering a terrifying burst of automatic fire. Robert could see bullets ricocheting off the metal skeleton of the Potez in a shower of sparks.

"For God's sake, lie still," Pierre groaned.

Having found no bodies, the enemy patrol would lose no time in hunting for survivors. Another flare, still burning, came to rest not far from their position. It sputtered and hissed as it burned a hole into the snow. Robert tensed for the Germans to head their way. He knew if that happened he could never leave his fellow airman, even though the consequences of capture would be so much graver for him. They had come too far together for him to abandon Pierre now.

To Robert's utter amazement the German patrol failed to turn in their direction. He and Pierre crawled ahead seemingly unnoticed by the enemy, who for some reason had taken their search farther toward the east. Pierre's grimaces and silent curses suggested that he was approaching the limits of his endurance. On the stroke of midnight — six exhausting hours after they had set out from the farmhouse — Robert glanced up to find that the wood was now a towering mass of darkness directly ahead of them.

"Almost there," he whispered. "A five-minute breather, then off again."

There was no response. Pierre lay silent and motionless beside him. Had his friend been shot by a sniper? Had he bled to death from his injuries? Had the physical and mental strain of this night proven too much for his overloaded system?

"Pierre! Pierre!" he whispered urgently. *Still no response.*

He reached across to the body and shook it by the shoulders. The Frenchman didn't lift his head from the snow, but he did speak — although in a voice so low that it was barely audible.

"Go on," he pleaded. "Go on alone. Leave

me. I'm finished."

"Nobody's leaving anybody," Robert retorted. "Either we both go forward or no one does."

He wasn't just angry that Pierre was giving up when they were so close to the sanctuary of the woodland; he was furious that his friend thought he was capable of abandoning him on a snowbound hillside in the midst of no-man's-land. But Pierre seemed immovable. Numbed by the freezing cold, his skin torn by ice and stones, his leg throbbing with a pain that he had never imagined possible, the tough Frenchman insisted he couldn't go another inch.

But Robert was having none of it. "When you feel me shove, make an effort to move forward. Like that we'll make it. We're nearly there."

He put his arm around Pierre's shoulders, thrusting a hand under his armpit and heaving him forward so hard that the Frenchman moaned in pain — yet at least it seemed to jolt him into action. Putting all his remaining strength into his one good leg, Pierre thrust forward, inching ahead. Robert remained at his side, heaving repeatedly as the injured man clawed at the frozen snow crust with his fingers and one good leg, thrusting himself onward.

Together, inch by agonizing inch, they crawled up the incline toward the dark wall of the woodland. It took a full forty-five minutes to reach the first tree. Robert staggered to his feet and dragged his friend behind that big, solid fir, putting him out of the reach of any sniper whose attention might have been attracted by the final moments of their flight.

Pierre rolled onto his back and promptly lost consciousness. Picking a tree beside him, Robert sank down with his back to the base of the trunk. Every muscle in his body was burning and the fire in his arms surged unbearably from shoulders to fingertips.

He fumbled for the zipper of his jacket, desperate to check that the breath hadn't been crushed out of the puppy in the last frantic yards. As he held the tiny dog before him, he saw that there was more life in his stick-thin tail than the two men seemed to have left in their entire bodies. It twitched elatedly to and fro in a somewhat premature celebration of their great escape.

Robert knew they were far from safe yet, but he craved rest. The last thing he saw as he drifted into an exhausted sleep was the little dog standing up on his hind legs to lick his chin.

■ ■ ■ ■

Robert was woken sometime later by a low whine. He looked around for the pup and saw him standing a few feet away, his legs stiff, his hackles raised as he stared intently at the undergrowth at the edge of the woodland. He had detected some kind of sound that his master couldn't yet hear, and all of his instincts screamed that a mortal threat was nearby. The growl he gave next was a warning both to the friends at his side and to whoever was approaching.

Robert grabbed the dog and covered his muzzle with his hand to stifle the puppy snarls. A twig snapped with a crack so loud that it could have been a pistol shot. It woke Pierre. He sat bolt upright, gazing around confusedly. Robert knew that it was too late to try to run, even if Pierre had been capable of moving. He felt for his pistol and readied himself for the final battle. At least their tiny companion had given them a few seconds' warning.

Figures loomed out of the shadows and were instantly upon them. Bayonets glistened at Robert's throat and at Pierre's chest. Yet more soldiers slipped out of the bushes. The two airmen were surrounded;

resistance was hopeless. Robert's disbelief that their epic bid for freedom should have ended in capture quickly gave way to despair. The German patrol must have followed their tracks in the snow. How else could they have found them so quickly?

"All right," he heard Pierre announce defiantly. "You've found us! So now what?"

Silence.

A flashlight was trained on their faces.

Then the tense and murderous atmosphere was transformed by the exclamation from the nearest soldier: *"Mon Dieu! Mais ils sont Français!"*

Barely able to believe his ears, Robert peered through the gloom at the men crowding ever more closely around him. French uniforms!

"Our plane . . . It crashed. Out there." He heard himself gasping out their story. He pointed at Pierre. "He's hurt. His leg. Help him."

A lieutenant wearing the uniform of the French infantry stepped closer. "Please, who exactly are you? Identify yourselves."

Pierre went first: "Sergeant Pierre Duval, French First Bomber Reconnaissance Squadron."

Robert found his voice, but it sounded faint and thin as if stretched to breaking point. "Sergeant Robert Bozdech, observer and air gunner. Same squadron. We were shot down this morning, sir. My pilot is wounded."

The lieutenant put a hand on Robert's shoulder. "Steady now. We know about the crash but we weren't sure about the aircrew. How the devil did you get here?"

"Crawled . . . every bloody inch," Pierre gasped. "Is there a doctor? My leg's buggered."

"Not here, and we can't do much this close to the enemy. We'd better carry you."

The French soldiers removed the bayonets from their rifles, lashed the butts and muzzles together to form a rough platform, and placed a greatcoat across it. Pierre was eased onto the makeshift stretcher and the party moved off through the trees.

"Is your pilot badly wounded?" the lieutenant asked Robert.

"A bullet through the leg, sir. He'll recover."

"Indeed. Anyone who can get up that slope with such an injury will surely recover . . . In fact, you're both to be congratulated. In the morning we'll get him to a hospital. In our frontline position we can at least give him first aid, plus you'll have a meal and a bed and you'll be safe there."

The small force made its way through the darkened woodland, until the first defenses of the Maginot Line hove into view. They entered a clearing where a blockhouse had been cleverly camouflaged to blend in with the firs. All around it Robert could see gun barrels poking out from hidden emplacements in readiness for the feared German onslaught. The lieutenant hesitated before the building as Robert unfastened his jacket and reached for the puppy.

"What's that you've got there?"

"A dog, sir. A puppy."

"Well, bring him in! Have you had him long?"

Robert grinned. "Long enough to make friends with him, sir."

A meal of bread and bully beef was being prepared, the mouth-watering aroma of meat and gravy hanging heavy in the air. The puppy stirred, took one sniff, and started whimpering in excitement.

"At least somebody appreciates the smell of Henri's cooking," joked the lieutenant. "Maybe the taste will change his mind!"

Secure in their quarters, the soldiers toasted the rescue of the two airmen with hot black coffee laced with French cognac. They demanded to know every detail of the crash landing and the airmen's escape to the woodland. But what they were most curious about was how, in the midst of the fight of their lives, the two airmen had ended up bringing a puppy with them.

"Poor devil, he looks half starved," Henri, the cook, remarked, once Robert had finished telling the story. "I'll mix him some gravy and bread. Perhaps he'll take it from you."

Sure enough, when Robert placed the bowl on the floor the puppy shot out from hiding and wolfed down every last morsel. He seemed to sense that if food came from Robert it was safe to eat. Wide brown eyes pleaded for a refill and a second bowl followed the first. Then, his tiny stomach swollen by the rich, unfamiliar fare, the puppy flopped down at Robert's feet and threw up violently. The room erupted with raucous laughter and fresh gibes about Henri's cuisine.

Robert lifted the exhausted pup onto his lap and stroked him to sleep. Soon he and Pierre were likewise dead to the world.

They were woken at dawn by the arrival of a field ambulance to take the wounded Frenchman to a hospital. Robert watched his friend being loaded aboard, before giving him one last grip of the hand.

"Get back to the squadron soon. We'll be

waiting."

Pierre seemed more concerned that his girlfriend's head might be turned by a rival while he was away convalescing. "Keep a close eye on the lovely Marie for me," he remarked with a wink, and then he was gone.

An hour later it was Robert's turn to take his leave. He thanked his rescuers, placed the puppy inside his jacket, climbed into a Renault van, and set off for the nearest airfield. There, an aircraft had been put at his disposal for the 215-mile flight back to the squadron's airbase at St. Dizier.

The twin-seat, single-engine training plane — a Potez 25 — was just the job to introduce an inexperienced flier to the air. The little dog trembled against his ribs as Robert started the engine, but a pat and a few gentle words soon calmed him. He behaved perfectly throughout the rest of the flight, and Robert felt a surge of pride in his new charge. What a team they made. Not only did they have their fighting spirit in common, but like him this little dog seemed born to fly.

While Robert and Pierre had dived through the fog over the German lines, the six fellow Czechs in Robert's squadron had been

70

flying high above them, battling a flight of German Messerschmitts. They had seen much of the doomed aircraft's desperate last moments, and they'd assumed that Robert and Pierre had perished as the Potez went down. Consequently, they had drunk heavily to help speed their friends' "journey upstairs," in traditional Czech style.

At first they were almost too hungover to take in the sight of Robert breezing back into the base, some twenty-four hours after they'd believed him killed in action. Then there were wild cheers, slaps on the back, and promises of a good many rounds of drinks that night to celebrate his great escape.

The Czech airmen had formed something like a close-knit family in exile. While serving in their own country's air force, they had bonded like young men do during wartime. But since Hitler's invasion had forced them out of their country, they had become united in one driving desire — *to kill Nazis.* Since they were stuck in France they had decided to adopt the motto of Alexandre Dumas's Three Musketeers: "All for one, one for all." And now they had an eighth musketeer joining their number in Robert's puppy dog.

Although they didn't know it at the time,

the lives of these men would be intimately bound up in the fate of their newfound four-legged friend. Robert's fellow Czechs were Joska, twenty-four, and Josef, twenty-six, both crack shots; Karel, a slim, twenty-three-year-old ladies' man; the avuncular Vlasta, thirty-five; Ludva, twenty-seven, nicknamed "Flame" for his red hair and fiery temper; and Gustav, at eighteen the baby of the party. All were single, and most importantly right now all were self-confessed dog lovers.

As they played with Robert's puppy dog the memories he evoked of family life reminded them of their loathing for the enemy that had driven them from their homeland. In no time each of the airmen had taken the little dog to his heart. No animal could have had more devoted protectors. The seven truly had become eight.

They would need a name for their new member, though. They debated long and hard. Such an obvious aristocrat of the breed deserved a noble moniker, they reasoned. Lord? Duke? Rex? All seemed a bit grand for a puppy that had yet to be house-trained. Karel lost the plot and suggested Emigrant; he was hit by a barrage of flying boots and books for his trouble. Then Joska, a handsome dark-skinned lad with a fine head of curls, had a brainstorm.

"I know," he said. "Remember that grand old plane we used to flog around the skies back home?"

"The ANT!" they shouted in unison, recalling the Russian Pe-2 dive-bomber they had all loved to fly. It had been designated the ANT by the Czech Air Force, and it was one of the best ground-attack aircraft then in service.

"That's it!" Robert exclaimed. "Joska, you've got it! We'll call him Ant in honor of our aircraft. Let's drink to it."

So it was that Ant was christened with all the exuberance of a baby in peacetime, except that he was toasted in beer rather than champagne.

The days passed. The rest of that winter of 1939–1940 was relatively quiet, for the "phony war" offered little chance of action or combat flying. Ant grew steadily and developed an assertive streak in keeping with a German shepherd's typically muscular physique. All the Czech airmen won his affection but there was only ever one master. When Robert was eating, Ant remained at his side patiently awaiting his turn. When Robert went to sleep, Ant curled up on the bottom of his bed and woe betide any intruders.

It was so cold that January and February of 1940 that the airmen's main preoccupation was keeping warm. The seven Czechs occupied one room in a blockhouse near the airfield and they slept in their greatcoats. Robert had the luxury of bedding down with Ant, a canine hot-water bottle with a fur lining. He was the only man never to wake with frozen toes.

Ant was quick to learn new tricks, and one in particular always drew a laugh. He became a one-dog welcoming party, greeting the Czechs as they returned from training flights or routine patrols by holding out his right front paw and "shaking hands" with each man in turn.

But this false peace couldn't last. On May 10, Robert and his friends heard battle commence at first light on a cloudless morning. German tanks thrust forward toward the French positions, heavy fire heralding the arrival of enemy bombers. French and Czech aircrew scrambled for their Morane fighters and the sky filled with raging dogfights. Six of the German bombers were brought down, but the euphoria was short-lived, as wave after wave of Panzer battle tanks punched through the French lines.

A plan was afoot for Robert's squadron to bomb a group of nearby bridges, in an effort to hold up the German forces massing there. Their Potez 63 bombers were the finest the French Air Force possessed, and all fourteen of them were ready for action, their crews raring to go. But the tension of waiting to be ordered into the air was unbearable, and when Robert spotted a soccer ball lying by one of the hangars, he proposed a quick kick-about to lighten the mood.

He booted the ball hard at Karel, who flashed a bright smile, trapped it deftly under his right foot, and kicked it back even harder. But it was now Ant's turn to shoot out from under the shade of a tree to intercept. The two men passed the ball to and fro, while Ant chased it down with relentless determination and unbeatable speed. In time soccer would prove Ant's favorite game, but all of a sudden the adolescent dog wasn't in a playful mood anymore.

Robert glanced up from the ball to see his young dog standing stiff-legged and staring at the horizon, hackles up and growling, just as he had done as a tiny puppy when two unidentified intruders had crept into his farmhouse. Robert scanned the skies to the southeast and could see nothing, but moments later the air-raid siren sounded.

Ant's early warning had just been confirmed: they were about to face a savage
onslaught from the skies.

Four

Ant proved to have a miraculous ability to sense enemy warplanes long before they were detectable by the human eye and ear, and sometimes even by radar.

Robert yelled for Ant to follow him. He turned to run, only to realize that for the first time ever since their chance meeting the dog had refused to obey. He seemed rooted to the spot, barking defiantly as a large formation of Dornier Do 17s powered into view. The Dorniers were known as "flying pencils," because they were so sleek, thin, and difficult to spot, and by the time you saw one it would be almost upon you.

Before they knew it, the first of the Luftwaffe's warplanes swooped in low and released its bombs. It scored a direct hit on one of the hangars, which exploded with a terrifying roar, shattered planking and galvanized iron spinning into the air. Two sharp blasts followed as the fuel tanks on one of the Potez fighter-bombers went up. A fireball punched above the roof, red-hot shards of metal raining down on the airmen.

Robert dived forward, bundled up his gangly dog into his arms, and sprinted hell-for-leather toward the far edge of the runway. The reverberations of the explosions were accompanied by the terrifying sound of heavy machine-gun fire as bullets tore up the ground at Robert's heels. The airfield was being strafed as well as bombed, and those few precious seconds spent rescuing Ant had left Robert hopelessly exposed.

As bullets kicked up the dirt all around him, Robert spotted a shallow slit trench beneath a row of trees right on the airfield boundary. He pounded forward and hurled himself headlong into it, landing in a heap on top of Karel. Ant was sandwiched between them, but he was still yelping angrily as the Dorniers thundered overhead.

The planes circled around and came back for another attack. Further explosions forced Robert to bury his head in his hands as debris thrummed through the air, smashing into the dirt just inches from where they lay. Bullets went snarling overhead. Ant wasn't making a sound anymore. His defiant barks and growls had given way to the fear that Robert could read in his eyes. Hugging him close, Robert felt his adolescent dog shudder with each new thud and snarl of an explosion.

The Germans turned their fire on a nearby group of aircraft, ones that had been left in the open on the edge of the airfield. As the bombs and bullets tore into those stationary warplanes, Robert could feel Ant's heart pounding like a jackhammer. Karel too was shaking and Robert slipped a reassuring arm around his shoulder. For two hours they huddled together — two men and one dog — as the enemy bombers tore the French airbase apart.

When finally they clambered out of the

trench they found that the Dorniers had done their worst. The hangars had been flattened and all fourteen of their Potez aircraft — the cream of the Armée de l'Air, as the French Air Force was known — had been blasted to smithereens. Nothing was left but smoldering wreckage and even the runway was filled with jagged craters. The squadron had ceased to exist, the airbase was finished, and the enemy's mechanized units were bearing down on them fast.

With the French Army in retreat, Robert and his companions were forced to move three times before they found a brief respite — and replacement aircraft — at the airfield at La Malmaison. Events were moving at such a rapid pace now that when Robert prepared for takeoff from their new base, he couldn't know for sure if he would be able to land in the same place afterward — and that meant he couldn't be sure of shaking Ant's paw at the end of the sortie.

What would happen to Ant if the German tanks appeared at the gates while Robert was in the air? The thought was unbearable. Robert risked his life every time he flew — that came with the territory. But the very idea of never seeing Ant again — that was a risk he wasn't prepared to accept. There was only one thing he could do: Robert decided that Ant would have to fly with him on each of his coming missions against the enemy.

Strictly speaking, it was against French Air Force rules for an animal to fly, which was why Ant had never joined Robert on a combat sortie. As a tiny puppy he'd been easily hidden for their one flight together, but not anymore. Yet the French were never famously rule-bound, and with their country ravaged by war Robert would have to gamble that a Gallic blind eye would be turned.

When he was scrambled for his next sortie, Robert whistled for his dog to follow. He ran for the hangar with Ant bounding along beside him. Before now Ant had been banned from the flight line, and there was something in the way he kept looking up at his master that suggested he expected to be ordered back to their quarters at any moment. When no command came, Ant wagged his tail into an excited frenzy, his eyes glowing with anticipation. The bond had grown so close between man and dog that Robert almost felt as if he could read Ant's thoughts. He knew that his dog was dying to get into the air alongside his master, and that he could barely believe that he was going to be allowed to do so.

Robert climbed into the waiting Potez 63

and called his dog's name. It seemed almost the most natural thing in the world for Ant to leap onto the wing of the aircraft and climb in beside him. The dog turned round and round in a tight circle, taking in the cramped confines of the glasshouse with the gunner's machine gun at the rear. He seemed to find the snugness to his liking, for he flopped down in contentment on the floor and curled up at Robert's feet.

Ant barely stirred when the twin engines roared into life. But as the plane taxied onto the runway, shaking a little from side to side as it crossed some rough ground, Ant raised his head and stared quizzically at his master. Seeing reassurance in the steady gaze that was returned, he dropped his head onto his outstretched forepaws and closed his eyes, content once more.

To Robert's surprise his young dog — still really a puppy at four months old — didn't seem to react at all on takeoff. A quick nuzzle of the hand that reached down to pat his head and Ant seemed happy. Even more extraordinary was the dog's reaction to combat: as the Potez dived, soared, and swooped to avoid the brown and white puffs of German antiaircraft fire that bloomed all around them, Ant seemed to doze through it all.

The perils of the mission didn't seem to worry him in the slightest. He showed little sign of alarm on hearing Robert's gun open fire at the German fighters that swooped to attack. His ears pricked up a little as the punching percussions of machine-gun fire filled the gun turret, his nose twitched at the thick cordite fumes that drifted all around him, but other than that he didn't seem inclined to stir from his laid-back position prone on the metal floor.

Whether their sortie had done much to disrupt the Nazis' lightning advance didn't seem to matter much to the war pup on his first foray into combat. As long as he was keeping his master company while he worked, Ant appeared blissfully happy.

As the mighty Wehrmacht war machine rolled onward, the dangers intensified. Hurricane fighters from the RAF's Advanced Air Striking Force joined the French Air Force in its desperate efforts to prevent the retreating British Expeditionary Force from being cut off. In the midst of this maelstrom, Robert and his fellow Czech airmen seemed to be leading charmed lives, for none had yet been shot down. The superstitious among them began to wonder if the presence of their cool and fearless canine mascot in the air had something to do with their good fortune.

On the morning of May 21, however, their run of luck came to an end. Accompanied by an escort of Hurricanes, the squadron set out to hit the German armored columns crossing the River Somme. As the fighter-bombers swept in to attack, a storm of antiaircraft fire blasted across the sky. It seemed to Robert that they were flying into a terrible wall of thunder and lightning, and for a fleeting moment he wondered if it had been right to bring Ant on such a seemingly deadly sortie.

They pressed home their attack and saw the German forces scatter in alarm beneath their bombs, but as Robert craned his neck to count his comrades during the climb away from the target, his heart missed a beat. Far below him he could see that Karel's plane had gone into a steep dive. Thick black smoke poured from the fuselage as the Potez dropped like a stone.

That night, in a bar in the tiny village of Amifontaine, adjacent to their airbase, the six remaining Czechs drank the traditional toast to a fallen comrade. No matter how familiar they were by now with mortal danger, it was hard to believe that the most carefree among them had been the first to perish. Each man had a fond memory of

Karel — more often than not of him persuading the prettiest girl to let him walk her home from a dance.

As the reminiscences poured forth Ant knew that something was wrong, though he had no idea what exactly. He wandered from man to man seeking an explanation. Then he gazed at the empty chair where Karel should have been sitting and whimpered softly, as if realizing that this was the cause of tonight's unhappiness. He crossed to the door and stood expectantly — waiting, it seemed, for their absent friend to return. Finally, with a look of puzzlement in his eyes, he lay at Robert's feet, his head resting on his master's boots. The shadow of death that had descended over the band of brothers had snuffed out even Ant's irrepressible spirit.

When they retired to their hut Ant seemed to sense his master's mood. The young dog tried to cheer him up in the only way he knew, by falling on his master's hands and face and licking every inch of exposed skin. That seemingly failed to do the trick, so he tried a little extra. He took his master's hand in his powerful jaws and squeezed gently, increasing the pressure little by little. When he removed his jaws the impression of his teeth showed like dimples in Robert's skin. Robert knew this play bite was his dog's way of trying to cheer his spirits, it being such a powerful demonstration of their mutual trust and love.

Still Ant couldn't settle down. He needed to carry out one last duty before sleep: his customary bedtime inspection. Ignoring the curses of the semicomatose airmen, he went from face to face, touching each with the cold end of his nose, as if to reassure himself that all his brothers were present and accounted for. The men had become accustomed to Ant's habit of checking on them all at the end of the day. They knew he couldn't be broken of it, no matter how annoying it was to be woken by a wet nose just as you were drifting off to sleep. But when Ant finally curled up beside Robert, his inspection done, he knew that one man was missing. That night would be broken by dark dreams of a stricken aircraft tumbling from a burning sky.

The next morning Robert was heading for the squadron office for a briefing when he heard a joyful shout from behind him. For a moment he thought he must have imagined it and kept walking, but then it came again.

"Hey, Robert! What's the big hurry?"

This time there could be no mistaking it. He turned to see Pierre hurrying after him, going as fast as his heavy suitcase would allow him.

"Pierre! I don't believe it!" Robert exclaimed, clasping his friend's hand. Ant caught the mood — *together again* — and despite his uncertain history with the French airman, he jumped for joy around them.

"I've been looking everywhere for you," panted the red-faced Pierre. "Can't you keep still for two days? It's high time you had a decent pilot again."

"Too bad, Ant." Robert grinned at his cavorting dog. "You've had your share of smooth landings. Now you'll have to put up with this bone rattler."

The leg pulling masked the intense emotion of their reunion. Robert had heard that Pierre's convalescence was going well, but being constantly on the move, he'd despaired of ever seeing him again. The return of the Frenchman softened the blow of losing their Czech brother airman, Karel, but only slightly.

As Robert and Ant took off for their first sortie with Pierre since their aircraft had been shot down, Robert struggled to banish from his mind the image of Karel's doomed plane smashing into the earth. It had never even entered his head that their dashing

Czech comrade might have survived. As for Pierre, he seemed to have lost none of his impulsiveness or his reckless bravery, and in a way Robert was glad to be flying with him again. He was the perfect pilot with whom to take the fight to the seemingly invincible German enemy.

But when Pierre brought them safely back to base after that first sortie together again, Robert was stunned to see a familiar figure waiting beside the runway. Ant bounded up to him, as if in recognition of a miraculous homecoming, offering an eager paw for the figure to shake. For a moment, Robert just stared in disbelief as Karel — the man they'd all given up for dead — bent to his dog and greeted him in the accustomed way.

After greeting Ant, Karel stood with his hands in his pockets and a cigarette dangling from his mouth, as if to say: *What's all the fuss about?* Seeming to revel in his comrades' obvious surprise and disbelief, he acted as if it was no big deal for him to have reappeared in their midst. He beamed and winked as if he'd just returned from one of his amorous nocturnal adventures, rather than a jarring impact with a furrowed field and a perilous escape in a French Army vehicle, which only just managed to keep ahead of the German armor.

"What I want to know," he remarked to Robert, "is what you lot were saying about me in the bar last night. Go on, don't be shy. It'll be like reading my own obituary."

Sadly, there was precious little time to enjoy the miracle reunion. The Wehrmacht's advance into France was overwhelming. As the Panzers rolled relentlessly toward Paris, Robert flew numerous, ever more desperate sorties, but always with Ant at his side. The young dog's boundless energy and apparent enthusiasm for combat gave Robert added strength and conviction, although Ant could have no idea whom they were fighting or why. *If my dog can fly repeatedly into the face of death undaunted, so can I,* Robert reasoned.

Reconnaissance flights confirmed that the enemy armor was blasting asunder anything that stood in its path. The squadron's few aircraft that remained serviceable had barely touched down before they were being refueled and flown to another aerodrome farther away from the German advance. The aircrew left behind had to follow in road convoys, and were forced to pick their way along routes choked with fleeing refugees.

The French and British Air Forces had fought courageously, inflicting heavy losses on the Luftwaffe, but the armies on the ground had been routed with bewildering speed. So many columns of French soldiers had been overrun that the Germans could not take them all prisoner. They were disarmed and turned loose to run for their lives along with the civilians.

Flying low, Robert could see that the roads were jammed with refugees fleeing Paris. He had no trouble telling them apart from others on the move, for plush cars carried the well-dressed Parisians in relative comfort. By contrast, most of the country folk relied on horses or oxen to drag ancient carts that groaned under the weight of their possessions. But both the city slickers and the fruit pickers had one thing in common: *fear.* Anxious faces scanned the skies for warning signs of an attack. Whenever German warplanes pounced, rich and poor alike scrambled into roadside ditches to take cover.

On June 14, the Germans penetrated the outskirts of Paris and thrust onward to find the city center virtually undefended. The remnants of Robert's squadron, complete with Ant, were withdrawn to a small airbase near the village of Le Breuil, far to the south of the capital, where it was hoped they might be able to operate for a while longer against the victorious enemy.

But a flight of ten Messerschmitts was to shatter that illusion once and for all. Pouncing without warning, they methodically targeted each of the surviving aircraft lined up on the airfield, their heavy machine guns spitting tongues of fire. By the time they had disappeared over the horizon, every last one of the squadron's warplanes was left a smoking, mangled ruin.

On the following day, June 17, the new French leader, Marshal Pétain, a hero of the First World War, made the humiliating announcement that France would sue for peace with Germany. It was the final hammer blow to an already fragmented war effort.

The last surviving members of Robert's squadron were summoned to a farmhouse garden to be addressed by the squadron's adjutant. His medals recalled days of past glory, but now he stood gray-faced before them and with shoulders bowed. No more than sixty men of all ranks mustered, including the seven Czechs with the obedient German shepherd in their midst.

As he called the roll, the adjutant's voice trembled and tears streamed down his face. He read Pétain's announcement and the men listened in stunned silence.

"My comrades," he concluded. "We are finished. The Boche already occupy Orléans and their Panzers are advancing. They are only twelve miles from here. The nearest railway station for trains south is Tours, twenty-five miles away. We can do no more. Save yourselves as best you can. Goodbye and God bless you all."

It was all the adjutant could do to call each man forward and hand him his papers. To Robert and the other Czechs he gave their French Foreign Legion pay books, the only identity documents they possessed. Finally, overcome with emotion, the adjutant retreated into the house. His country had been betrayed and the world as he had known it was obliterated.

It was obvious to all that if they stayed together, then sorting transport and food while remaining hidden from the omnipresent enemy would be impossible. Their only chance was to split up. The seven Czechs were joined by Pierre and his closest French friend, Jacques Chevalier, with Ant of course completing the party.

The sound of a tank column drawing nearer, its guns blazing, spread panic among local villagers, who fled with what possessions they could. The nine airmen tried to talk things over more calmly. Since they regarded Pétain's order to lay down arms as unacceptable, their aim had to be to fight on. They needed an objective and a destination, they reasoned. If they could not fight in France, their destination had to be the one place that might help them lift the iron heel of oppression from their homelands. They would head for the one country still holding out against the Germans — Great Britain.

Making that decision was the easy part. The challenge was working out how to get there. Not a man among them would ever think of abandoning his flying kit, and they could barely move with each of them having a pair of bulging leather suitcases. As airmen, they naturally planned to beg, borrow, or steal a plane that would take them to the English coast, from where they would carry on fighting the Boche as warriors of the air.

A rapid search confirmed that everything on wheels in the immediate vicinity had already been pressed into service. They were almost resigned to making their flight on foot, laden down with their baggage, when they came across a large, brightly lit house on the edge of Le Breuil. It made an incongruous contrast with the dark and deserted dwellings all around it. Not only were lamps blazing in every room, but the sound of laughter spilled out of open windows. And was that singing? On closer inspection the men saw that a party was in full swing, and the partygoers appeared to be celebrating the imminent arrival of the Germans.

Collaborators!

Cold fury concentrated the minds of the airmen. Apparently, this champagne-swilling fifth column had arrived in dozens of cars of all shapes and sizes, betraying that a wide variety of renegades had been willing to deliver their country to the enemy, no doubt in return for positions of petty influence under the coming occupation. The vehicles were parked in a large courtyard inside the gates. Standing watch over them was one guard, with a revolver tucked in his belt.

"Keep moving," hissed the tall, fair-haired "Uncle" Vlasta, the oldest member of the group. "Don't do anything suspicious. If we can fix him, we can help ourselves to some transport."

The friends walked on for a quarter of a mile before halting to discuss how to do away with the guard. It was Uncle Vlasta, the most experienced and battle-hardened of the Czechs, who came up with the plan — one in which Ant, predictably, was to play the pivotal role. Vlasta stressed that whatever else, the guard must not be allowed to fire his revolver or raise the alarm in any way.

When they were all clear on the plan Robert turned back toward the house, Ant trotting happily beside him. As man and dog moved along the road, the redheaded Ludva — "Flame" — vaulted over the hedge so he could sneak into the grounds of the house, accompanied by Pierre's friend Jacques. Both men could barely contain their anger at what they had seen of the partying collaborators, and they were a natural choice for what was coming.

Robert noticed his dog's tongue flicking from side to side, as if in eager anticipation of what lay ahead. In some uncanny way he sensed that Ant knew they were embarked upon a vital, life-or-death mission. He felt sure his dog understood he had a crucial part to play in whatever drama might unfold.

Show me what to do and I'll do it, Ant's determined expression seemed to say. *I won't let you down.*

FIVE

The final leg of Robert's epic flight from France was via a convoy sailing from Gibraltar, although it required ingenious subterfuge to smuggle Ant aboard.

Robert and Ant pressed ahead, trying as best they could to give the impression of a man and dog out for a relaxed evening stroll. Robert threw a stick so Ant could chase after it. He pounced on the wooden snake, tail erect and flicking back and forth excitedly as he grasped it in his jaws. They kept the game going until the brightly lit house hove into view once more.

As they neared the gate the guard stationed there spotted them, but he didn't appear to suspect a thing. Robert threw the stick so it landed near him. The guard picked it up and threw it back to Robert in an effort to tease the prancing dog. As Robert tossed the stick back to the guard, Ant found himself bounding back and forth playing monkey-in-the-middle.

"Evening!" the guard called over. "Nice dog you have there. A *German* shepherd if I'm not mistaken. That's the kind of breed that will endear us to our new masters." A pause. "Want me to find him a good home?"

"Well, it certainly looks as if *you've* found yourselves a good home," Robert replied, feigning nonchalance. "Seems like the good old days, what with the music playing and the partying."

The guard tapped his temple as if to say *there's a brain in here.* "Ah, well, some of us have used our heads." With a smug grin he pointed at Robert's uniform. "Tell you one thing, pretty shortly you'll be wishing you didn't have that on."

"Maybe you're right," Robert mused.

He whistled for Ant and scooped him up, stroking him thoughtfully as if he was seriously considering giving him up. Over the guard's shoulder, he caught a glimpse of Ludva and Jacques creeping out of the bushes.

He held the dog out before him, as if showing him off to the guard. "Perhaps he might just be in need of a new home. What'll you give me for him?"

The guard shrugged. "I was thinking less of a payment, more of me doing you and the dog a favor —"

His words were cut off as Ludva struck from behind, snaking his arm around the guard's neck and pulling hard to choke any attempt to cry out, while his other hand smothered the mouth. Robert saw the guard's eyes bulge in alarm as Ludva tightened his hold, and at the same time Jacques secured his revolver. It was all over in seconds. Bound and gagged, the guard was thrown into the back of one of the vehicles. Theirs had been a plan built on a deception and it was one in which Ant had played his part perfectly.

A soft whistle from Robert summoned the

others. A whispered discussion ensued. Ludva wanted to take the sportiest car for the speediest escape. Cooler heads were drawn to the cart standing to one side of the courtyard: it could be removed with no noise and pulled off the road whenever the way ahead became congested. It would also help them blend in with the scores of rural refugees. There wasn't time to steal the pony as well, but the trap was light and the men were strong. They could haul it themselves.

Dusk had turned to darkness by the time seven Czechs, two Frenchmen, and a German shepherd joined the column of refugees heading south. Two men pulled on the cart's shafts, and seven pushed from behind. As for Ant, he rode atop the heap of suitcases and gear, looking as proud as an Indian raja with his nine bearers around him.

They had resolved to head not for Tours, as the adjutant had suggested, but for the smaller town of Blois, on the Loire, which was closer. There was precious little time if they were going to beat the Germans to it, but if they succeeded they should be able to take a train from there to the southern coast. The south of France had yet to be occupied by the enemy, and there were rumors of evacuations being organized from the Mediterranean ports. Allied soldiers fleeing the German advance were being urged to get there as quickly as possible.

But the progress of the cart, first on crowded roads, then on rutted tracks, was anything but swift. Every time it tilted, Ant clawed furiously at the suitcases but rarely could he keep his balance. He tumbled off repeatedly and whined miserably when he was lifted back on. Not yet fully grown, the puppy didn't have the energy or the endurance to make the journey on foot. He would have to ride the cart or be left behind. Nerves frayed with each delay and for the first time Ant became a source of division among the men.

"This is no bloody good," the hotheaded Ludva snorted as Ant fell yet again. "At this speed we'll all see the firing squad before morning."

When Ant tumbled from the cart for the umpteenth time and howled out in pain, Vlasta's composure deserted him. "He's not hurt — he just wants to be carried! The enemy patrols will hear him. We've got to get rid of him."

Without a word Robert scooped up the gangly pup and tucked him protectively under one arm while continuing to push the trap with the other. He was determined to carry Ant all the way to England if necessary. The dog's whining ceased, and after a few minutes Uncle Vlasta fell into step beside Robert.

He glanced across at him, sheepishly, then down at the dog. "Sorry about that . . . I don't know what got into me."

"Forget it," Robert replied. As for Ant, he turned his soft eyes on Vlasta and nuzzled his arm. "See." Robert smiled. "Ant's forgiven you already, so there's no harm done."

Without another word Vlasta took the puppy from his master, hoisted him onto his broad shoulders in a fireman's lift, and carried him for the next hour or more, after which another of the airmen took his place carrying the dog.

It was well after midnight when they heard the sound of a railway engine pulling out of a nearby station. It looked as if they'd just missed one of the last trains heading south. They roused the stationmaster by hurling stones at his shuttered window, only for him to confirm somewhat grumpily that there would be no more trains that night. He seemed deeply suspicious of their party. It was hardly surprising in a country that was rife with collaborators, turncoats, and quislings.

Pierre explained that they were French

airmen fleeing the Boche, and that the enemy was close on their tail. If they had to spend the remainder of the night waiting for a train, it might well prove the death of them. The stationmaster seemed finally to relent. He directed them to a short stretch of track two miles farther on, where he thought they might find one of the last trains preparing to steam south — that's if their luck held.

The airmen pressed on into the night, heaving the cart over muddy ruts and rough ground, their exhaustion temporarily forgotten in the chase after this elusive night train. Behind them they could hear the growls of heavy engines in the distance and the odd burst of gunfire as the German panzers ground onward. It was deeply ominous.

They were on the verge of giving up hope when Ant's hyper-sensitive hearing detected something. He leaped off the cart, leading the men toward a shadowed ravine. It turned out to conceal a deep railway cutting. Hidden within its depths were thirty railcars, with three engines coupled to the front and working up a head of steam in preparation for imminent departure.

The entire train was full to bursting. Still, a mob of desperate servicemen and their families besieged it, demanding to be allowed onto carriages that could hold no more. As the nine airmen surveyed the scene, it looked pretty hopeless. On a first-come-first-served basis they were at the very back of the line, and there was no way that they would push women and children aside so as to claim their own place on this train ride to safety.

It was then that Ant took the initiative. Steering a path through the crowd, he headed toward the rear of the train, with Robert following. The final few cars were cattle cars, which the airmen presumed had to be crammed full of livestock. Unlike the passenger cars, there were few if any people milling around, and the rear of the train was a place of relative calm.

Ant reached the very last of the cattle cars, plunked down his rear, and glanced back at his master, his eyes aglow. *There's a gorgeous smell in here. Irresistible, actually! Open up and let's see what it is!*

When Robert tried to slide the door aside it failed to move. He banged on it a few times, but with little hope that the animals he presumed were inside would respond. Then, miracle of miracles, the door slid open a crack. A well-dressed woman poked out her nose, peering guardedly at Robert. An instant later her face lit up when she saw the puppy sitting obediently at his side. She slid the door open wider and beckoned Robert and his dog to enter . . . perhaps not gambling on the eight fellow airmen who accompanied them!

Robert and Ant took a place in one corner of the carriage. It was devoid of livestock, and apart from the woman and her two teenage daughters, plus a large quantity of luggage, it was completely deserted. Hardly daring to believe their luck, the nine airmen piled in their own suitcases and slid shut the door.

With the car door firmly closed and bolted, the girls revealed the source of the smell that had drawn Ant to them. They had been feasting on a bar of chocolate. Noting how the puppy eyed it hungrily, the older girl broke off a piece and offered it to him. The ravenous dog needed no coaxing with fingers dripping in melted chocolate this time; instead, he took the piece gently from her hand and wolfed it down.

"Mais il est mignon!" she exclaimed, breaking off another square of chocolate — *but he is so cute!*

With Ant having broken the ice, the woman explained that her husband was a publisher in Brussels, but that he had been called up by the Belgian Army. She had heard nothing of him for two months, and so was fleeing the family home for the south of France, where she hoped to find sanctuary. Her daughters were delighted to be able to make a fuss over Ant, and the woman seemed happy enough at the extra company.

The elder of the two girls let the tired dog rest his head in her lap. She soothed him to sleep with a soft Belgian lullaby, one that partially drowned out the shouts of people farther up the track fighting for seats that did not exist. Just before dawn the overloaded train finally lurched into motion, using the only undamaged track going in the direction of intended travel — south to safety — and leaving hundreds of desperate would-be passengers behind.

But so great was the weight of those who had squeezed aboard that at the first gradient the long line of cars broke apart in the middle. Those cars nearest the break lurched backward into the cattle cars at the rear, Ant being buried under a heap of falling suitcases.

His yelping was pitiful. *Hey! Hey! I'm here! Get me out of here!*

As the airmen pulled the suitcases off him Robert dragged the puppy clear. The engineless railcars gathered speed, careering backward down the incline, with those in the runaway part of the train fearing that they had been abandoned. How could the drivers know that the rear section had become uncoupled? Fortunately, the train's conductor had been alerted, and once the runaway train came to a standstill the errant cars were reattached.

But their onward progress was dogged by delays. An axle snapped, and they were forced to stop for repairs. There were frequent halts due to air-raid warnings — for a train steaming at speed would make an irresistible target for marauding German warplanes. They also seemed to stop at every station — not that the train was capable of accommodating any more of the desperate people who thronged the platforms. Finally they reached a section of track that had suffered such serious bomb damage as to make it impassable, and long hours were spent repairing it.

In three days they covered just sixty miles. Progress was barely faster than walking pace, and all the while they feared being overtaken by the German forces at their rear. The nine airmen had been reduced to a starvation diet by now: all they had to feed themselves and their dog were a few tins of sardines and bars of chocolate. Ant was becoming listless due to the lack of proper food: his eyes had dulled, his nose had gone dry and flaky, and his coat was losing its customary luster.

After a twenty-hour delay for no discernible reason in the midst of a town, it was almost a relief to come to a halt in open countryside due to yet another air-raid warning. Pushing the door open to let in some fresh air, Robert spotted a herd of cows grazing nearby. He seized the opportunity.

"Come on, chaps," he called. "Here's our chance to get some milk. Ant, stay."

The airmen needed little encouragement, not least because their beloved canine companion looked to be in such a bad way. The Belgian woman fished around in her bags and pulled out a baby's bottle, which she said would be ideal for feeding Ant the cow's milk. But the herd was understandably wary at the sight of nine wild-eyed airmen dashing toward them, hunger burning in their eyes. Their attempt to corral the cattle only caused a stampede. Just one of the beasts failed to join the mad dash away from the direction of the train. She strolled over to the hedge, stood ruminating for a moment, and was cornered.

But the question was, who would milk her? In Czechoslovakia, milking was considered woman's work and none of the men knew what to do. Urged on by the others, Robert tried his hand. Four of his comrades held the cow, two at the head and two at the rear, as he positioned the bottle directly beneath the udder. But no matter how he might pull on her teats, he failed to coax a single drop of milk from them.

Laughter came from behind a nearby hedge. Two elderly French-women were watching the performance in something close to astonishment.

"She's the grandmother of the herd," announced one, stifling a giggle. "She's dry! Her milking days are long gone."

Then her friend spotted the bottle and seemed to take pity on them. "Oh, is it for the baby you need the milk? Wait, we have plenty for a little one."

She held out her hand for the baby's bottle, which Robert passed across to her wordlessly. She vanished into a nearby cottage and reappeared holding it aloft, brimful of milk. She had filled a wine bottle with some more and sealed it with a stopper. Back in the train car, Robert offered Ant the bottle, having first squeezed out a few drops onto the rubber nipple. The dog took one sniff, his eyes brightened, and he began to suck greedily. Robert felt a flood of relief wash over him.

So a pattern was established. Whenever the train stopped, Robert had only to show the baby's bottle at the doorway of the cattle car for some kindly soul to fill it. Anyone who inquired after the infant's welfare was left with the impression that "baby Antoine" was bearing up admirably under the circumstances.

The milk proved a lifesaver for Ant, who began to strengthen, which in turn proved a major morale booster for the men. But when the train finally reached Montpellier, on France's Mediterranean coast, the nine were to lose two of their number. Jacques and Pierre felt unable to abandon their families to the vagaries of the German occupation: they left the train, vowing to the Czech airmen to be reunited one day when all of Europe would be free again.

Pierre and Robert shared an especially emotional parting. *"Vive la France,"* Robert announced, shaking the Frenchman's hand for what he feared was the last time.

Pierre smiled through the tears in his eyes. *"Vive l'Angleterre."*

As for Ant, he was sad to see the French pilot leave. Together, the three of them had survived so much, and had Pierre not chosen to fly his aircraft low over the German lines on their doomed reconnaissance mission, Ant would never have been discovered and rescued by his master and protector.

From Montpellier the party made for the port city of Marseilles. The scene all around them was chaos, with French servicemen discarding their uniforms and declaring that any further resistance against the Boche was futile. But the seven stoic Czechs ignored the febrile atmosphere that swirled around the city and made directly for the docks. There they were able to catch one of the last ships bound for the nearest free British territory — Gibraltar.

"Gib" lay nearly nine hundred miles along the Spanish coast. Spain was in theory a neutral party in the war, so at least the voyage wouldn't be menaced from the Spanish coastline. To the Czechs, the last leg of their epic journey to freedom — one that would enable them to continue to take the fight to the loathed enemy — seemed the least daunting. But for Ant, one of the greatest dangers of their perilous flight was still to come.

They reached Gibraltar on June 30, 1940, after a largely uneventful voyage. As luck would have it, a convoy was preparing to set sail for Britain. Gibraltar was the airmen's first-ever taste of British territory, and they learned that they would be transferred to the British collier ship, the *Northmoor*. She lay at anchor one hundred yards offshore, and final preparations were being made for her departure for England.

A ferryboat was shuttling back and forth to the busy vessel, and as the seven men shuffled up the gangplank they felt overcome by the sheer thrill and exhilaration of having pulled off a seemingly impossible escape. But Robert's joy was to be short-lived. As the servicemen operating the ferry checked over their papers, one spotted Ant waiting patiently at Robert's heel.

He gave a curt shake of the head. "Sorry, no dogs allowed. Captain's orders."

Robert tried to reason with the man but he was adamant. "Sorry, my friend, but we've had to stop a full colonel for the same reason today. You haven't got a hope." Seeing Robert's face fall, he tried to console him. "He's a good-looking animal; plenty of people ashore will be glad to have him. Gibraltar is British territory, and the people here are dog lovers. Rest assured he won't starve."

Robert understood that the man had his orders, but no way on earth was he about to leave Ant behind. After all they had endured — and after the many ways in which Ant seemed to have safeguarded their journey so far — Robert was not about to be parted from his dog. He handed his gear to Joska and headed back down the gangplank to shore.

Robert and Ant sat side by side on the quayside, the airman resting on a heap of timber, Ant lying in his customary position at his master's feet. Robert stared out at the *Northmoor. So near and yet so far.* He could see their six friends waving to him across the short stretch of water as they neared the vessel. Robert was not only the master of this adolescent pup: he felt as if he had become its father figure, and as if the fates of man and dog were inextricably intertwined.

He felt his dog's eyes upon him. Ant was scanning his face with a searching look. *I thought we were on our way out of here, Dad. So, what's happening?*

Robert reached down and ruffled his dog's ears. "I'm not sure, boy. Give me a few minutes to think up a plan. But one thing's for sure: there's not a hope in hell I'm leaving you behind."

Ant's tail made a few reassuring thumps as he wagged it back and forth, banging it against the woodpile. Then he got to his feet, galumphed over to the water, seemed to gaze from it toward the waiting boat for several seconds, before turning back to the woodpile. Robert watched, fascinated, as the dog chose a piece of wood, pulled it free from the pile, turned back to the harbor, and launched it into the water in the direction of the ship. The current carried the length of wood out toward the vessel, until finally it was lost from view.

Ant turned his head, fixed his master with an intense look, and barked, once, excitedly. *See, Dad, it's not so far. If that dumb lump of wood can make it, so can I!*

"By Christ, you're right," Robert muttered, shaking his head in amazement. "Now, why didn't I think of that?"

The one hundred yards would be an easy swim for Ant. Robert could board the ship, telling the ferry crew that he'd left his dog to be adopted by a local family. Once safely aboard, he could whistle for Ant, who'd be sure to swim out to the ship following his master's call. There was just one problem: fierce arc lights lit up the entire harbor. His dog was bound to be visible in their glare as he waited patiently by the dockside, then dived into the harbor.

For the first time in his life Robert found

113

himself longing for an air raid — for then the arc lights would be extinguished, enabling him to smuggle Ant across the darkened water unseen. Robert reflected upon the incredible closeness that had formed between him and his dog, one that made him actively wish for enemy warplanes to attack. He chided himself for doing so. Good men might die under the German bombs. Their transport to Britain might even be sunk. But such was their bond that he would have welcomed a flight of Dorniers right now.

Robert squatted down and took Ant's head in his hands, staring into the depths of his eyes in the hope of finding some added inspiration there. Ant it was who had first thought up the idea of swimming across the harbor and sneaking aboard the ship, so why not a plan to avoid the arc lights too? But the dog returned a gaze that was as empty and desperate as Robert's. It was as if he was saying: *Search me, Dad. On that one I haven't got a clue.*

Robert let his eyes rove around the dockside. They came to rest on an old and blackened cinder bucket. Now here was a possibility. It was a good two feet high and had a coiled rope attached to it. A plan began to form in his mind, and the more he mulled it over the more plausible it seemed. By the time he got to his feet he was very much a man with a mission. He couldn't be sure it would work. It would be the ultimate test of Ant's obedience, loyalty, and training.

But right now it was the only hope he had of keeping his dog at his side.

SIX

Sailing aboard the Northmoor, *Robert and his stowaway dog were menaced by German U-boats and warplanes, not to mention discovery by the ship's crew.*

Making sure he couldn't be seen from the ferryboat, Robert coaxed Ant into the bucket and carried him across to the quay's edge.

"When I whistle, you come," he whispered to his dog. "But only when I whistle, mind. Then it's time to swim hell-for-leather across the water to that ship. Got it?"

Robert could have sworn he saw his dog nod agreement, and he felt certain Ant had understood. Using the rope, he lifted the bucket, then lowered it from the jetty until it was floating in the water. He could hear the faint slap of seawater against the iron sides as it bobbed about on the calm surface. Tying the rope to a bollard on the quayside, he whispered a soft but firm "stay" to the pair of gleaming eyes gazing up at him. With a whispered farewell, Robert made his way to the waiting ferryboat.

"Sorry I had to refuse your dog, mate," the soldier remarked. "But you know how it is. Orders is orders. Hope you fixed him up all right?"

Robert made no reply, and thinking that he must have been silenced by the sadness of losing his pet, the soldier waved him aboard. As the ferry set out for the ship, Robert cast his mind across the water to his dog. He hoped to God that he wouldn't start howling or crying, as he had done when Robert had once truly tried to abandon him, back at their first meeting in no-man's-land.

Curled up in his floating bucket, Ant would find his world reduced to a small circle of dark sky high above him. Robert heard the sharp cry of a gull echo around the docks, and he prayed that Ant didn't mistake it for the whistle that he was awaiting — the one that would signal him to start his swim to the ship. If Ant set off prematurely there would be no one there to greet him or help him aboard, and the puppy might well drown.

As soon as he had clambered aboard the *Northmoor* Robert hurried to the stern. There a ladder descended into the darkness, where a wooden platform set just above the sea enabled sailors to take a dip after a hot day's work. Robert went down to join them. He waited until the coast was clear, then gave a soft, low whistle across the water — the signal that he hoped and prayed Ant was straining to hear.

Minutes passed and still Robert could detect not the slightest sign of a dog anywhere out in the dark stillness. He was about to give a louder whistle, when the faint but unmistakable sound of a puppy's frantic dog-paddling reached him on the warm night air. First sight of his beloved Ant was a streamlined muzzle sucking in greedy lungfuls of air as it plowed a V-shaped furrow toward the ship's stern.

Robert let out a second soft whistle, to guide the swimmer directly toward him. Seconds later he was able to reach down, grab the dog's collar, and help the dripping animal from the water, whereupon Ant shook himself from head to tail, a shower of water like a breaking wave drenching Robert's uniform. He didn't mind. He was overjoyed to be reunited with his beloved dog of war.

Tucking Ant beneath one arm, Robert carried the dripping hound up the ladder. The deck was packed with refugees from just about every country in Europe, but man and dog soon found their Czech comrades. They were celebrating an unexpected reunion with a dozen fellow members of the Czechoslovakian Air Force. The entire party greeted Robert and his stowaway dog warmly.

"Will you look at that!" Karel exclaimed. "What did you do, bribe the ferryman?"

Robert laughed. "Not a bit of it. You'll get the full story later. For now the question is, where can we hide him?"

It was Karel's turn to smile. "We've thought of that. We've got the perfect place."

Wrapping Ant in a greatcoat to conceal him, Karel led Robert forward to the bow and pointed into the dark and gaping cavern of the ship's hold. "Welcome to Ant's new home," he announced. "With hundreds of people and all their luggage aboard, we won't be carrying much cargo, so there's little fear of him being discovered."

While the others milled around the entrance providing cover, Karel slid Ant out of the bulky greatcoat and handed the sodden dog to Robert, who was waiting at the top of the iron ladder. With the trusting animal slung over one shoulder, Robert disappeared from view. In the darkest corner of the smelly hold the friends had already made Ant a bed. Certain that Robert wouldn't leave him alone down there, they had fixed one for him as well. Ant took one look at the two beds and promptly curled up soggily on the larger of the two, which was Robert's!

The half-grown puppy glanced up from the nest of old sacking and gave a wide yawn. All of that swimming seemed to have tired him out, and he was soon fast asleep.

As the convoy readied itself to sail, Robert kept Ant constant company in the hold.

Each of the Czech airmen set aside a portion of his food so it could be lowered to them by bucket, and Ant was never hungry. But coal dust from earlier cargoes lay everywhere, and even the air was thick with it. Man and dog were used to rough quarters, yet Robert received frequent ribbings from his friends whenever he went on deck. The thick coal dust had formed dark rings around his eyes, making him look as if he'd been in an endless round of brawls.

On the third morning Robert was awakened by the sound of the engines throbbing powerfully through the ship's hull. He hurried up the ladder to find the crew making final preparations for departure. The *Northmoor* moved into its allotted position in the convoy and at 10 a.m. sharp, twenty-eight merchant ships and four destroyers steamed out of Gibraltar harbor. On board were hundreds of ship's crew, thousands of refugees escaping the Nazis, plus one stowaway — the dog that was hidden in the *Northmoor*'s hold.

The steady throbbing of the *Northmoor*'s engines and the thump of the propellers reverberated through the echoing hull. For a man and dog hidden belowdecks it was like being incarcerated inside a giant drum. The noise took some getting used to during their first hour at sea, so much so that when Robert finally pulled his fingers out of his ears he expected to find blood.

The coal dust was getting deep into his lungs and it made him retch. He knew it would be weeks before he shook off the hacking cough that he was developing. Yet while Ant's glossy brown coat had become matted and rough with dirt, he seemed happy enough. He amused himself by rummaging through heaps of debris in the hold and retrieving pieces of wood that he could proudly present to his master.

Ant's golden eyes gazed up at Robert playfully as he darted stiff-legged from side to side urging the game to commence. *Throw it, then! Come on! Cheer up! This is fun!*

On the second day out from Gibraltar the ship's alarm pierced the steady beat of the engines. Warning Ant to stay put and keep quiet, Robert clambered onto the deck. The ship's crew had donned life jackets and were already at their battle stations, scanning the choppy gray waters for the enemy. Uncle Vlasta warned Robert that they were facing a suspected U-boat attack. He could see the destroyers steaming around the fringes of the convoy like sheepdogs shepherding their flock, trying to safeguard the ships from an unseen threat.

The Czech airmen stared at the sea apprehensively, trying to spot any trails of turbulence that might betray an inbound torpedo. As for Robert, he was trying to work out how he could save himself and his dog if a torpedo did tear into the *Northmoor*'s hull. His dog couldn't climb the ship's ladder, so Robert would have no option but to shimmy down and rescue Ant, very likely as torrents of icy seawater poured into the ruptured hold.

Robert's mind was pulled away from such dark thoughts by a muffled explosion that rent the air. One of the destroyers was circling a particular spot in the ocean, violent spouts of white water erupting in her wake. It looked as if one of the U-boats had been cornered. As the *Northmoor*'s passengers cheered, the destroyer continued to unleash her depth charges, but Robert's attention was back to belowdecks again. There, a six-month-old German shepherd with large, pointy ears was secreted in a steel hold that would be ringing horribly from the subsurface explosions.

Robert hurried below. At the bottom of the ship's ladder he found his dog pawing desperately at the steel rungs to escape what had become a clanging metal coffin. Robert rejoined him just as a noise like a thunder-clap punched through the hull. His fingers clamped tight into the dog's thick hair as he clasped Ant closer to him. A rapid series of further detonations followed as a second string of depth charges sown by the de-stroyer churned the ocean into a boiling mass of foam.

Robert knew it was crazy to remain in the hold. If a torpedo did strike the *Northmoor,* the best — perhaps the only — chance of escape lay with those on deck. Down here man and dog would be trapped like the liv-ing dead in a steel tomb. Those belowdecks were always the last out and the least likely to survive. As the ship keeled and buckled under the torpedo's impact, the ladder might sheer off in a cascade of sparks, and there was no other way out. Robert and Ant would be imprisoned together, facing a tor-rent of water as cold as the grave.

But what fate would await his dog if Rob-ert did get him out on deck and the ship's crew spotted him? He was a stowaway, pure and simple. For an instant the ferryman's words echoed through his mind: *We've had to stop a full colonel for the same reason today. You haven't got a hope.* While Robert doubted the *Northmoor*'s crew had the heart to throw his dog overboard, he didn't doubt that Ant's discovery would lead to the two of them being parted, perhaps forever. There was no other option: they'd have to take their chances in the hold.

At least Ant's fear and panic at the underwater explosions seemed to have subsided. The dog he held in his arms seemed completely unperturbed by the ongoing blasts. There wasn't the slightest whimper or tremble as Ant waited patiently for the unearthly clanging to stop. Robert caught his dog's eye, their faces close together in the semi-darkness. The look his dog returned him seemed to say: *it's dark; it's noisy; but as long as you're here with me, Dad, I know I'm safe.*

It was hours before the all clear was finally sounded. It seemed as if the destroyers' spirited action had driven off the German sea-wolves. But no sooner had Robert begun to relax, letting the stress and tension drain out of his system, than the ship's alarm sounded once again. Semaphore signals flashed from the escorting destroyers, ordering the merchant ships to spread out so as to present more difficult targets for the coming attack. A squadron of the Luftwaffe's dreaded Junkers 88 *Schnellbomber*s — so called because they moved too fast to be intercepted by most Allied warplanes — were inbound.

By now Robert had had enough of sitting out such dangers in the hold. He clambered up the iron ladder and emerged on deck, with Ant wrapped around his shoulders. He'd had a bellyful of crouching in that dark and echoing steel sarcophagus, blindly waiting to die. From the southeast, six of the twin-engine fighter-bombers hurtled out of the gray horizon in an arrow-shaped formation. As Robert flicked his gaze over the *Northmoor*'s deck, ship's crew and passengers alike had their eyes cast skyward as the enemy warplanes thundered in to attack. As long as their focus remained concentrated on the heavens, Ant's presence among them should remain undetected.

The destroyers' antiaircraft guns opened fire, peppering dark splotches of flak across the horizon. The black smoke of the exploding shells erupted in the *Schnellbombers*' path. Glowing red trails of tracer threaded a seemingly impenetrable web of fire between the warplanes and the ships. For an instant Robert's mind was back in France, as his Potez 63 dived over the German lines, flying into a terrifying storm of explosions and bullets — yet he felt little sympathy for those German pilots. As they had been back in his native Czechoslovakia, the Germans

126

were the aggressors here, and he wanted nothing more than to see them blasted out of the sky.

After two failed attempts to break through, the Junkers returned for one final effort. This time they swept in low across the waves, in an attempt to remain hidden from the British guns until the very last moment. Wild cheers erupted from the decks of the *Northmoor* as one of the sleek aircraft faltered for an instant, a thick trail of black smoke erupting from its port engine. Ponderously, and chased by fire as it went, the crippled *Schnellbomber* turned for France, its sister aircraft following in its wake. For tonight at least, the German enemy seemed to have decided that discretion was the better part of valor.

But the relief of those aboard the *Northmoor* was to be short-lived. As she'd steamed at full speed to avoid the attacking aircraft, the collier had developed engine trouble. All passengers were to be transferred to a sister ship, the *Neuralia,* for the *Northmoor* would be a sitting target for U-boats if her engines failed completely. Of course, this didn't present a massive drama for all but one of the *Northmoor*'s passengers: Robert. How on earth was he to transfer his beloved dog from one vessel to another without him being discovered?

He settled on a simple solution. He got Ant up on deck again, where man and dog were surrounded by a screen of Czech airmen. Robert knelt down, emptied his kit bag of its contents, which were distributed around the others, grabbed Ant, and lowered him into the bag. With a reassuring pat and a few comforting words he drew the cord tight and tied it off so that Ant couldn't be seen, but had an airhole through which to breathe.

The *Neuralia* pulled alongside and a gangway was lowered, linking the two ships. As swiftly as possible the *Northmoor*'s passengers made their way across to the sister vessel. This was the most dangerous of moments, for the two vessels would make a juicy target for any hidden U-boats. All was going smoothly until Robert reached the gangway. He sauntered across to the *Neuralia,* trying to act as relaxed as he could, but just as he stepped onto the waiting ship his dog chose to wriggle his head out of the opening.

Robert and his dog found themselves face-to-face with three British naval officers and one Czech interpreter. Ant gazed at the four of them happily, his tail thumping out a wag of welcome deep inside the bag. They stared back at him dumbfounded, glancing from dog to Robert and back again. He knew this was it: he'd been caught red-handed trying to smuggle his dog aboard the ship. A sharp reprimand and confiscation of his beloved Ant were sure to follow.

But the reaction of the British officers could not have surprised him more. One of them let out a loud guffaw.

"By Jove! A stowaway!" He reached forward for the dog. "Come on, old chap, out you come! Let's have a look at you, you handsome beast!"

The officer eased Ant out of the bag and gave him a comforting pat. He glanced at Robert, amusement creasing the lines around his eyes.

"You'll have to feed him up a bit . . . He's a right bloody skinny-ribs!"

It was true then. What Robert had heard so many times was indeed the case: the British were a nation of hopeless dog lovers! Robert did the only thing he could think of, so overcome was he with relief: he snapped off his smartest salute to the British officer, then went to join his friends, with Ant trotting at his heels.

In contrast to the *Northmoor*, the *Neuralia* — a former cruise ship — offered real comfort, in spite of the fact that her cabins were so overcrowded. For Robert and his dog — who no longer needed to remain hidden — the onward passage to Britain promised to be one of luxury compared to the *Northmoor*'s sooty hold. Or at least it should have been, had it not been for the other stowaway on board — a monkey!

The *Neuralia* was already carrying twenty-two Czech airmen who were likewise fleeing France, and the new arrivals were reunited with many old acquaintances. One was a good friend of Robert's called Anderle. As matters transpired, Robert and Anderle shared an extra bond aboard the *Neuralia:* each had an animal stowaway in his charge. But for Robert's dog and Anderle's pet monkey it was to prove hatred at first sight.

From its perch above the cabin door the monkey leaped upon Ant as soon as the dog entered, shrieking, clawing, and biting at him for all it was worth. Ant seemed so astonished to be challenged to his first physical fight — and this from an animal the likes of which he had never laid eyes on — that all he was able to do was charge around the cabin with the monkey clinging on like a rodeo star, howling for his master and protector.

By the time Anderle had managed to grab

the monkey's leash and drag the animal off, both Ant and Robert had been bitten. They headed for the bathroom to clean their wounds, only to find that Anderle and the beast had got there ahead of them. A second skirmish ensued, after which Robert decided to settle for the deck. He and Ant ended up taking a position in the open air adjacent to a gun mounted on the stern.

For much of the rest of that day Ant peered over the side of the ship in fascination as dolphins rode the waves churned up by their passing. He seemed to appreciate their company far more than he had the psychotic monkey. That night he slept curled up with Robert, keeping both of them warm as they dozed through the coldest hours. Occasionally, Ant woke Robert with whimpers as he dreamed, and Robert figured evil primates very likely loomed large in his nightmares.

Two days before the *Neuralia* was due to dock in Britain the owners of all animal stowaways were called before the ship's captain, to be informed via an interpreter about the fate of their pets. In addition to Ant and the mad monkey, Robert noticed that several more dogs appeared to have been smuggled aboard.

"Before you land," the captain warned

them, "all animals must be handed over to the ship's authorities. They will be cared for properly. Provided you can pay the fees, they will be sent into quarantine for six months. After that you can reclaim them."

This was the first Robert had heard about Ant's probable fate, and the first inkling he had of a *six-month* separation, not to mention any fees.

"What happens if we have no money, sir?" asked a soldier, pretty much speaking for them all.

"Then I'm afraid your pet will have to be destroyed," the captain replied. Seeing the shock on the faces ranged before him, he added in the most sympathetic voice he could muster: "I can assure you it will be done in a humane manner."

Robert checked with his fellow animal smugglers on the likely quarantine fees. He consulted his fellow airmen and between them they could muster only a few French francs, plus the ten shillings each had been given by the RAF's welfare people upon arrival in Gibraltar. Even after passing a hat around for donations, Robert garnered barely enough to pay the fees for three weeks. He couldn't believe the situation he and Ant found themselves in: having survived so much together, and coming so close to Britain, was his dog to be destroyed for want of money to pay *quarantine fees*?

It was such an ignoble fate for Ant — who in Robert's eyes was truly the world's most fearless dog, not to mention a flying ace, a war veteran, and an aristocrat of the breed. No way could he — or any of his fellow Czech airmen — let this happen. Seated in a circle on the open deck, they kept their voices low as they discussed their options.

"The dog's one of us," Joska reasoned. "He's an *airman*. And his circumstances are utterly different from any other animal aboard this ship. He's the squadron's dog and a fellow flier, and for all we know we eight are all that's left of the squadron. We stick together, come what may."

Uncle Vlasta nodded gravely. "Absolutely. All for one, and one for all."

"Count me in," Karel confirmed.

The others added their words of support.

"But how can we stick together?" Robert asked. "They know I have him, they've read me the rule book, and they'll be watching."

The discussion went around and around. Ant sat with them, cocking his head to one side and then the other and thumping his tail on the deck every time his name was mentioned. Robert could sense how confident his dog was in their collective ability to

133

save him — if only his master shared such confidence.

They had been discussing various stratagems, but nothing seemed to offer their dog even the barest chance of escape. Robert cradled his head in his hands for a moment, resting his face against that of his dog. He stared into the trusting eyes of his faithful companion: *My boy, I do not have the slightest idea what we're going to do with you now.*

As if in answer Ant rose to his feet, wandered over to Robert's kit bag, and started to root out the contents. He crawled inside and glanced back at his master, and in that instant he seemed to communicate to Robert the beginnings of a plan: *Remember — all for one, and one for all.*

"Hold on a minute . . ." Robert glanced at the others, the germ of an idea making his eyes sparkle. "Correct me if I'm wrong, but isn't there a huge pile of our luggage waiting to be off-loaded?"

Karel nodded. "There is. What're you thinking?"

Robert beckoned his fellow conspirators closer, lowering his voice as he outlined a plan. An hour later Ant had vanished completely from view. His protectors had decided to defy the British authorities and to break the law of the country to which they were headed, and upon which they had pinned their hopes of further resisting the enemy. They knew it could jeopardize their future in Britain if they were caught. They might even be arrested or refused entry: but that was a risk they were willing to take to save the eighth member of their fellowship.

All for one, and one for all: that had been the trigger that had set Robert's synapses sparking. Toward the stern of the ship were several large heaps of luggage. They constituted the passengers' worldly possessions, separated out by service and nationality. The Czech airmen's pile was netted down and sheeted over with a tarpaulin. On arrival at the dock, their heap of suitcases and kit bags would be raised up in its net by a quayside crane and lifted ashore.

It was within that netload of luggage that one dog's promise of escape and survival might lie.

Seven

They'd smuggled Ant onto the ship and had to smuggle him off again — for pets were bound for quarantine or destruction upon arrival in the UK.

Under cover of darkness Robert and his fellows mined out a tunnel leading to the very center of the luggage mountain. They removed one large case and placed it on top of the others, replacing it with one dog trussed up in Robert's kit bag, and with only a thin passage leading to the outside. It was too narrow and dark for anyone to see into the center, but wide enough to pass food and water to Ant, depending on how long he needed to be kept hidden in there.

The hiding place complete, Robert urged Ant to stay silent and still, for his very life might depend upon it. That done, they left their dog in the midst of the luggage mountain and prepared for stage two of their plan: outright defiance of British law.

At two o'clock the following afternoon the ship's crew began a final inspection of the *Neuralia*'s quarters, with a view to taking into custody all animal stowaways. When they tallied up at the end of their search, one was missing. Sergeant Robert Bozdech's young German shepherd — the handsome dog with a distinctive black streak running down his backbone — seemed to have disappeared. Robert was called before the ship's officers, but there was little sign now of the amusement that had greeted Ant-the-stowaway's arrival aboard.

"Sergeant Bozdech, we note you have failed to hand over your dog," one of the officers began. "We made it quite clear what the rules are, so where is he?"

The Czech interpreter translated, and Robert gave the best shrug he could muster. "Sorry, sir, I haven't seen him for a good twenty-four hours or more."

The officer fixed Robert with a withering look. "This is a ship. There's not exactly far he can go, is there? So, presumably you must know where he's likely to be?"

Robert shook his head. "Sorry, sir, I couldn't tell you."

The officer paused for a long second, letting the silence hang in the air between them. "Quarantine laws in Britain are strictly enforced, Sergeant. Breaking those laws is a very serious offense."

"I'm not committing an offense, sir. I just can't seem to see my dog."

Robert was choosing his words carefully. Strictly speaking it was true that he couldn't *see* his dog, for right now he was concealed deep within a mountain of luggage.

The officer stared at him as he pondered his next move. "Very well, but don't try to tell us that you didn't know the penalty when your dog is found . . ."

The ship's crew searched the vessel from end to end, flinging open lockers, rifling through closets, lifting containers, and peering behind doors, but no sign of the errant

German shepherd could be found.

Later that afternoon Uncle Vlasta briefed Robert that a Lieutenant Josef Ocelka would be meeting them upon arrival at the Liverpool docks. He was to be their liaison officer for further processing into Great Britain. Lieutenant Ocelka had been persuaded to appoint Joska and Robert himself as the party in charge of disembarking the Czech airmen's luggage and ensuring its safe transfer to the railway station for transport to their new home — Cholmondeley, just outside Liverpool.

"You've been put in charge of *all* luggage," Vlasta repeated, looking Robert meaningfully in the eye. "All luggage is to be disembarked safely from the ship."

"Understood," Robert confirmed.

On the dank early evening of July 12, 1940, the convoy steamed up the Mersey and docked at Liverpool. Thunder rolled over the city as the Czech airmen were separated from the other passengers for their deployment instructions, and rain started to pelt down from a glowering sky. Welcome to Britain. On the quayside a crane creaked and squealed as it took up the strain and then jerked a netload of luggage into the air. Robert gazed up at the load's seemingly perilous progress, wondering what on earth he would do if the cable broke and Ant was plunged into the cold waters of the harbor.

Lieutenant Ocelka, having been tipped off about the smuggling operation, ordered Robert and Joska to move the baggage double-time onto the waiting truck, before the rain soaked it completely. He wanted it out of sight and out of mind before a hidden dog started yapping. By the time they had most of the luggage loaded, Robert had detected not the slightest sign of life from the bulging kit bag in which his dog was concealed.

The last suitcase thrown onboard, he leaped onto the truck's rear and settled down next to the kit bag. He slipped his fingers through the semi-open top, murmuring quiet words of reassurance, and was rewarded by a good few licks from the hidden animal. So far, all was going to plan.

After a short journey they unloaded the luggage and prepared to board the train. But the station platform was milling with British policemen, and worse still, eight of the dreaded Red Caps — British Military Police — were scanning the assembled throng. Few of the airmen doubted that news of a stowaway dog trying to evade British quarantine laws had been passed around the assembled forces of law and order. It was now that Ant — secreted in the kit bag perched beside the Czechs' luggage, and emblazoned with the name *R. V. Bozdech* — had to play his part to perfection.

Just minutes before the Cholmondeley train was due in at the station, a platoon of British soldiers marched onto the platform. They came to a halt in unison right next to the pile of luggage and lowered their rifles with a sharp clatter. The butt of one inadvertently struck a kit bag labeled *R. V. Bozdech,* and a loud and startled yelp issued forth from within. The Czech airmen froze. The British soldiers stared about themselves confusedly. But the Red Caps had also heard the mystery whine, and half a dozen of them began to close in.

The Czech airmen sprang into evasive action. As if eager to be of assistance they started flinging bags to either side, acting like they were searching for the source of the mystery noise. Under cover of the general confusion, one bag marked *R. V. Bozdech* was flung rapidly from hand to hand until it was well clear of the Red Caps' focus of attention.

By the time the military policemen had completed their search, not a sign of a dog was there to find. But they weren't about to be put off that easily. The Red Caps started to fan out across the platform, like dogs on the scent of their prey. Sensing disaster, one of the Czech airmen — the real joker of the pack — went into action. He stepped into plain view, slapped himself hard on the thigh, and let out a yelp like a dog that had just been kicked. He repeated the performance, howling like a beaten puppy as the Red Caps stared at him in consternation.

Eventually one of them turned to the others. "See that bloody Johnny Foreigner taking the micky out of us lot! I've had enough of this lark." He stomped off the platform in disgust, and the other Red Caps followed.

So it was that the search for the contraband canine was abandoned, and Ant was able to finally set foot on British soil. He did so upon arrival at Cholmondeley Castle, in Cheshire, a rest camp for foreign servicemen coming from the chaos and bloodshed of continental Europe.

Cholmondeley Castle was everything that Robert had imagined Britain might be: a vast and rambling mansion complete with turrets, towers, and gargoyles, and surrounded by rolling green hills and verdant woodlands. The tented camp was temporary home to some four thousand non-British

142

servicemen, including those Czechs who would go on to form the Free Czechoslovak Forces — a body of men-at-arms determined to fight the Nazis and liberate their homeland.

Emotions ran high as brother was reunited with brother and soldier with fellow soldier. Ahead of Robert and Ant lay eighteen days of rest and recuperation — time in which to wash and darn their battered uniforms, and for Robert to take Ant on long walks through the grounds, which turned out to be a rabbit-infested paradise. In the evenings Ant insisted on cold-nosing each of the seven airmen's faces, to check that the brotherhood was present and accounted for. Then he'd fall into a contented sleep alongside his master, one punctuated by a snapping of jaws and twitching of limbs as he dreamed of hunting rabbits.

These were good times, but each man sensed that this was a temporary lull — the calm before the coming storm. They had been at Cholmondeley barely a week when the camp was visited by Dr. Edvard Beneš, the former president of Czechoslovakia who was now setting up a government-in-exile. On a misty July morning all present at the camp — including 120 Czech airmen complete with their war dog — assembled on parade, to hear Beneš's speech about the Herculean struggle that lay ahead, one that would surely end in the liberation of Europe.

A week later the first of the Czech airmen received their marching orders. Thirty-six of them — Robert and Ant included — were being posted to the Czech Air Force Depot at RAF Cosford, near Wolverhampton. The remaining ninety formed a cordon of honor around the chosen as they were reviewed by the senior Czech commander at Cholmondeley, a colonel and distinguished veteran of the First World War.

"I envy you the chance you are about to be given," the colonel intoned, his gravelly voice thick with emotion. "Fight for the honor of the Czech motherland, for Great Britain — your adopted home — and strive with all your power to vanquish the Nazi enemy."

The colonel shook each man's hand as he marched past, the seven Czech airmen who made up the original brotherhood forming the head of the column, with one very proud war dog and quarantine buster taking up the lead.

This was a moment of mixed emotions for some. Halfway down that column a gray-haired veteran of the First World War marched with ramrod-straight pride in perfect step beside his two sons. At the front gate he stepped out of the file and, struggling to hide his emotions, smartly saluted his departing boys as they boarded the waiting trucks. He had only recently been reunited with them, but he knew they had to answer the call of duty. He could not have known that before the leaves on the trees had fallen that autumn, both would be dead.

Late that evening the trucks reached RAF Cosford, where the rebirth of the Czech Air Force and its integration into the RAF was being masterminded. Cosford exuded discipline and studied purpose. Two thousand airmen were housed in a large, modern barracks formed of serried rows of wooden huts. A hospital with specialist facilities stood in one corner, flanked by ornamental flower beds. The scale and sophistication of the base convinced the Czechs that the RAF had what it would take to stand against the mighty Luftwaffe.

While Robert was preoccupied with his first assignment — studying a little red book entitled *Fundamental English* — Ant went about befriending as many as possible who might make life as pleasant as it could be in this brave new land. By now he was growing into a magnificent specimen. The black splash down his spine stood out dramatically from his smooth, golden-brown coat, and he carried his head with real pride. His flanks were lean and he moved with the fluid lope of his lupine ancestors. It was perhaps inevitable that he'd make a lot of very useful friends at RAF Cosford, aided in no small part by his master.

One morning shortly after their arrival a member of the Women's Auxiliary Air Force (WAAF) found Ant sitting in her doorway with a letter in his mouth.

"Young lady," it began. "My name is Ant. Will you please shake hands with me?"

Penned by Robert with the aid of his little red book, it was testimony to how well his written English was progressing.

Ant stretched out a paw and made an instant friend in one of the most important places in the camp — the cookhouse. From then on, whenever his nose appeared around the door he could be sure of a warm welcome and some special tidbit. Ant next befriended the two young ladies who called each morning at the base, driving a green van filled with meat. As soon as they'd shaken hands with Ant, a bone fit for a hungry dog was added to their daily deliveries.

Ant's third target was the nurses' quarters.

He soon discovered that the pockets of their starched white uniforms invariably hid the kind of treat that he'd first tasted as a lost puppy on the ends of his master's fingers. *Chocolate!*

One afternoon Robert broke off from his English studies and whistled for his dog to go "walkies," but was surprised to see him bounding over with a pillbox gripped in his mouth. Inside were six of Ant's milk teeth — removed courtesy of one of the nurses — and a note of advice about future dental treatment.

"You know, Robert," one of the Czechs joked, "you should go say thank you to the nurse who cares for your dog. Look — I bet it's that girl with the gorgeous brown hair."

Robert looked where his friend was indicating and felt his heart skip a beat. There, framed in the window, was in his eyes the prettiest woman on the entire base. The Czech airmen had met her earlier, when they'd had their medical examination to ensure they were fit for duty. Her name was Pamela. Her father was English but she had inherited her Spanish mother's olive-skinned beauty. Ever since then they had admired her from a distance, but none had plucked up the courage to approach her.

Robert waved to catch her attention. He

smiled and saluted, and she rewarded him with a brief nod. He gestured at his dog — who was sitting at his feet wondering what had happened to walkies — showed his teeth, and mimed as if pulling one out. Pamela shook her head in amusement, which was all the encouragement that Robert needed.

"Well, come on," he muttered to his Czech friend, "let's write her a note. How do we start?"

"How about 'Dear Nurse'?"

"No, let's promote her," Robert suggested. "Let's put 'Dear Sister.' She'll like that."

A few minutes later Ant trotted over to the window with the note gripped in his jaws.

"Dear Sister," it read. "I am deeply obliged for the service you so kindly gave my dog, Ant. I should be glad if you would give me further advice regarding his health. Yours truly, Robert."

Soon the dog was on his way back with a reply that was both short and sweet: "Very well: 7:30 tonight, here. Pam."

So it was that Ant, barely eight months old, played Cupid for his master and introduced him to his first English girlfriend.

Under Ant's tutelage the romance flourished. Whenever Robert thought it too wet to go walkies, Ant only had to scratch at Pamela's door to summon her, and off they went for a long and romantic stroll in the rain. What Ant particularly liked about those evening sojourns was that Robert was so engrossed in his girlfriend that he forgot all about training his dog. While they held hands and strolled through the lush summer woodlands, Ant was spared the tedious exercises in discipline that his master had started submitting him to, and he could hunt rabbits to his heart's content.

Robert knew that such intensive training would not normally begin until a dog was one year old. But Ant had more experience than most fully grown dogs, and Robert was sure he was ready. He also sensed the need. This quiet period at RAF Cosford couldn't last. Sooner or later they would be moved on to an operational unit. Once Robert took to the air, Ant would be left without him for long periods of time. Absolute obedience while he was away flying sorties was going to be essential, for unlike the French Air Force, the RAF was beset with rules and regulations that were as rigidly enforced as Britain's quarantine laws.

Robert had taught Ant to "sit" and to "stay" at an early age, lessons that had proved vital in the bucket smuggling operation that had gotten Ant safely aboard the *Northmoor.* But to "stay" for a prolonged period of time in his master's absence was a different discipline entirely.

Over fine summer evenings Robert and Ant walked for miles through fields teeming with rabbits, but with Ant forbidden to leave his place at his master's side. At first Ant tired of such exercises, and scampered off for a chase in the undergrowth. But over time he began to master the art of patience, something he would become famous for before the war was over. Eventually, the young bunnies grew so confident that they sat smugly on their haunches, as if to taunt him.

Man and dog reached the stage where they could complete the entire walk without Ant once stepping out of line: his bond with his master had trumped his innate hunter instinct. But whenever Robert stopped for a rest and a smoke, Ant would sit in front of him, whimpering and shuffling his bottom around in such a frustrated way that Robert could not resist. A slight nod, and a muttered *"Rabbits!"* and Ant would turn on his rear and fly, his tail trailing like a flag behind him, and the fields emptying in a flash of white tails.

Their idyllic existence at RAF Cosford ended with a second visit from Dr. Edvard Beneš, who by now had been recognized by the British government as the Czech president-in-exile. The Czech airmen were duly sworn in as serving members of the Royal Air Force and issued their spiffy new uniforms. Their deployments followed. Sadly, the Original Eight were to be split up, the brotherhood of all for one and one for all finally being broken.

Uncle Vlasta alone was to remain at RAF Cosford. Joska, Karel, Gustav, and Ludva were off to join No. 311 Czech Fighter Squadron, based at RAF Honington, in Suffolk. Robert was being sent with Josef — the twenty-six-year-old crack shot of the squadron — to join No. 312 Czech Fighter Squadron at RAF Duxford, in Cambridgeshire.

"It can't be helped," the ever-jocular Joska told his disconsolate brother airmen. "In any case, we're all going to stay in touch, aren't we? How about getting together in London at Christmas?"

A rendezvous was fixed: they'd all meet up on December 23 at the Czechoslovak National House in Bedford Place, in London's West End. Each pledged that nothing would keep him away — but it would turn out to be a rash promise indeed for men heading into mortal combat.

For Robert, the time had come to bid farewell to his sweetheart as well as his five close friends. He and Pamela said their lingering goodbyes in the quiet of an English country lane. Like millions of young couples parted by the war, they were grateful for the magical days they had enjoyed together but terrified that they might never meet again.

So great was the pain for Pamela that as Robert and Ant stood waiting for their train the following day, she appeared on the platform in the hope of snatching a final few moments. Robert could tell by her eyes that she had been crying all night and was struggling even now to hold back the tears. He wanted to take her in his arms and comfort her, but the presence of the others on the crowded platform restrained him.

Pamela did her best to hide her pent-up emotions by taking Ant's shaggy mane in her hands and speaking softly to him, but Ant seemed about as uncomfortable as his master with all the heavy emotion. He shook his head free and bounded about as if seeking one last chance to play. Pamela took Robert's hand, and he felt her grasp tighten as the train rolled in. There was a brief embrace, before man and dog turned away and boarded the train.

"Write to me as often as you can, Robert," she called after him. "Write in your own language! The interpreter will translate for me!"

Touched more deeply than he had thought possible, Robert waved at the forlorn figure until she had disappeared from sight. That image of her would be a constant comfort during the savage months that lay ahead. In the meantime, he soothed his own fevered thoughts by whispering sweet nothings into the ear of a young dog who didn't seem to mind — uttering the kind of words that the airman wished he'd found the time and the opportunity to say to the girl he'd left behind.

The Battle of Britain was nearing its climax by now, and Robert and Josef were expecting a busy time of it at their new base. They had been assigned to a squadron flying the Boulton Paul Defiant fighter, one similar to the Potez 63 warplanes they'd flown over France in that it had a gun turret mounted to the rear of the cockpit. As a gunner, it was Robert's task to operate the turret, and after the long months spent fleeing from France and retraining, he was desperate to get into the air and into action. But there were just two Defiants available at RAF Duxford, and both were presently unserviceable.

RAF Duxford had been hit repeatedly in Luftwaffe bombing raids and aircraft kept getting destroyed or damaged on the ground. All the newly arrived airmen could do was acquaint themselves with the Defiant's turrets and her Browning machine guns, in the hope that they would soon get a chance to use them. Come sundown they had to be ready to sprint for the air-raid shelters as flights of German bombers seemed to fill the skies over Cambridgeshire from dusk to dawn.

The majority of those warplanes were en route to hit the industrial heartlands of Birmingham, Coventry, or Liverpool. Even so, as they roared overhead in the darkened skies Ant demonstrated once again his uncanny powers for sensing distant danger — for he'd cast his eyes skyward and whimper and growl at those roaring monsters of the air.

With Robert and Josef spending a great deal of time in the base armory studying the guns, Ant became a good friend to the armorers. Robert took to leaving Ant there whenever he had to attend briefings — not that they had any aircraft they could yet fly.

One evening the armorers were going about their business with Ant in his customary position — belly-down and dozing beneath one of the workbenches — when all of a sudden the dog rose to his feet and began to whimper.

Ant started to walk backward and forward down the length of the building as if he were somehow trapped, his taut tail whipping to and fro in a clear sign of distress and alarm. The armorers had heard rumors of the dog's incredible early-warning abilities, and they stopped what they were doing to listen for any signs of approaching aircraft. But all they could hear were the throaty tones of a Hurricane's engine being tested nearby.

As they turned back to their work Ant's body went rigid. He unleashed a low, rumbling growl, baring his teeth at the heavens. Finally he lunged at the nearest man, grabbed at his pant leg, and started tugging hard. Ant seemed to be trying to drag the man toward the door, and the armorer could sense the creature's exasperation and near panic. He glanced at the others, anxious not to make a fool of himself over a false alarm. After all, Ant was only a dog.

Finally one of the men suggested they had nothing to lose in heading for the shelters. The man whose pants had been gripped allowed Ant to drag him outside, whereupon they all ran for the nearest shelter. At that moment a lone Dornier *Schnellbomber* came tearing out of the clouds above in a shallow dive, its engines screaming at full throttle. Before the armorers or their dog could reach cover, the *Schnellbomber* leveled off at treetop height, roared across the base, and released its bombs.

Six black objects tumbled end over end, looping their way toward the airfield. Ant could have no idea what they were exactly, except that they had been released by his master's sworn enemy, and that they presaged mortal danger. He raced ahead several paces in front of the armorers, and the last they saw of him was a black streak diving into the bomb shelter. At that moment the bombs struck, the *Schnellbomber* having sown a stick of high explosives across the runway.

Fierce blasts tore across the airfield. Miraculously every bomb missed its target, but for the armorers a vital lesson had been learned. Never again would they ignore RAF Duxford's phenomenal "radar dog." The main impact of that air raid would be on Ant's reputation. Word of the radar dog — who was more attuned to the dangers of approaching German aircraft than the sophisticated tracking systems British scientists had invented — spread like wildfire.

The name of Ant the canine radar was beginning to be heard far and wide.

EIGHT

Several weeks later Robert was transferred to RAF Speke, in Liverpool, to help strengthen the city's defenses against the fearsome nightly bombardment from the Luftwaffe, but still he had no aircraft to fly. Confined to so-called desk duties — and separated from all of his original Czech flying brotherhood — he became disillusioned and listless.

Two things served to break the monotony of those early days at Speke, but neither was particularly welcome. First, a decision was made of necessity to change Ant's name. He'd chosen to chase a black cat up a tree in a nearby terrace of houses. Robert had shouted at and scolded his dog, but the cat's owner had somehow mistaken Robert's calls of "Ant, you fool!" to refer to her — as in "Aunt, you fool." Apparently, the way the Czechs spoke the dog's name it sounded more like the British pronunciation of

"Aunt." The lady cat owner had taken real umbrage and had ended up yelling angrily at Robert.

Everyone had grown very fond of his name, which many took as being short for Anthony. But even so, the last thing Robert wanted to do was rub his English hosts the wrong way. Reluctantly, with the help of his fellow Czech fliers, he decided to change the dog's name by adding "is" on the end — so it became "Antis." It was a minor enough change so as not to confuse the dog, but should avoid any unfortunate misunderstandings in the future. Henceforth that was how he was known.

Second, Robert was involved in a minor car accident and injured his wrist. It wasn't in any way serious, but it meant that he was most definitely grounded. He whiled away the hours with his nose stuck in his *Fundamental English* manual and he found himself daydreaming of Pamela.

The summer nights were starting to grow shorter, and as rain swept over the city from the Irish Sea, Robert's mood grew blacker. He began to neglect even Antis's daily walks. He paced to and fro in their hut with the little red book grasped in one hand, muttering to himself in a variety of tenses as he rehearsed the words he might write to the girl he'd left behind.

"I think I'm getting the hang of this," he'd murmur as he tried a certain English phrase, his spirits rising for a moment. Then he'd glance at Antis slumped in one corner, and as the dog's eyes flicked up from where his head rested on his forepaws, Robert could see more than just a hint of reproach in his look.

"All right, all right — we'll go for a walk tomorrow. Can't you see I'm busy studying?"

It all came to a head a few evenings later, when Antis — hungry for just a sniff of fresh air — gently touched Robert's hand with his paw, as if to remind his master of his existence. Robert responded not by fetching his lead but by wandering across the room, his nose still in his book, and absentmindedly opening the door onto the rain-lashed darkness.

"Go on, then, if you want to go out," he gestured, returning to his seat at the table.

Antis refused to give up. Wagging his tail in hopeful anticipation, he picked up Robert's leather flying gloves in his teeth and placed them in his master's hands. They were the gloves Robert always wore on a cold and wet evening when out walking. His hazel eyes gazed up at Robert anxiously as he tilted his head to one side, trying to fathom what could have so dimmed his master's spirits, and stressed that special bond that existed between them. In truth, Robert was at his wits' end. He lived for one thing only — other than his dog, and Pamela — which was to take the fight to the German enemy. Yet ever since reaching England, he'd not fired a single shot in anger.

Antis gave a few good nuzzles with his nose at Robert's hand, as if to try to dislodge his grip from the hated red book. *Come on,* his expression seemed to be saying, *let's go! Give yourself a break. We both need to get out of this stuffy room.*

"Can't you see it's raining?" Robert remarked. "Anyway, I'm busy. You go. Good dog."

Antis returned to his blanket, which lay at the side of Robert's bed, chased his tail around a few times, then lay down. If his master had been watching more carefully he might have noticed that Antis's eyes came to rest on the little red book, which he was staring at with a resentment bordering on hatred. His mind was made up: *The book has to go.*

The following afternoon Robert returned from lunch in the mess with a plate of food for his dog.

"Looking for someone?" he called as he stepped through the door.

Those few words — first spoken when Robert had turned back to save the no-man's-land puppy dog — had become his and Antis's catchphrase. But instead of the usual bark of welcome there was only an ominous silence. Robert glanced around the room. The place that he had left so neat and tidy that it could have passed an im-promptu inspection looked as if it had been hit by a whirlwind. Strewn around the floor were half-chewed and clawed-up scraps of paper, and Robert quickly realized where they had come from.

His little red book lay in tatters. Its hand-some cover had been torn in half and was streaked with drool, almost as if Antis had spat on it in disgust. Robert stared at his dog for a long moment, struggling to calm himself. Antis was pretending to be asleep, but Robert knew by the twitching of one ear that he was paying attention to his master's every move. Antis opened one eye a fraction to assess his master's mood, but closed it again in a hurry.

"Come here," Robert ordered, in as level a tone as he could manage.

Antis rose awkwardly, the ultimate hangdog expression on his face. He walked slowly toward his master, his paws dragging reluctantly and his tail between his legs. He offered a conciliatory paw to shake, but to no avail. Instead, Robert thrust the wastepaper basket at him.

"Look what you've done," Robert announced. "Look at all this mess." Antis's eyes followed the finger as it traced a 360-degree circle around the room. "Bad dog."

Antis cast his eyes at the floor. It was an extremely rare occasion when his master scolded him. *I know. I have been a bad dog. Very bad. But all I wanted was a walk.*

"Now, Antis, you're going to pick up every scrap of paper and put it in this basket."

To reinforce what he meant, Robert banged the basket on the floor so hard that it made Antis jump.

"Like this." He picked up a piece of paper, held it out to Antis, then dropped it in the basket. "Come on. Every single scrap in here. No food until you're done."

With that, he picked up his gloves and waved them in front of Antis's face, as if hinting that the reward when the task was completed might be walkies as well as dinner. With a deep sigh Antis tried to pick up the nearest scrap of paper in his jaws. Instead, it stuck to his nose. He leaned his head over the wastebasket, flicked out a pink tongue to try to lick it off, but the shredded page of *Fundamental English* was stuck fast. Next he tried to scratch the scrap of paper off with a paw, but he kept missing. This promised to be a long and painstaking process.

Robert meanwhile was watching closely and trying not to laugh. Finally, as more and more of the torn pages got stuck to Antis's nose, Robert's composure failed him.

"What do you look like?" He chuckled. "Have you seen yourself lately, boy? I guess I'd better lend a hand, before those pages stuck on your nose start to suffocate you!"

As Robert bent to the task alongside his dog, Antis vowed he would never again take his frustrations out on one of his master's possessions. But it was to be his unerring ability to sniff out danger and save lives that would fully redeem Antis in the eyes of his master, and that before the very day was out.

After the big cleanup Antis offered his paw to Robert as a gesture of reconciliation. He was not only forgiven, but he was taken on his longest Liverpool walk yet, in spite of the incessant rain. Then came a surprise that banished from the minds of both man and dog any thoughts of *Fundamental English*'s unfortunate fate. Back at their hut Robert wrapped Antis in a warm towel, and he was shuddering with the pleasure of a vigorous rubdown when a messenger called to say there was a visitor at the main gate. It was a lady, she had come to see both master and dog, and as if to deepen the mystery she had refused to give her name.

Mystified, Robert hurried to the entrance with Antis at his heel. He was not expecting a visitor; nor did he know of any Liverpool lass who would be calling at the airfield to see him, for he had barely been at Speke a week. Before he realized what was happening, Antis had dashed ahead of him with an eager yelp. The next thing he knew, his dog was dancing around a woman standing in the shadow of the gate.

As she turned in his direction Robert realized who it was. Pamela. He sprinted over, taking both her hands in his, and stood gazing at her, momentarily lost for words.

"What's the matter?" She laughed. "Aren't you pleased to see me?"

Robert had written to her several times, but he'd never expected anything like this — a visit from out of the blue.

"Is it really you?" he said at last. "I can barely believe it's for real. How did you manage to get here?"

She smiled mischievously. "When I got your letter about the accident, as chief medical adviser to the pair of you, I thought I'd better check out the damage myself, in person!"

A few days ago Robert had written to Pam about the car accident, but it was of so little significance that he'd forgotten all about it. Yet for Pam it had clearly offered the excuse she needed to come looking for them.

"Fair enough, Dr. Pam. We place ourselves — excuse my English — in your disposal. But I hope you haven't run away from your important duties just to see us."

She laughed. "I had a few days' leave owing and I've got a cousin in the area — so here I am."

As the pair chatted, searchlights began to finger the sky above them and an air-raid siren started its banshee wail. A bunch of WAAFs ran past en route to the air-raid shelters. Such alarms were a regular occurrence at RAF Speke, and rarely had the base itself been attacked. The German bombers seemed to be concentrating on the Liverpool docks, several miles away.

Robert and Pam strolled into town arm in arm, with Antis trotting happily at their side. The sirens faded behind them and the searchlights were extinguished. It had been a false alarm. They were halfway to Pam's cousin's house when Robert was distracted from the lady at his side by a whine from Antis. He paused and bent to give his dog a reassuring pat, but recognized instantly the look he saw in those eyes. Antis had sensed danger in the dark skies above them.

There had not been any raids for several nights — only false alarms. But when the sirens had sounded earlier Robert had sensed this might signal the return of the German warplanes. Antis's whining grew louder and he shuffled back and forth anxiously, shaking his head from side to side and staring into the sky. Finally, Robert figured he could hear a faint droning in the distance.

Moments later, as if in confirmation of Antis's early warning, the shriek of air-raid sirens rose above the streets of Liverpool, rebounding off the walls and windows of the empty offices all around them, and searchlights lanced the night. Robert did his best to play down the threat. He didn't want anything to ruin this precious evening. The sinister rumble of the approaching bombers was drowned out by the ack-ack guns on the edge of the city, but Robert remained convinced the bombers would be targeting the docks.

Even so, Pamela seemed mightily relieved when they reached her cousin's house and they were able to duck inside. Several hours and a few good pots of tea later they emerged. The streets seemed utterly deserted, but the angry red smear on the horizon confirmed that Robert had been right. The docks were burning, and anyone who had been living anywhere near them would have been lucky to survive.

They began to retrace their route to the airbase. Halfway there Robert heard an incongruous sound — giggles coming from beneath a viaduct. It was followed by a raucous burst of singing — in Czech. Robert recognized the voice of Stetka, a Czech airman who had joined them at Speke, plus one or two others. Stetka was renowned for spending all of his money in local pubs, and tonight he seemed to have managed to drag most of the other Czech airmen with him.

They, like Robert, Pam, and Antis, were now heading back to base. Detaching himself from his drinking buddies, Stetka crossed the street and bent down to whisper something to Antis. But one gust of his whiskey-laden breath in the dog's face was enough to set off a sneezing fit. Antis backed away, shaking his head to get the alcohol out of his senses.

An instant later, like a gun dog pointing at game, Antis was standing stock-still, head thrust upward and eyes raised to the sky. Robert knelt to pat him but Antis resisted and began to whimper. Then he broke free and performed the back-and-forth shuffle, the one that meant *danger.* When Robert, Stetka, and Pamela failed to react as Antis wanted, he began to dart between them, tugging at their shoes.

"Don't worry, boy," Robert tried to soothe him. "It's the docks they're after. We're safe enough here."

Even as he spoke, he spotted a gasworks some two hundred yards away, the huge tanks silhouetted against the sky. Several times the Germans had tried to bomb it on their way back from the docks. They probably hoped they would incinerate an entire Liverpool suburb if they scored a direct hit. The locals had seen buildings wrecked and families suffer wounded due to the bombing, but so far the gasworks had remained intact.

Robert nodded in the direction of the enormous tanks. "You know, Stetka, I get worried every time I pass this place."

"Me too," his friend replied, instantly sober. "The people who live round here are either ballsy or bloody bonkers."

Even before the sentence was finished the whipcrack of a nearby artillery gun firing rang out, reverberating around the terraced houses. Robert ducked instinctively. He was rattled, but he tried his best not to show it.

"That's got to be Thin Bertha," he shouted to Stetka, recognizing the throaty roar of the artillery piece as it fired again.

Thin Bertha was an antiaircraft gun sited at their airbase. The fact that the gunners were opening fire had to mean there were German aircraft somewhere overhead. Antis was tugging frantically at Robert's heel now. Robert could sense the imminent danger, and he knew that his dog was calling for his master to lead them to safety.

"Come on!" Robert shouted, grabbing Pamela's hand and starting to run. "Into the nearest shelter! No time to get to camp now!"

High above him in the sky he sensed the hollow pop of flares bursting. Moments later the flares were hanging from their parachutes directly overhead, swinging gently to and fro as they burned with the light of a million candle flames. The streets all around them were lit up in a sharp, blinding glow. It reflected off the dull gray of the gas tanks ominously. The German

170

aircraft dropped such flares to light up their targets, which meant that bombs were bound to follow.

In the harsh, ghostly light Robert could see scores of people, their faces contorted with fear, running for the shelters, some with terrified children clutched in their arms. The flares drifted lower, until they were hanging a few hundred feet above the rooftops, throwing the red brick terraces into knife-cut light and shadow.

"We've got to get to the shelter!" Robert roared.

He was unable to conceal his worry any longer, but even as he yelled he heard the high-pitched scream of the first stick of bombs plummeting out of the darkness. With no cover in sight, Robert threw himself flat on the pavement, drawing Pamela down alongside him. Then he grabbed Antis, and pinned the dog beneath his body to shield him from the blast. No way was he about to let the Germans kill or injure his dog, not after all they had survived together. They'd have to get through him first.

To the left and right Stetka and the other Czechs rolled into the gutter, praying that a curbstone no more than four inches high might protect them. The screeching of the bombs turned to a deep-throated roar as the first to strike tore through roof tiles, penetrated ceilings and bedrooms, and smashed into living room floors, before detonating. Dropped with delay fuses, they exploded deep inside their targets, punching out walls in a whirlwind of shattered brick and masonry, and firing debris at the speed of bullets over the heads of those lying prone in the road.

The ground shook horribly as Robert pressed Antis deeper into the gutter, calling soft reassurances into his dog's ear. The raid was over in seconds, though it felt as if it had lasted a lifetime. As quickly as they had appeared, the bombers vanished into the distance. The flares drifted to earth, their burning light replaced by an impenetrable darkness, lit here and there a fierce orange by the fires that had ignited in the ruins of people's homes.

For a moment, all was quiet. Stumbling to their feet, the airmen saw that where three houses had stood before them, only shattered stumps of walls remained. Cries for help mingled with the crashing of falling masonry and the hissing of sparks from severed electrical cables. There were injured in those ruins, and they were screaming for help. They were also in danger of being crushed or burned to death where they lay.

With Antis leading the way, the Czechs ran to the rescue, Robert having sent Pamela off to get help. Choking and gasping, he stepped, half blinded by the dust, into the rubble of the first building. He scrambled over broken walls and splintered furniture, the adrenaline surging through him and numbing any fear he might otherwise have felt: buildings were collapsing all around them. He forced his way toward the direction of the nearest voice, trying to ignore the agonized cries coming from all sides.

We can only help one at a time, Robert told himself.

Antis was scrambling ahead of him, paws scrabbling in the dust. The dog paused atop a mound of rubble, his taut body silhouetted against the glow from a burning building. He dropped his head and let out a sharp bark, which echoed around whatever lay below him. Seconds later Robert had joined his dog. Below was a narrow hole, leading to what Robert presumed was the cellar of the house. The cries were coming from down there.

Using his bare hands, Robert began to scrabble at the smashed brick and tiles, tearing great handfuls away to enlarge the opening. Antis watched him for a few moments, before he too began to paw and scratch away at the smaller stones. From behind them an army officer in uniform appeared with a flashlight. Peering into the hole, by the light of its beam they could see a man at the bottom, trapped by a timber that had fallen across his legs. They dug more fiercely now, calling for Stetka and the others to help. When they finally reached the wounded man it took all of their combined strength to lever the weight off the victim and lift him free. Three of the airmen carried him to a waiting ambulance.

The army officer tapped Robert on the shoulder and pointed farther into the ruins. "Good work, but there's more to be done. Get your dog searching in there."

It seemed as if the officer had mistaken them for a professional man-and-dog search team. Dogs can be trained to search for just about any scent — including buried people — using their noses, which are infinitely more sensitive than a human's. Robert lacked the English to explain to the officer the truth of the situation. In any case, how could he refuse? He looked at Antis for a moment, then nodded his acquiescence. After all, the dog had already proved himself by rescuing the first victim.

Robert took Antis's head in both his hands and gazed deep into his eyes. He gestured first to the hole, then to the rest of the wrecked buildings with an expansive sweep of his hand, trying to convey what he wanted and the import of the task.

"There are lives to save here, boy," he whispered. "Let's go find them."

Antis let out a short, sharp bark of understanding. It echoed across the ghostly wasteland that they were now tasked to search. Taking a leather lead from his pocket, Robert fastened it to Antis's collar and led him farther into the heart of the destruction.

Antis's hypersensitive ears homed in on one sound. It was the pitiful plea for help from someone buried somewhere beneath his paws. Groping his way through a cloud of dust, and with brickwork falling all around, Antis pressed onward. As they crunched their way across a carpet of shattered glass, Robert dreaded to think what it would be doing to the pads of Antis's paws.

Robert caught a barely audible moan now. It sounded like a woman's voice. He couldn't be sure from what direction it came, but Antis was in no doubt. Dragging his master by the lead and keeping his nose to the ground, he came to an abrupt halt and began yelping and clawing at a dusty heap of stones. Robert called for Stetka, and in no time a passage had been cleared. The injured woman was lifted out of a collapsed cellar and carried to the ambulance.

She was scarcely breathing, but at least now she stood a chance. A few minutes later Antis found another victim. A tug on the lead, a sniff, a bark, and a pawing of stones, and that was where they knew they had to dig. In no time, another man had been released from a hole in the ground that could have been his grave. By now, all the assembled rescuers were watching Antis like hawks, for they knew he would lead them to where the next casualty was to be found.

Another rescue followed, and another, each as dramatic as the last. But then came disaster. Antis's instincts had just led him to discover his sixth survivor, and he was sniffing and snuffling at the ground for more. Robert had him on a loose lead so as not to inhibit the search. But as Antis thrust forward several feet ahead of his master, there was an almighty crack. Before Robert knew what was happening, a wall had collapsed straight ahead of him.

As Robert went to try to drag his dog back, the lead came away in his hand. It had been sliced in two by the falling masonry. For several seconds Robert stood there dumbfounded, the severed strap dangling from his hand. He was dazed by the speed of the calamity. One moment, Antis had been just in front of him. The next, he had vanished and all Robert could see was a heap of bricks and mortar.

Dropping onto his already shredded knees, he seized the first brick in a hand that was gashed and covered in blood and began to dig, frantically tossing bricks to either side. Stetka knelt beside him, scrabbling at the heap in a frenzy. Robert felt certain that his dog had been crushed. If the weight of the falling masonry hadn't killed him, the lack of oxygen under all that rubble certainly would. The very thought seemed to drive him out of his mind.

In answer to an unspoken prayer, Robert heard a faint bark. The airmen tore at the bricks with a redoubled effort, and finally a pointy nose came into view. It was dusty and flecked in shattered masonry, but it was definitely still twitching. As they pulled more debris away, Robert was overjoyed to see Antis turn his head his way, shaking the dirt and dust from his ears as he did so. The next moment Antis gave an almighty sneeze, and he leaped to his feet, seemingly unharmed.

Robert began to sob. He didn't care who saw the tears coursing through the dust that coated his cheeks. Antis was alive and that was all that mattered.

He was more than ready to call it a night after such a miraculous escape, but Antis had other ideas. He insisted their job wasn't done. He was going to follow the trail he'd picked up just before the wall collapsed, no matter what.

Antis stepped ahead, nose down and nostrils puffing away like a pair of bellows as they vacuumed up the dusty scent. At his side Robert had hold of the frayed remains of the severed lead. Antis came to a halt beside a small bundle of clothes. He had sniffed out a tiny toddler, no more than a year old. Nearby lay the child's mother. There was nothing that anyone could do for her, but the little toddler seemed as if she might live. Once again, due to Antis's incredible canine abilities, hope flared among the ruins and the fearful darkness.

It was well after midnight when an exhausted Robert arrived back at camp. For the last few hundred yards he'd had to carry his dog, so painful had his paws become to walk on. They went straight to the sick bay, where Robert began to painstakingly clean his dog's cuts and bandage his bleeding paws. He spoke softly to him throughout, telling him what a good boy he was and how well he had done, and that he was a lifesaving hero. Not until he'd finished tending to Antis did Robert accept any treatment for his own gashes, scrapes, and bruises.

Robert's malaise had truly been broken. This dark night had reminded him how he needed to put his dog first, every time.

NINE

Ant became 311 Squadron RAF's official mascot. But when German aircraft bombed the airbase he was blown up, lost and buried in debris for several days.

The remaining few days that Robert and Pamela had together were spent attending to Antis's recovery, with plenty of romantic interludes. Her departure hit Robert harder than he had expected and he began to wonder if he was falling in love. But the shock of that was as nothing compared to the hammer blow of the letter he received the following day, from RAF Honington.

His old friend Karel had written to tell him that Joska, the bright young flier who had first thought up Antis's name, and helped him to evade the military police upon arrival in Britain, was dead. He had been crewing a Wellington bomber that was hit by enemy fire. The aircraft had burst into flames and become a funeral pyre for Joska, plus the five other Czech aircrew, as it plummeted from the heavens.

Joska it was who had pledged to organize the Christmas reunion for the seven Czech airmen and their war dog — the Original Eight. *All for one, and one for all.* But like many such pledges during the war, it had proved impossible to uphold. Joska would not be the only one to miss the party. Just days later Robert received a second letter, this one informing him of the seemingly impossible. Karel — the handsome Casanova of their party, and the one who had come back from the dead once before — had vanished, likewise killed in action. He had exulted in life's pleasures for just twenty-four years and now he was gone.

In their candlelit hut, Robert and Stetka,

plus Jicha and Mirek, two fellow Czech airmen, held a customary wake as they speculated about how many of their number might survive the horrors of this war. One operational tour of duty constituted two hundred hours of flying, and neither Joska nor Karel had reached the halfway point of their tour. For Robert the news of their deaths brought one emotion that overrode all others: in spite of the seemingly unbeatable odds, he hungered to get into the air and take the fight to the enemy. The eight had become six, and he burned to avenge the deaths of his fellows.

Antis dozed at his master's feet, lulled by the somber hum of the conversation and keeping no more than half an ear alert for trouble. But suddenly it was as if a pistol had been fired next to his head. The comatose dog sprang to his feet, and dashed to the door with ears pricked forward. Cocking his head, he listened intently, raising nervous eyes to the sky. Apparently satisfied that he wasn't mistaken, he hurried across to Robert, whining in what had now become an all-too-familiar fashion.

But Robert and his friends were absorbed in their somber conversation and burdened with the news of the deaths of their comrades. In any case, the air-raid sirens had sounded at about this time for several days in a row now, and the target had always been the docks. Why would it be any different this evening?

Robert reached for his dog and gave him a reassuring rub around the ears. "It's all right, Antis," he soothed. "They're not coming here."

But his dog shook his head free and fixed his master with an electrifying look: *It's not all right. It really is not. Trust me, the monsters of the air are coming.*

He pushed his nose under Robert's hand and pressed his trembling body against his thigh, trying to shove his master into motion. Robert focused his senses on the skies above and listened hard for a moment, but he could hear nothing out of the ordinary.

"Don't worry, Antis. I'm telling you — they're miles away."

In answer, Antis seized Robert's hand in a near-painful grip and forced him to look into his eyes. The magnitude of the alarm the dog was feeling was palpable.

Robert sighed. "Okay. All right, boy, you know best." He turned to his friends. "I think we'd better go. Antis seems too convinced to have got it wrong this —"

The words froze on his lips as a thunderous roar vibrated the hut's flimsy wooden walls. Every one of the airmen knew that sound. The engines of a Dornier Do 17 bomber — the "flying pencil" — had been opened to full throttle, indicating that it had just leveled out from a dive and was coming over the airbase at low level.

No siren had sounded.

No gun had been fired.

The only warning had come from Antis.

The pitch of the engine noise changed slightly. "He's already dumping them!" Stetka shouted, but his voice was drowned out by the detonations of a stick of bombs.

The force of the explosions rocked the hut on its foundations as if it had been hit by a tornado. Stunned and half deafened by the blasts, the men and their dog had been flung across the floor. The candles had all gone out, and Robert heard Antis yelp as someone fell on top of him in the darkness.

"Antis, I'm here!" Robert cried, crawling on all fours toward his dog.

Antis rushed toward the sound of Robert's voice and the two of them had a head-on collision over the floorboards.

"Into the shelter before he comes back," one of the others shouted.

By the time they had rushed for the door, they could hear the faint roar of the Dornier inbound toward them once more. Worse still, the door had been warped by the force of the explosions and would not open. They tugged and shoved at the handle but it refused to budge.

"Stand clear," Stetka ordered.

He was the biggest and burliest of them. He charged at the door, shoulder down, and tore it from its hinges, landing in a heap outside. By now the bomber was coming in on his second run. The airfield's guns were in full cry and the searchlights had swung into action, but on the ground there was scant relief or shelter.

In the brilliant glare of the searchlights Robert spotted the Dornier in silhouette, racing toward them. The last he saw of Antis he was one hundred yards in front, tearing toward the shelter. But then he halted and began searching all around in confusion, seeking his master.

"Get in the shelter, boy!" Robert yelled at him. "The shelter!"

The pilot of the Dornier was clearly a highly experienced combatant. He'd flown in for a second attack knowing the base's defenders would be ready and waiting, but with his aircraft down to no more than fifty feet. At that altitude the aircraft would be over the airfield and gone almost before the gunners on the ground had time to open fire. The bomber skimmed the very treetops as it roared in, the dark night lit up by the aircraft's 7.92mm machine guns spitting fire.

Robert, Stetka, Jicha, and Mirek urged their legs to move faster as the bullets tore up the ground all around them, but it was clear they weren't going to make the shelter before the Dornier unleashed its bombs. With six dropped already, it would have up to fourteen more fifty-kilogram high-explosive bombs to deliver. If they were caught in the open as blasted shrapnel tore across the airbase, the Czechs were dead men.

"SHELTER, ANTIS!" Robert roared, trying to make his voice heard above the cacophony.

He gesticulated wildly at the gaping mouth of the underground shelter, which lay one hundred yards away. The dog was right next to the entrance. If only he would stop staring at his master and look to his side, he'd see safety. He could be in there in a flash.

The Dornier's nose dipped a fraction and for an instant Robert thought the pilot had miscalculated: it looked as if he was going to crash into them. Robert hurled himself flat, fearing that he was about to be smashed apart by the body of the warplane, or sucked into the vortex of fire that would result if it plunged into the ground. He dug his fingers into the juddering earth as the Dornier went howling over his head, bracing himself for the blasts he knew were coming.

As the Dornier powered away, the stick of bombs it had dumped in its wake hit. For a second or so nothing happened. The delay fuses had been triggered, but not yet detonated. Then the first blast erupted from the direction of the hut they'd only just vacated, forcing Robert to try to dig his body deeper into the earth.

The second explosion was closer still, and with each the danger seemed to be drawing nearer. He tried to calm his mind with the image of a bushy tail vanishing down the shelter's steps and out of sight. But the force of the final bomb blast was so intense that he felt as if giant needles were being driven into his eardrums, and as if his eyeballs were being crushed in their sockets.

Moments later there came a flash so brilliant that even though his eyes were screwed shut, the light bled through and half blinded him. He was plucked into the air, as if by a giant hand, flipped over, and flung back to earth. A nearby fuel dump had gone up. The sensation of flames roaring overhead faded as Robert sensed himself slipping into a dark abyss.

"Robert! Robert! Are you all right?" It was the voice of Jicha, who hailed from a neighboring village back home in Czechoslovakia.

There was a terrible ringing in Robert's ears and a painful throbbing in his temples. He felt horribly confused. If that was Jicha's voice, was he in his native Czechoslovakia? Were the Germans bombing his village? If so, where was his mother? As he opened his eyes and the confusion began to clear, he realized where he was. He had only one thought burning through his mind now.

"Has anyone seen Antis?" he blurted out.

"Never mind your dog, how the devil are you?" Jicha replied. "You were tossed into the air like a rag doll . . ."

Robert was so deafened that he could see Jicha's lips moving, but he couldn't hear the words.

"Have you seen Antis?" Robert repeated. "Is he okay?"

"He'll be fine," Jicha answered. "That one's a real survivor." He spat out some more of the soil he'd been forced to swallow as the blast washed over him. "I'm sure Antis is okay. I think I saw him dashing into the shelter."

"No wonder he left us to it," said Stetka, holding a blood-soaked handkerchief to his forehead. "Serves us right for refusing to listen to him in the first place!"

"He didn't leave us," Mirek remarked gravely. "He wouldn't do that. I was watching him. He got to the shelter entrance and then he came running back toward us, like he was trying to show us the way. He couldn't have been more than ten yards away when the last bomb went off."

The airmen stared at one another in a worried silence. Robert rolled onto his side and hauled himself painfully to his feet. He'd understood the gist of what Mirek had said and he felt overcome by a heavy sense of apprehension. He and his friends had suffered nothing more than sprains, bruises, and cuts as a result of the attack. But their hut had been reduced to a pile of smoking matchwood. And as for Antis — the hero dog who had warned them to save themselves — there was no sign of him.

Robert staggered across to the nearest shelter, dreading that at any moment he might stumble over a deadweight of mangled flesh and fur.

He leaned into the entrance. "Has anyone seen my German shepherd?" he called.

A face appeared. "Sorry, mate, hardly

189

anyone down here. I'd definitely know if we had a dog."

Robert felt real fear — icy and raw — tearing at his guts. Mirek was right about one thing: Antis hadn't made it into the shelter. If Mirek had been right about that, maybe he had seen what he said he'd seen. Maybe Antis had been caught in the Dornier's blast as he was running back to join them.

With the adrenaline surging through him, Robert ran toward a second shelter a little farther on. Antis was a regular visitor there, for this was the shelter most frequented by the women of the base. He loved their company not only for the fuss they made over him, but also for the American sweet cookies they kept as doggie treats. If there was one place he would have felt safe, it was here.

But even as he hammered on the thick steel door, Robert sensed that his efforts were going to be in vain. If Antis had reached this shelter, his scratching and barking would have been drowned out by the roaring of the Dornier's engines and the barking of the guns, not to mention the explosions. Finally the door swung wide. Robert was mystified to see that the lady who'd opened it didn't seem to recognize him.

"Excuse me, have you seen Antis?"

"Robert? Is that you?" she gasped. "My goodness, your face is cut to shreds."

It was the first he knew of it. "Antis," he repeated, not bothering with an explanation. "Have you got him?"

"He hasn't been here tonight. The last I saw of him was earlier this evening. But come inside and let me clean up your poor face."

Robert raised his fingertips to his chin, which was scraped raw. He felt blood trickle down from his nose, which was bleeding profusely. But as long as his injuries weren't life threatening, he didn't really give a damn. He refused the offer of first aid, turned away, and went back to the search.

It was well after midnight by the time the last of the German raiders had been chased from the skies above Liverpool and the all clear was sounded. A thick veil of smoke lay across the airbase, but the extent of the devastation was revealed here and there by the light of a pale moon. Full of grim forebodings, the four comrades continued the search by picking through what was left of their hut. Perhaps Antis had ended up there, searching for his master and his friends in the place where they'd last been together?

But in among the mangled wreckage there was no sign of their dog.

The ruins of neighboring buildings were searched next. The airmen picked their way through twisted door and window frames, shattered masonry and brick, and splintered wooden planking, but not so much as a clump of hair was to be found. They were about to move on to their third mound of wreckage — all that remained of another of the huts — when a cry went up.

"Bomb! Unexploded bomb! Move right away!"

Before they knew it, they had been ordered to abandon their search, and the area had been cordoned off.

"Don't worry, he'll turn up," said Mirek, trying to comfort a distraught Robert. "He always does, doesn't he?"

"Perhaps the explosions frightened him off," Jicha added soothingly. He swept his arm across the fields on the outskirts of the base. "He's probably out there somewhere hiding in the countryside. He'll calm down and come back, you'll see."

Robert knew that they meant well but he didn't share their sense of optimism. Air raids were nothing new to Antis and he had never deserted his master before. Robert allowed himself to be led away to some emergency accommodation, but all the while he couldn't help wondering whether Antis was lying somewhere amid all the destruction, alone and wounded and unable to move.

The thought was unbearable.

Once Robert had been patched up he ignored the nurse's advice to rest and began to jog around the fields, calling and whistling. He was dying to hear that familiar hearty bark that he knew so well, without really expecting to. He felt a dark foreboding that his dog was in real trouble — the worst that he had ever been in, including being abandoned in no-man's-land as a tiny puppy.

After fruitless hours of searching he ended up outside the NAAFI building (the base's Navy, Army, and Air Force Institute's shop and bar), cold, exhausted, and close to despair. He was certain that Antis had to be somewhere within the cordoned-off area of rubble and debris, for it was the only part of the base that he hadn't checked. He was growing more and more frustrated that the white ropes meant that he couldn't look, and he was tempted to go in anyway — unexploded bombs and all.

The shadows deepened and the dank autumn air chilled him to the core, but still

Robert rejected his friends' pleas to go inside for something to eat and to get warm. The thought of both food and comfort turned his stomach, when his dog was out there somewhere cold and hungry, and possibly dying.

"Suppose Antis does reappear," he told them. "What then? The hut's been flattened and he won't know where we are. I'm going to wait for him."

He was still at it at first light, quizzing the bomb-disposal team and anyone else who came near whether they had seen his dog. At long last the unexploded bomb was removed. In spite of the torrential rain that had begun to fall, a party of volunteer airmen descended on the area, working systematically and searching it from end to end. No sign of Antis could be found. Filthy, sodden, and exhausted, they tried to comfort Robert, but he was inconsolable.

Antis seemed to have disappeared off the face of the earth and it tortured Robert to have lost him. How could it be possible? he wondered. He was a big, strapping German shepherd, and approaching fully grown now. Even after a direct hit there was still much of a human body that would remain. People — and dogs — didn't just get vaporized.

Robert managed no more than two hours

of fitful sleep that second night. He kept reaching out to the blanket that lay beside his bed — Antis's blanket, which he'd retrieved from the wreckage of their hut — hoping beyond hope to discover a warm and furry body lying there. But of course there was none.

At first light the following morning he sat in the dining hall with breakfast uneaten, trying to come to terms with the fact that he would very likely never see his dog again. To make matters worse, he would likely never know what had happened to him, or even be able to give him a proper burial. He had rescued the dog from no-man's-land, but ultimately he had failed to save him from enemy action.

He would never be able to forgive himself, no matter how long he might survive this terrible war.

Ten

"Bozdech!" a voice shouted from the doorway of the mess. It was one of the squadron sergeants, and Robert feared he was wanted for some inane duty or other. "Bozdech!" the voice cried again. "There you bloody are! Why didn't you answer?"

Robert sighed. He'd been spotted. There was no escape now.

"You're wanted outside, Bozdech," the sergeant added. "Look lively."

Leaden-footed, Robert reached for his gas mask and cap and shuffled toward the door. If he hadn't been so downcast, he might have noticed the excitement in some of the faces around him. The sergeant walked ahead of Robert so that he would not miss the scene that was about to unfold.

The first thing Robert saw when he emerged from the hall was a large group of men and women, standing around in a circle, smiling. When he looked down, he gave a strangled shout. There, sprawled on a mat, sodden, mud-caked, and so weak that he could barely raise his head, was Antis, whimpering at him.

Where were you, Dad, where were you? his eyes seemed to say. *I waited and waited and waited . . .*

Robert fell to his knees before his dog. Oblivious to those around him, he clutched Antis to his chest, murmuring choked words of reassurance in the dog's ear.

"I couldn't find you, Antis . . . I looked everywhere." He was fighting to keep his emotions in check in front of so many people, but it was no good. Throwing his arms around his dog's neck, he buried his face in his sodden hair and felt his tears flow.

As word of Antis's miraculous return spread, the mess hall emptied so all could cheer the reunion. But when they saw the outpouring of emotion from the Czech airman, and the pitiful state of the dog, they fell respectfully silent. One by one they paid their respects and drifted away, the toughest warriors among them profoundly touched.

Robert ran his hands over every inch of Antis's body to check for broken bones. He received a perfunctory lick for his trouble. It was all Antis could manage. Relieved that there was no obvious sign of injury apart from the many cuts to his legs and head, Robert gathered his dog in his arms and took him to the sick bay. Only as he carried him across the airfield did he notice the tears in the sensitive pads of his paws.

The following morning he finally felt able to leave Antis to rest. He returned to the bombed-out ruins to investigate what might have happened to his dog. Paw marks in the mud led him to a deep crater thirty yards from the air-raid shelter. It had been made by a bomb dropped from the Dornier on its first run, while Antis and the Czechs were still in their hut. Yet on one of the heavy chunks of concrete at the bottom of the crater Robert found a handful of dog fur and dark smears of blood. From there he began to piece together the mystery of Antis's fate.

The explosion that had lifted Robert off the ground on the Dornier's second run must have blown Antis high into the air — high enough in fact to blast him over the roof of a nearby hut and into this crater. When that hut had been blown up, debris from it had been blasted on top, covering but not quite suffocating the dog. That was how he had come to be so totally hidden from view.

Robert tried to imagine what it must have been like for him, lying dazed and frightened in the darkness. With no room to move, he must have felt walls of mud were pressing him into his grave. He would have been fighting for breath and struggling to rise to his feet, only to realize that the weight of the rubble pinning him down was too great.

Robert had never once seen Antis panic, but had he sensed in a moment of claustrophobia that he was about to suffocate? He must have pushed again with his head and legs to create the smallest of breathing spaces, even as the earth forced its way into mouth and nostrils. He would have heard Robert and the others whistling and calling his name as the buildings were searched all around him, but he must have been so crushed as to be unable to respond.

It would have been a nightmare for the dog, and doubly so when he heard his master and his friends giving up the search. How he stayed alive there for two whole days Robert couldn't imagine. Perhaps an occasional draft of fresh air had filtered through. Some of the drizzle that had fallen the first night might have permeated the dog's would-be tomb, providing the odd lick of moisture. But he would not have survived without being able to draw on the extraordinary inner strength that Robert had always known his dog possessed. In fact, he'd sensed it from his very first sight of the dog, as a tiny, growling puppy in no-man's-land.

Antis's will to live — the thing that had attracted Robert to him in the first place, in that war-blasted farmhouse in France — must have somehow seen him through. Maybe the heavy rain that had fallen had dislodged some of the debris, allowing Antis to breathe more easily and to lap up some much-needed moisture. Or perhaps he had finally realized that nobody was coming for him, and that only he could save himself.

Either way he must have mustered all his remaining strength for one last super-canine effort. The marks on his paws indicated that he had scratched, kicked, and clawed his way to the surface. There, he had been spotted by a couple of passing mechanics. He was so thin and his coat so matted with mud and blood that they had thought he was some stray dog that had wandered onto the base.

"Hang on a minute," one of them had said. "Isn't that Antis?"

"No way," his companion had replied. "Antis's much bigger and nowhere near that dark."

It was only when the dog had limped

toward them, his tail wagging feebly, that they had realized who exactly they had found.

Robert nursed Antis back to recovery, rejoicing in each sign of his return to good health. The wounds healed quickly enough and the spring gradually returned to the dog's step, boosted by scraps of meat from his many admirers in the mess hall, plus even more sweet cookies than usual from the NAAFI.

The less Robert worried about Antis, the more he yearned to get back into the air. Thankfully, the long wait to go into action against the German enemy was almost over. Everyone knew that the ranks of Allied Bomber Command were dwindling fast. As the RAF's raids on enemy territory intensified, their losses climbed at a dizzying rate. Bold, brave airmen were needed to fill the vacancies, and Robert had no hesitation in putting himself forward. Along with Stetka and Josef, he volunteered to join No. 311 (Czech) Squadron. Their base would be Honington, in Suffolk, where both Joska and Karel had served before they were killed. Their volunteering for duty would be driven in part by a desire to avenge the deaths of their friends.

The rules dictated that Bomber Command volunteers be given forty-eight hours with their wives or sweethearts before they moved to their squadron. Robert leaped at the chance to pay Pamela a surprise visit. He hoped the delights of an unexpected two days together would soften the blow she would doubtless feel when he told her about his new assignment. The dread would remain with her every day until the end of his tour, but he felt certain she would understand.

Robert and Antis arrived at Lime Street Station in high spirits to catch their train to Cosford, in Shropshire. But as he paced up and down the platform, Robert was disappointed to find that there was little chance of getting a spot on the train where his recently injured dog would be out of the way of other passengers. The corridors as well as the carriages were full to bursting, with dozens of soldiers and civilians still pressing to clamber aboard.

Resigning himself to an uncomfortable journey, he headed for the baggage car, where at least Antis would not prove a nuisance to any passengers who disliked being smeared with dog slobber. Before he could follow Antis into the car, however, Robert was stopped by a porter. At first he thought he was going to be told that the car was out of bounds for passengers, let alone dogs. But the porter smiled in friendly fashion, beckoned him to follow, and led him to the far end of the platform, where the first-class cars awaited.

Turning his back to the crowd so he wouldn't be seen, the porter thrust two first-class tickets into Robert's hand, and with a raised finger to his lips — urging silence — he turned and walked away. Astonished, Robert stood there for a moment, fearing it had to be a case of mistaken identity. He tried checking the names on the tickets, but of course there were none — just the seat numbers. Feeling uncertain whether to board, he was startled by a voice as sleek and smooth as satin, speaking to him in his own language.

"This way, my friend," the voice purred. "There's plenty of room for you and that handsome hound of yours."

Robert turned to see a young woman with striking, almost haughty features and perfect white teeth smiling down at him as she leaned from the carriage. Whether by luck or design, her cashmere coat had parted at the neck to reveal just a glimpse of her femininity. Robert's gaze fell momentarily on her tight, white blouse — he couldn't help himself — before he flicked his eyes up to meet hers. He couldn't quite fathom her mischievous expression and the heavy makeup, framed by chestnut-colored hair with the show-pony sheen that only a well-groomed woman can achieve by brushing one hundred times a day.

He opened the door and followed her swishing skirt as she led him up the aisle. What really entranced him, though, was the *click, click, click* of her black heels. If Robert was honest he liked a nice pair of heels, and these were high — much higher than anything he had ever seen on Pamela. As she seated herself opposite him in the plush compartment, he saw that those distinctive clicks had come from the type of shoe that was all the rage right then, called "peep toes." The red polish on her immaculate toenails matched her perfect lipstick.

Robert felt an illicit tingle burn through him. He was about to introduce himself when Antis poked his head around the compartment door.

Forgotten someone?

"Antis," Robert remarked, spreading his arms wide in welcome.

The dog barged in, took a couple of steps toward him with tail down, and flopped huffily onto the floor.

You! You left me on the platform. What's going on? Who's she? She's not our Pamela, I know that much.

"Antis, I'd like you to meet . . ." Robert began.

"Ann Arbuthnott." The woman stretched out a manicured hand and Robert shook it gently. Warm, smooth skin. Dazzling red nail polish, the same as the toes. He was going to have to contain himself. It felt like such a long time since he had touched a woman.

"Robert Bozdech." He treated her to his most charming smile. "Thank you so much for the tickets . . . I presume you —"

"It's nothing," she interrupted, brushing his thanks aside with an elegant wave of the hand. "In any case I must confess to an ulterior motive. You see, I spent eleven years living in Czechoslovakia. My father worked at the British embassy in Prague. When I saw the Czech flashes on your shoulders, I couldn't resist the chance to show off my knowledge of your language."

Robert smiled. "Fair enough. You do speak beautifully." He hoped this did not sound too forward.

"I wish I could trust what you are saying is true," she murmured.

Was she being coquettish? Fishing for compliments? He could only imagine that

205

she was; her Czech was near perfect. In any case, he wondered, was this really all about a bit of impromptu language practice? After all, even if he said it himself, he did look rather dashing in his uniform, the one he had ironed specially for his forthcoming visit to Pamela. Plus Antis remained as handsome as ever, in spite of having been blown up and buried for several days in a bomb crater, one that by rights should have been his grave.

Normally, Antis proved an irresistible source of fascination and a draw to pretty women. On that note Robert decided introductions were long overdue. "This is Antis. Antis, meet Miss Arbuthnott."

Ann reached out to pat the dog's head and Robert waited for Antis to put on the killer show that he always did when he met an attractive woman. But instead of sitting up and offering his paw — which in turn gave Robert the chance to utter a few well-rehearsed jokes — he stared coldly at Robert's new acquaintance with her peep-toe shoes. He flung his master a momentary look, one full of accusation and almost . . . of loathing.

So, I figure you've made no mention of who we're actually off to see today — of PAMELA.

Ann tried to laugh it off, as did Robert,

but she was clearly unaccustomed to being treated with anything other than rapt attention. She must have decided to bribe her way into Antis's affections. Pulling a chocolate ration from her bag — something doubly precious in the midst of this interminable war — she slit the wrapper with one of her red nails and peeled a piece away.

But it was as if the smell of the chocolate and the swaying of the railcar transported the dog instantly back to the south of France and the long and dangerous stop-start train journey he, Robert, and the other Original Eight had shared when they were fleeing from the Germans. He snorted in disgust at the slab she offered him, turned his head away, flopped onto his outstretched forepaws, and pretended to go to sleep.

Got the message, lady?

Robert flushed with embarrassment, like a father whose adolescent son has just been rude to a new acquaintance. He resolved to make up for his dog's indifference by being as attentive as possible, but a part of him almost felt like laughing at his dog. *What is it, Antis?* he felt like saying. *Surely you can't be jealous?*

He recounted to Ann their French escapades fleeing from the Germans in such a way that he hoped it would half explain his dog's behavior. For two hours the pair of them swapped stories in Czech, each warming to the other's tales. The war had forced both of them to leave a country that they loved. They had led very different lives at opposite ends of the social spectrum, but they shared a deep affection for that country. Neither knew what the future might hold for Czechoslovakia, but they relished the chance to reminisce and to dream dreams of hope.

Antis kept snuffling and snorting as if in disgust at the growing closeness between them. *Please, get me out of here.* He tried whining softly, hoping to attract his master's attention, but Robert was in no mood to indulge him.

"Be a good dog and keep quiet," he said, turning back to Ann.

Antis's whines increased in volume. *No, seriously — get me out of here. I need to go for a pee.*

There was no response. Robert was so wrapped up in Ann that he was ignoring his dog. Antis loped off up the corridor of the first-class compartment, his tail hanging unhappily between his legs, but there was nobody to heed his needs as his master should have done. In any case, the train was hurtling through the countryside, and there was no chance of stretching his legs until the next stop, or of taking a pee.

A few minutes later he was back at their seats, whimpering at his master with added urgency, and staring with renewed resentment at the woman who monopolized his attentions. He pawed at Robert's hand, hoping that the deeply troubled expression in his eyes would elicit some kind of notice. But the woman was laughing at one of her own jokes, and Robert was joining in the laughter. Then he said something about her joke that made her laugh all the more.

Antis made one last go of it. He let out a long piercing whine — the one that meant *do something, now, or else* — but Robert didn't break off the conversation for a moment, or even glance at him.

That's it. I've had enough.

For Robert the first sign that anything was amiss was when Ann's smile vanished from her face. The perfect white teeth disappeared behind ruby-red lips that were curled in horror. The sparkle in her eyes was replaced by shock. She was staring down at her fabulous peep-toe shoes, and Robert was forced to follow her gaze, dreading what he was about to see.

Sure enough, a pool of steaming yellow fluid was spreading around Ann Arbuthnott's shoes. The toenails had suddenly lost their luster. The click-click heels were half submerged. Those shoes had been Ann's pride and joy, but now she couldn't get rid of them fast enough. She snatched one of them off, only to give a little cry of frustration as she stepped with her stockinged feet into the puddle.

"For God's sake, Antis, get out! Out!" Robert cried.

The dog raced out of the door so fast that his claws scratched on the floor as he turned sharply into the corridor. But Robert could tell that his dog was far from ashamed. The tail that had been jammed between his legs was now being carried high. It was a sure sign that, if anything, he was rather pleased with himself. As far as he was concerned, this woman was his — *and Pamela's* — bitter rival, and if he'd managed to throw a monkey wrench in the works, so much the better.

Incredibly, Ann seemed to take the dousing in fine spirits. "Don't punish your dog," she implored. "He did his best to warn you he needed to go. Anyway, no harm done. I've another pair of stockings in my handbag."

"But, Ann . . ." Robert stammered. "He's never done anything like this before . . .

How can I make amends?"

She laughed. "Forget it. Though I have to say it's the first time anyone's thought my legs looked like a lamppost!"

Ann vanished into the ladies' room leaving Robert astonished that she could be so cool and understanding. She was truly one in a million. Antis's attempt to sabotage their budding romance had backfired. Rarely had Robert met such an easygoing type. After all, how many other girls could have his dog pee on their legs and shrug it off with a joke and a smile?

Ann was back a few minutes later, the damage done by Antis fully repaired. They laughed and joked until the train reached Wolverhampton, where Robert had to transfer. Once man and dog arrived at RAF Cosford, Pamela was quick to get herself a pass. Soon the three of them were strolling through the gentle countryside, Robert regaling Pam with the tale of Antis peeing on the shoes of the girl he had met on the train.

Pamela paused to ruffle Antis's neck. "Serves her right, eh, boy? Good old Antis — he even protects my interests when we're far away from each other."

ELEVEN

The airmen's huts were horribly crowded, but Robert made sure that Ant — now renamed Antis — always had a blanket bed on the floor by his master's side.

It was a dull and cloudy day in mid-November when three men — Robert, Josef, and Stetka — plus one dog showed up at the guardroom of RAF Honington, in Suffolk. They had their worldly possessions crammed into the same battered suitcases with which they had fled from France, and there was a feeling among them as if they were fresh arrivals at a new school. They were here to receive flight and gunnery training, in preparation for joining 311 Squadron proper.

Robert was sharing a room with Stetka, and of course their dog. They'd been allocated one on the ground floor, close to a side door, which suited Robert. It made it easier to let Antis in and out to pee during the night. One of the first things Robert did was pay a visit to station headquarters, to speak to the station warrant officer (SWO), to make the standard application necessary to keep a dog on an RAF camp.

The SWO was also the chairman of the sergeants' mess, and unbeknownst to Robert there was a diktat in the mess rules that no dogs were allowed to be kept in the rooms. There was a note to that effect pinned up on the notice board, but Robert hadn't seen it. He'd made up Antis's bed as usual, laying his blanket on the floor next to his own.

The SWO at Honington was called Meade. He had nineteen years' service with the RAF, and wore the long-service ribbons to prove it. He was tall, thin, and ramrod straight. His hair was cut razor short, his mustache was bristle thin, and it sat atop a mouth like a slit trench. He had no other duties than to be the station disciplinarian, and he was the equivalent of a regimental sergeant major in the army. The SWO ranked next to God on the base, and this one acted very much as if he knew it.

Robert and his dog's first meeting with SWO Meade didn't go terribly well. As soon as Meade laid eyes on the dog, his face was like a storm cloud. Muttering something about "damn foreigners turning the place into a menagerie," he told Robert to get the dog out of his office. Robert did as he was instructed, leaving Antis with Stetka, and then returned to the business at hand of seeking a permit. But he had little doubt already that SWO Meade was far from being a dog lover.

On seeing Robert's return sans dog, SWO Meade greeted him with a thin, wintery smile. "Now, what can I do for you?"

Robert laid his letter of application on the SWO's desk. "Permission to keep a dog on the camp, sir."

The SWO ran a gimlet eye over the paper. "I would have preferred 'RAF Station,

Honington,' not 'camp.' But I suppose it will have to suffice."

He jabbed a bell push beside him. A bespectacled orderly came running.

"Take that along to the squadron leader for onward transmission." The orderly scurried out again. "All right, Sergeant, see the orderly room sergeant tomorrow, by which time he'll have your answer. In the meantime, keep that dog of yours under control."

"He's never been a nuisance to anyone, sir."

"Maybe not to you," the SWO scowled. "That will be all."

The following morning Robert called on the orderly room sergeant and found that his request had been granted. Antis was now formally permitted to be at RAF Honington. But when he returned to his room, Robert found an official-looking envelope had been pushed under the door. It had his name, rank, and number written across it in a spidery hand. He opened it to find a typed note on sergeants'-mess-headed paper.

It drew his attention to Mess Rule No. 18, which stated that it was forbidden for any animal to sleep in quarters. He'd been given two hours to get Antis out of his room and to find him alternative accommodation. The note was signed by SWO Meade,

Chairman of the Sergeants' Mess. Robert had known already that he had no friend in that man, but now he could see how determined the SWO was to make life difficult for his dog.

There was no getting around it. Robert was a foreigner who had sworn an oath of allegiance to Great Britain when he joined her armed forces, and as such he had to abide by orders and the law. And this rule, petty though it might at first seem, had the full force of law behind it. Cursing to himself, Robert prepared to search for alternative quarters. He was forbidden to keep Antis in his room: ergo, both of them would have to find somewhere else to billet themselves.

It was a bitter November day as he, Stetka, and Josef scoured the base. They swung past station headquarters, and Robert threw a dark look at the window of the SWO's office. Keeping his dog with him had never been an issue on any base before, but for some reason it was here. So be it. They passed the hangars and reached the tarmac of the airfield. They passed the hulking forms of the Wellington bombers they were soon going to be flying, their airframes staked to the ground in case of strong gusts of wind, their guns covered to stop the rain from getting into them.

They reached the long grass that grew up around the airbase's perimeter and the rolls of barbed wire raised up on wooden platforms that marked its very boundary. In the distance was a group of derelict-looking huts. They looked as if they might well be out of bounds, but as foreigners, the three Czech airmen wouldn't know this. They approached the first and peered inside. The hut was empty of every scrap of furnishing possible, but there was still a stove inside it, with a metal pipe going up through the ceiling.

The door proved to be unlocked. It creaked open, and Robert made a rapid inspection. There was a pile of old newspaper in one corner, which would help with lighting the stove.

He turned to Josef and Stetka. "Well, it's hardly Prague Castle, but it'll do."

Josef and Stetka stared at him, as if he was going a little mad.

"But surely —" Josef began.

Robert cut him off. "Do you have a better idea?" He glanced at his watch. "The two hours are almost up, so it will have to suffice." He turned to his dog. "Antis, my boy, this is our new home."

The three men collected some firewood

from the adjacent woodland, piled it beside the stove, then returned to their quarters to get Robert's belongings and some blankets.

Once they were done settling man and dog in, Josef ran his eye around the bare hut. "Well, there should be enough blankets to keep Antis warm, at least," he joked.

Stetka, meanwhile, was bent before the stove trying to kindle a fire. At the third attempt it began to smolder. Josef went outside to check that the chimney was drawing.

"That's not much of a fire for one hell of a lot of smoke," he remarked. "They'll spot it a mile off."

"They can spot whatever they like," Robert snapped. He was angry and upset at the treatment he'd received, and the rebel within was coming to the fore now. "I was ordered to get my dog out and get him out I have."

"You'll probably get murdered in your sleep," Stetka teased.

"Probably," Robert confirmed. "I don't give a damn."

Oddly enough, Robert found himself quite happy in his new digs. He dared not light a fire during the day, for fear the smoke would be spotted. But it got dark early in the British winter, and from five o'clock on he had the stove roaring, and he could snuggle up close with his dog. More to the point, he was flying again. He might not have gone into action against the enemy yet, but he was learning to fight from a warplane that he sensed could do the Germans real harm.

The Vickers Wellington was a twin-engine, long-range, medium bomber. It was used mainly for night bombing raids, hitting targets in occupied Europe and in Germany itself. A sturdy workhorse of an aircraft, it had already earned a reputation for being able to take incredible amounts of punishment and still limp home to base. It possessed self-sealing fuel tanks and armor to protect the cockpit and other key areas, and it could survive the kind of damage that saw similar aircraft go down.

Robert had started flying "circuits and bumps" at RAF Honington, thereby mastering takeoff and landing. Soon they'd be on to "cross-country," when they would fly simulated long-distance bombing missions. He worked hard on his gunnery, and studied English in the long evenings alone in his hut with his dog. When Robert was in the air, Antis made himself at home with the sergeant in charge of the armorers. The only drawback to their new existence was that Robert's greatcoat and three-blanket bed would get horribly cold in the early hours of morning, and then he'd have to cuddle even closer to his dog.

Two weeks prior to Christmas, SWO Meade was once again appointed head of the roster duty for inspecting the base. It was a task that he performed with a thoroughness and relish that none could match. He had a finely honed instinct for seeking out the blanket not folded neatly enough, the shelf not dusted properly, or the supposedly forgotten corner used to hide some broken teacups that a trainee was loath to own up to having smashed. His death-gray eyes missed nothing.

At midnight SWO Meade set out, with his long-suffering orderly corporal in tow, to check on the aircraft. "We'll have a look around dispersal, shall we, Corporal?" the SWO remarked, sniffing the air in anticipation. "We'll soon find out if those lazy deadbeats picketed the kites properly. There's a gale warning and woe betide anyone who hasn't."

The orderly corporal would far have preferred to be sleeping in a warm bed, but his was not to reason why. Together, they crossed the airfield and bent to examine the corkscrew picketing irons that tethered the

Wellingtons to the ground. They were almost done with their work when the SWO stiffened for a moment. His head came up like a dog sniffing an unexpected scent.

"I say, do you smell that, Corporal?" he barked. "Smoke. I smell smoke. Where the devil's smoke coming from out here and at this time of night?"

The orderly corporal yawned. "Sorry, sir, can't smell a thing."

"Well then, you're clearly not sniffing hard enough. Sniff again, Corporal. Sniff again, and deeply. If that's not smoke then I'm a Chinaman."

"Well, now I come to think of it maybe there is a bit of a peculiar pong . . ."

"Exactly!" the SWO exclaimed. "Now to track it. It seems to be coming from the direction of those old transit huts. We'll cut over and have a look, catch whoever's up to whatever funny business at it."

The SWO and the corporal were soon at the door of the offending hut. With a flashlight gripped in one hand, the SWO swung the door open violently and shined the flashlight around the room. There in the center by the stove were the unmistakable forms of the Czech airman Bozdech and his damn dog.

"Well, well, well . . ." The SWO's pencil-thin mustache bristled. "Mind explaining what you are doing here, Sergeant?" He was barely able to keep the glee from his voice. "A Czech foreigner and his damn bloodhound, and both camping out where they shouldn't be."

Robert was half awake now, rubbing the sleep from his eyes. Beside him Antis was instantly alert, and he hadn't appreciated the two strangers bursting into their room, or the tone the taller one of them was using to address his master.

The dog rose to his feet, his ears flat against his skull and his hackles raised. He was more or less fully grown now, and once roused to anger he would be a real force to be reckoned with. His lips curled, his canines began to show, and he let out a menacing growl, one that reverberated deep in the dog's throat. The orderly corporal tried to utter a few words of appeasement at the dog, but the SWO wasn't so easily scared. He flicked the flashlight directly into the dog's eyes, which served only to enrage Antis more.

Robert reached out a restraining hand. "Easy, Antis, easy, boy."

"Rather than pandering to that feral dog of yours, do you mind answering my question, Sergeant. Who gave you permission to take up quarters here?"

"You turned us out of our room," Robert replied, "so obviously we had to find ourselves somewhere else."

"Correction, Sergeant," the SWO barked. "Nobody turned *you* out of anywhere. You were simply asked to comply with the rules regarding your dog."

Robert had been woken from a deep sleep in the middle of the night, only to face an unwanted interrogation by a man he was truly starting to hate. He was sitting in his underclothes, with only a blanket to cover him, and it was clear who had the advantage. He was having real trouble keeping his temper in check.

"Where my dog goes, I go," he grated.

"Is that so? Is — that — so?" The SWO spat out each of the words slowly and with real vitriol. He jerked his head toward his orderly corporal. "Take this man's name. To report to my office after parade tomorrow morning. I've a mind to put you under open arrest. Make no mistake, Sergeant, we will fix you properly this time."

The two men gone, Robert sat awake in the darkness, his face and that of his dog lit only by the glow of the stove. What did "fixing" him mean? he wondered. Was he to lose his dog? Was he to be thrown out of the

RAF? Was he to lose his chance to take the fight to the enemy, the one thing more than any other that he burned for? Out on that airstrip was a Wellington in which he'd gotten accustomed to slipping behind the twin Browning machine guns as he scanned the skies for enemy warplanes.

Was all of that at an end now, and all due to the petty attitude of a dog-hating, and apparently xenophobic, British SWO?

Robert was damned if that was to be the case. His mind drifted through the months that Antis and he had shared together. This extraordinary dog had come to him as if by a miracle. From the very first he had felt as if the two of them were fated to be together. Ever since that chance meeting he and his dog had acted pretty much as free agents, going where they pleased and taking to the air, to train, to cart, or ship more or less at will. Their lives together had been defined by rule-breaking wherever necessary: after all, their very arrival in Great Britain had involved smuggling Antis past customs and quarantine. Throughout all of that Robert had forged an unbreakable bond with his dog.

For many an evening here at RAF Honington the two of them had sat together in their otherwise deserted hut, Robert with his arm around the German shepherd's thick neck as he talked to him in low whispers. He'd shared with Antis his innermost thoughts, emotions, and concerns. His homesickness for his native country and for family and friends he'd left behind. His growing affection for Pamela — was this the big Love? His fear for what the future months might hold — for few of Bomber Command's aircrew ever completed a tour of duty unscathed. As he'd sat there and talked, Antis had growled and snuffled his soft responses, showing that — to Robert's mind at least — he understood.

No. There was no way that Robert was going to allow the SWO to hurt, harm, or disrespect his dog. It wasn't going to happen. Instead, he knew exactly what he had to do.

Very early the next morning Robert went and sought out the station's Czech translator, Flight Lieutenant Divis. They were old friends, and Divis knew well how much Antis meant to his master. Robert discovered the flight lieutenant in his room having an early-morning shave. He blurted out the story of what had happened between him, his dog, and SWO Meade.

"All right, all right," Divis told him, "calm down a little. I'll go see the station adjutant this morning, over breakfast, and maybe the CO if I can grab him. I reckon the CO's taken a fancy to Antis, whenever he's seen him around the base. Don't worry — I've no doubt we'll think of something."

Thanking him profusely, Robert went to stand that morning's parade, after which he headed straight for the SWO's office. He knocked on the man's door determined to fight for his dog every step of the way, no matter what it might cost him. He had almost abandoned Antis once before, back in a shell-torn French farmhouse. He wasn't ever about to do so again.

"Ah yes, Sergeant Bozdech, do come in," SWO ·Meade greeted him. Robert could have sworn he detected a forced air of bonhomie about the horrid man. "Now, I've seen the CO and it has been decided — just this once, mind you — to take no further action in this matter. You're to report for your duties as normal."

"Thank you, sir," said Robert, almost choking on the words.

"Not at all, not at all. But you chaps must realize, of course, that the RAF has its standards to keep up, and people in my position are the standard-bearers. We have a job to do and there's nothing personal about it, of course. Yes, yes. What's right is right, and what's wrong is wrong, and I daresay there's not a man among us would argue with that."

"Understood, sir."

"Now, there is a general mess meeting this week, and it may be possible — only *may*, mind you — to rescind that particular order about animals in sergeants' rooms, but it's up to the entire mess as a whole —"

"Please, sir, don't bother, not on my behalf," Robert interrupted. "I'm grateful, of course, but Antis and I are quite happy where we are."

"As you wish, Sergeant," the SWO remarked, picking up a file from his desk. "Now, if you'll excuse me, I'll wish you good morning."

"Good morning, sir."

As matters transpired, the CO had given SWO Meade a ten-minute lecture that morning on the proper treatment to be accorded England's gallant Czech allies. "For pity's sake, Mr. Meade, bear in mind those poor bastards have come one hell of a long way to fight in our cause, and it behooves us to show some forbearance and a proper sense of an English welcome . . ." Hence the remarkable turnaround in the SWO's attitude.

That evening, when Robert returned to

his derelict hut, he found it transformed. There was a pile of freshly cut wood by the stove, plus a bucket filled to the brim with coal. Under one window was a brand-new desk and chairs that must have come straight from stores. There was also a camp bed, and on top of that a pile of neatly folded blankets. Maybe SWO Meade wasn't such a bad sort, Robert reflected.

Maybe he'd teach the man to become a dog lover after all.

TWELVE

With Bomber Command launching sorties far into occupied Europe, and even into the German heartland itself, the Luftwaffe had redoubled its efforts to smash the British bomber squadrons wherever it encountered them — on the ground or in the air. RAF Honington had so far escaped largely unscathed. But during those dark December days, when thick banks of cloud lay low and glowering over the airbase, it would be easy enough for the Germans' fighter-bombers to sneak up unseen and launch their attacks.

A few days before Christmas the first of the enemy came. Robert was making his way to the cookhouse one lunchtime, hoping very much for a hot meal for himself and his dog. In spite of the SWO's improvements to their hut, it was still like an icebox in the midst of a freezing British winter. Antis was hurrying ahead of him, sensing the chance of a good hot feed.

Suddenly, the dog stopped and assumed a pose that Robert had gotten to know well . . . and fear. Head raised and limbs trembling, he was staring toward the distant, cloud-enshrouded horizon, a low growl beginning in the depths of his throat. Robert knew instantly what it signified: they had an enemy aircraft inbound.

As he sprinted for the nearest shelter with Antis hot on his heels, he spotted a group of WAAFs chatting and giggling. Robert could hear the deep throb of the aircraft now, and he figured it was less than a mile away. He recognized it as the engine beat of a Dornier Do 17 — a "flying pencil" sneak raider that would drop without warning out of the cloud base. At its top speed of 250 miles per hour, it would be over the base within a matter of seconds.

He yelled over at the WAAFs: "For God's sake, get down! Get down!"

Having paused to warn them, Robert knew he'd never make it to the shelter in time. He threw himself flat on the frozen ground. But the WAAFs must have assumed he was joking. The Dornier had beaten the camp's defenses, for no warning siren or firing of defensive guns could be heard, and presumably the girls figured this foreign airman was playing some distasteful joke on them.

They waltzed away several paces, noses held disdainfully in the air, and then the flying pencil came tearing out of the clouds. Stunned by its sudden appearance, the women stood as if frozen. As the sleek bomber leveled out and prepared to release its bombs, Robert jumped to his feet and rugby-tackled the lot of them, the thin blanket of snow that lay across the airfield cushioning their fall. One tumbled on top of Antis, but his howls of distress were drowned out by the deafening explosions as the first of the bombs struck.

The Dornier had strung out its twenty fifty-kilogram bombs like a necklace across the entire length of the runway. The explosions tore over Robert, his dog, and the WAAFs, as if a giant hand were trying to rip them from the earth. In among the deafening roar of the detonations and the snarl of the Dornier's twin engines, Robert detected the whistling of the last of the bombs. It seemed to be coming directly at them.

The blunt-nosed bomb plowed into the ground barely yards away, bounced up, tore across their prone forms, and exploded on the far side of the runway, flattening the station's clothing store. Out of the corner of his eye Robert saw a figure blasted into the air, and he knew instantly that whoever the victim was he had to be finished. It was an eighteen-year-old trainee airman, and sure enough he was dead by the time his body hit the earth.

The Dornier was climbing away now, making for the safety of the glowering clouds. But before it could reach them, a streak of silver flashed above Robert's head as the sleek form of a Spitfire howled past, right on the German's tail. An instant later Robert saw the British fighter's guns spitting fire, and the clear impact of cannon rounds sparking all along the enemy aircraft's fuselage.

Moments later, with its twin engines trailing tongues of flame, the Dornier's nose dropped and it plowed into the earth. A mushroom cloud of dark smoke punched upward from the impact point, and Robert felt a surge of elation that the Dornier had been taken down. The bodies of the German airmen would later be found in the tangled heap of wreckage, the knowledge of their deaths only strengthening Robert's hunger to get airborne and into action.

Christmas 1940 came, marking the end of

their training at Honington. In a matter of days now, Robert and his fellow Czech airmen would be moved to 311 Squadron's operational airbase at nearby RAF East Wretham, just a dozen miles across the Suffolk–Norfolk border. The base had been hastily pressed into service at the start of the war, and the runways and aircraft standing areas consisted mostly of stretches of mown grass, ringed with trees.

The Christmas celebrations were to be the last at Honington for Robert and his fellows. The beer flowed freely in the mess, and the only sign that this was a British airbase ensnared in a bitter and bloody war was the four airmen wearing their white pullovers and heavy flying boots, the only ones who were abstaining from alcohol. Since dusk they had been standing by in readiness, just in case the enemy should violate the spirit of Christmas, during which hostilities between the warring parties were traditionally put on hold.

At around ten that evening Robert carried a full roast dinner across the airfield to the distant hut so that Antis could have his festive meal. While his dog enjoyed the food, Robert surveyed their quarters. On the desk provided by the SWO stood a small Christmas tree, around which were arranged photos of his parents and his sisters, plus one of Pamela. Earlier that evening she had phoned to wish him and his dog a happy Christmas, which had been a wonderful surprise. It was good to know that she was thinking of them at this special time.

Robert was lost in thoughts of his girl and reminiscences of home, and he completely forgot his promise to his brother airmen to return to the party. It was an hour after he'd left the mess when he heard the stamp of heavy boots outside and the sound of raucous laughter. As their friend hadn't seen fit to rejoin them, Robert's brother airmen had come to join him. A dozen piled into the hut, each bringing with him an armful of bottles. As Antis moved among them, sniffing at familiar figures with his tail wagging happily, the drink started to flow.

There was something about the candlelit hut set far from the main base that was strangely conducive to partying. As drink followed drink and the singing became ever more rowdy and spirited, Robert worried for a moment about the possible consequences of having an illegal party in his only recently made legal quarters. But he was soon caught up in the swing of things, and Antis, it seemed, had also embraced the party mood. He moved around quietly, his nose sneaking into various glasses placed absentmindedly on the floor, until finally he stumbled into Stetka's legs and half tripped him.

Stetka gave a drunken cry of alarm, and Antis reacted by barking loudly and chasing his own tail. So fast was he spinning round and round that it looked as if three or four dogs were whirling madly in a blur.

"Antis, have you gone barking mad?" Robert exclaimed. He'd never seen the likes of this before from his dog.

At the sound of his master's voice Antis tried to stop and move toward Robert, but he got his legs and tail all tangled up and ended up in a mess on the floor. When he tried to stand again, all he could manage was a halfhearted stagger and a weave across the space between them. For the first time in his life Antis was drunk as a lord.

Robert had no idea what time the party must have ended. The next thing he knew he was awake, lying on the hut floor with the camp bed above him. He was even more astonished when he wriggled out from underneath it only to find his dog sleeping soundly on top and all tucked up in the blankets!

Thankfully, there were no duties to attend to that day. By lunchtime Robert was feeling a little recovered, but Antis lay on the bed snoring. He didn't even wake up when Robert lifted him off and put him in his rightful place — on his blanket on the floor. By that evening Robert was getting worried. He tried toweling his dog down with cold, wet cloths, but the only reaction he got was a series of disgruntled snorts and growls.

In the early hours of the morning Robert awoke to discover Antis asking in his normal way to be let out — by scratching at the door. The dog came back, went over to a fire bucket that was kept ready in case of a blaze in their hut, and almost in one gulp he drained it of its water. Come dawn he seemed to be back to his normal self, and it was as if the great Christmas drinking binge had never happened.

On New Year's Day three aircrews, including Robert, Josef, and Stetka, flew into East Wretham. It was a fine, crisp morning. After all the snow and sleet the air seemed to have been scrubbed clean and clear. A light snow had fallen overnight, and from the air the gently rolling landscape glittered with a dusting of silvery white, interspersed here and there with darker patches of woodland.

As they circled the airbase in preparation for landing, Robert could see tractors towing bomb trailers toward the runway. He spotted camouflaged Wellingtons dotted around the fringes of the airfield, and they were clearly getting bombed up ready for a coming mission. The last time he'd seen live ordnance being loaded aboard aircraft — ones that he might soon fly into combat — was back in northern France, almost a year earlier. As he gazed down on the familiar sight he felt the thrill in his stomach that always accompanied imminent combat.

Shortly after dusk, one by one, those Wellingtons would trundle from their dispersal points, taxi along the perimeter track, and take up their positions for takeoff. Then, one after the other, they would nose forward onto the grass, turn their heads into the wind, and weighed down with their heavy bomb load, they would bounce and thunder their way toward takeoff. With their throttles fully open they would gain momentum until each became airborne, leaving behind their ungainly earthbound existence and becoming things of agile poise and power in the air.

Robert couldn't wait.

As soon as their aircraft had landed and come to a standstill, they were surrounded by a sea of familiar faces. First to greet Robert and Antis were Gustav, Uncle Vlasta, and Ludva — three of the Original Eight.

Antis was going wild with excitement as he recognized his old comrades — the all-for-one-and-one-for-allers. He pranced and leaped about, then dashed in a complete circle around and around the group of airmen.

"Look!" cried Vlasta. "Look at Antis! He's doing a war dance for joy!"

Once he was done dashing about, Antis went from familiar face to familiar face, seemingly checking that all were present and accounted for. He ended up gazing about forlornly and whimpering, as if searching for someone he couldn't see. He gazed at Robert, then turned his head to each man in turn, as if counting them: *One, two, three, four, and five with you, Dad. So where are the others?*

He seemed to be asking for Karel and Joska, the two of the Original Eight who were missing.

"Sorry, Antis, they're gone," Robert told him softly. "We won't be seeing them again."

"They never came back," Uncle Vlasta added. "Never mind, old boy. Plenty of rabbits to chase around this place to perk up your spirits."

"We've booked you and Antis into a tent," Ludva added, trying to lift everyone's spirits. "It's pretty basic after Honington, but we've coped fine and we've been here all through the winter! Anyhow, you'll be too damn tired to care where you sleep when you start flying ops!"

As luck would have it, Robert and his dog were billeted in the tents only a matter of days. A local farmhouse had been requisitioned to house some of the Czech airmen, and Robert and his dog were relocated there. Manor Farm was still a working farm, so the yard was full of scratching chickens and gobbling turkeys. You'd have to go a long way from the farm to realize there was a war on. It was as peaceful and pleasant a place as they could have wished for, and Robert sensed that he and his dog were going to be very happy at Manor Farm.

He and Ludva took the top floor along with Antis, while Gustav and Josef took another. The farm lay at one end of the tiny village of East Wretham, with the church next to the farm and a scattering of cottages farther on. The airfield was a good mile away, and Robert managed to buy himself an ancient bicycle to make the daily journey to and from the base. It gave Antis great exercise as he trotted by his side.

The only trouble with their new existence was that the flying was almost nonexistent. The day after their arrival a thick fog descended on the airbase. It lasted for three weeks during which time Robert only managed to get into the air once or twice. New airmen undertaking their first bombing missions were known as "freshmen," and they were normally allocated a "soft" target in nearby France — one that involved minimal flying over hostile territory.

Such missions were a comparatively gentle baptism by fire, before longer-range missions over Germany herself, and the far more intense air defenses that they'd encounter. Thus all Robert flew that fogbound January were a couple of "easy" operational sorties, in the aircraft that he was to come to know and love well — a Wellington with the call sign "C for Cecilia." He had yet to get a feel for the cut and thrust of a long-range bomber squadron at war, but at least he'd "broken the operational ice," as Vlasta put it.

In their enforced inactivity the airmen used whatever means they had — bicycles, old motorcycles — to make the journey to nearby Thetford of an evening, where the bars of the Bell and Ark Royal hotels were the draw. As often as not they'd be joined by the RAF's liaison officer to the Czech squadron, Squadron Leader "Pick" Pickard, a British pilot with a soaring reputation.

Pickard would come on the invitation of Wing Commander Ocelka, the Czech pilot in command of 311 Squadron.

Both men liked nothing more than to mix it with "their boys," and over time the British commander had warmed to the quiet determination and stoicism of the Czechs. Pickard had in turn won the Czech pilots' undying affection and admiration for a recent stand he had taken against the enemy. The Germans had threatened to execute any Czech airman they captured. Pickard — who flew often on active operations — had reacted to this by sewing Czechoslovak shoulder flashes onto his flying tunic. There could have been no greater gesture of solidarity, no finer indication of how all were united against a common enemy.

Standing at the rear of the bar, half hidden in a cloud of aromatic smoke from his pipe, Pickard would laugh and joke with all and sundry while keeping half an eye on the men. He understood the frustrations of being grounded by bad weather, and the incredible stress and tension of flying repeated combat sorties. He knew well the value of relaxation and letting off steam.

When he judged the time was right he'd get the party games going, and few could resist joining in. As for Antis, his Christmas booze binge seemed to have left him with a strong aversion to the evil brew. All he'd ever take was half a pint of Bass and no more, which was supplied to him free by the landlord.

During daylight hours Robert spent much of his time teaching Antis the golden rules of behavior on an active airbase. With the help of a friendly ground crew and pilot, he arranged to get his dog blown over a few times by the slipstream of a Wellington's propellers. The first few times that the dog was bowled over by the invisible but immensely powerful blast, he couldn't work out what had hit him. But he soon learned to give any warplanes a wide birth, at least until they had powered down.

Robert also taught Antis to avoid crossing the runway at East Wretham. He cycled the perimeter track with his dog, and whenever Antis tried to take a shortcut over the grass, Robert warned him off with a sharp "No!" He soon learned which parts were out of bounds and to stick to the track. Such lessons were vital, for soon Robert would be taking to the skies for hours on end, and his dog would have to behave impeccably in his absence.

■ ■ ■

January rolled by and February blew in, bringing with it a period of clearer weather. It was time to start flying the nightly bombing raids again. C for Cecilia was made ready by her ground crew — a group of hardworking and dedicated men led by a cheerful Czech named Adamek — and now all Robert and his fellow airmen needed was their mission.

On the night of February 5, six Wellingtons took off to bomb the Channel ports on the French coast. Robert's wasn't among them, and when dawn came only five aircraft had returned. Aircraft 7842-T had been shot down. The crew had managed to bail out. Among them was Robert's great friend Gustav, a fellow gunner and one of the Original Eight. He had been captured by the Germans, and so the original fellowship was now reduced to five.

It was a sobering moment for Robert. No one knew Gustav's fate, but the twenty-year-old had been captured by an enemy that had vowed to execute any Czech airmen who fell into their hands. It was also the first time that Robert had been part of an active combat squadron in which one of his close friends had — more than likely — been killed. Moreover, Robert, like Gustav, was a Wellington gunner, and he was painfully aware that if ever he failed to return from a mission he would be leaving behind one traumatized and orphaned dog.

The squadron's targets for the next two nights called for real precision bombing, which was something close to the limits of the technology the Wellingtons possessed. Anchored at the French port of Brest, on the extreme west of that nation's northern coastline, was the prize German battle cruiser, the *Prinz Eugen.* At some eighteen thousand tons displacement and with 1,382 officers and enlisted men aboard, *Prinz Eugen* was a prime target. Moreover, the battle cruiser's presence at Brest menaced all shipping to and from Britain via the Atlantic and the English Channel.

It would be a real blow to the German war effort, not to mention a morale-boosting victory for the Allies, if 311 Squadron could sink or seriously disable her. 1958-C, to use the aircraft's formal flight number — otherwise known as C for Cecilia — was one of eight aircraft selected to carry out the first raid. C for Cecilia's crew consisted of six. The aircraft's pilot and captain was a sergeant called Capka, with Sejbl as second pilot, Lancik as navigator/bomb aimer, Kacir as radio operator, and Gruden and Robert serving as gunners (in either the nose or rear-gun position, as need dictated). Capka had served as a second pilot until recently, and with his extensive combat experience the crew had absolute confidence in his abilities.

The stocky Adamek — C for Cecilia's ground-crew chief — was known as "Little Adam" to the men. During the coming sorties he was to become Antis's greatest friend and companion. As Robert prepared to get airborne, his dog seemed to sense that his master was about to take to the skies on a life-or-death mission. The ground crew had its own tent pitched by some woodland on the far side of the perimeter track, and it was there that Robert took his dog as he and his crew began their final flight checks.

Robert had noticed how Antis was naturally drawn to Adamek. He asked the sturdy Czech to keep his dog safe for him, to shelter him in the tent, and to keep him warm and fed until his return. Adamek was more than happy to oblige. Ahead of him and his men lay hours of boredom as they played cards and chatted and waited for the aircraft to return.

During the long hours of darkness and

uncertainty that lay ahead, Antis would be welcome extra company.

THIRTEEN

Robert trained Antis never to cross the runway or approach one of their Wellington bombers when the engines were running — crucial for a dog on duty.

Having watched his master disappear up the front steps leading into the belly of the Wellington, Antis stood trembling on the edge of the dispersal area, his eyes glued to the warplane. He tracked the heavily laden aircraft as it taxied toward the end of the runway. One by one the bombers took off, but Antis seemed to know exactly which was the one that contained his master. As C for Cecilia turned ponderously, accelerated, and became airborne, clawing into the dark sky, his mournful gaze remained fixed on the warplane.

He couldn't pull his eyes away until the last speck of the Wellington had disappeared into the southern skies. Even then, as the ground crew gathered up their tools in preparation for returning to their tent, Antis's focus remained on the dark horizon, his ears pricked forward to catch the last vestiges of sound. Finally, with a drooping tail, he turned from the runway and joined Adamek and the others as they headed for their tent.

But Antis stopped short. He found a place at the side of the dispersal area, sank onto his haunches, and made it clear to all that that was where he was going to stay. No amount of entreaties could persuade the dog to join them in the shelter, and so the warmhearted Adamek opted to remain with Antis, at least for the first hour or so. Adamek was a natural-born optimist, and while he knew from sad experience how often crews failed to return from missions, he never once allowed himself to think that C for Cecilia might suffer such a fate.

There would be no end of volunteers at 311 Squadron to take the dog, were Robert to be captured or killed. At the front of the line would be Adamek himself, Squadron Leader Pickard, Wing Commander Ocelka, and of course Uncle Vlasta and Ludva. That wasn't the worry. The worry was whether a dog who was so intimately bonded with his master could ever recover from losing him. Adamek didn't allow his mind to dwell on such thoughts. There was enough darkness in this war without worrying about grief and loss that would perhaps never happen.

After a good hour with the dog, Adamek went to get a hot meal. He returned to find Antis stretched out with his head resting on his forepaws, sound asleep. He had brought Antis some food, but when the dog awakened he absolutely refused to eat. This would become his unbreakable habit: whenever his master was away flying, not a morsel of food would pass his lips.

As the first faint skeins of a duck-egg blue shot through the sky to the east, presaging dawn, Adamek sensed the dog's growing excitement. It was almost as if he knew that this was the time when the warplanes would return, and when all those waiting would know for sure if one had been lost. Adamek placed a powerful arm around the dog's shoulders, whispering words of comfort to him — that his master would be home soon.

Antis whimpered softly, all of his senses focused on the skies now, his ears straining to hear the first sounds of a Wellington powering in to land. As Adamek watched the dog carefully, he suddenly saw a change come over him. The whining stopped and Antis cocked his head to one side, every molecule of his being concentrating on the noises in his head.

Antis had caught the distant sound of a Wellington's twin Bristol Pegasus radial engines. In fact he could hear several. He was sifting those various sounds, searching for the one that he'd learned to recognize as C for Cecilia's signature engine beat. As his excitement grew, the first black specks appeared, silhouetted against the barely nascent dawn. Suddenly, Antis was on his feet and he barked loudly, beginning the wild war dance for joy that Uncle Vlasta had first noticed, tearing around and around the group of waiting men as if he'd gone half mad.

At last C for Cecilia touched down. As the Wellington taxied across to her dispersal point, Antis could hardly contain his excitement. But the lesson he'd learned never to approach an aircraft with engines running held him back, right until the moment the hatches opened and out stepped the crew. Antis bolted forward, so he was waiting at the bottom of the ladder as Robert climbed down.

Robert's welcome back to East Wretham after the mission to bomb the *Prinz Eugen* was to be half bowled over by one crazy-happy dog.

As it turned out, the raid had been only a partial success. All aircraft had reached the target and completed their bombing runs. But C for Cecilia's bomb load had fallen just to the west of the target, where they'd counted six blasts on what had to be the quayside. They had been close, but not close enough. Their munitions had overshot. Still, Cecilia's crew had proven they could navigate to a specific point, carry out near-precision bombing under heavy fire, and return to their airbase, which was about as good as it got for a freshman crew.

They'd only get a damage assessment on the *Prinz Eugen* once the local cells of the French resistance had managed to set eyes on the ship and radio through a report on what bombs may have hit. In the meantime breakfast called, and Robert felt ravenous.

As he ate he could feel the adrenaline of the night sortie bleeding out of his system, to be replaced by a leaden fatigue.

He cycled back to Manor Farm with Antis running happily at his side. By now it was broad daylight. Robert closed the curtains in their room and lay down to rest. Antis settled on his blanket beside him, head on his paws and eyes fixed on his master's prone form. Only when Robert's breathing became regular and easy did Antis decide that the time had come for him too to get some sleep.

So the pattern was set, as C for Cecilia began to fly nightly sorties, making the most of the fine weather of the first days of spring, while Antis stood his dark vigils on the dispersal area waiting for his master's return. With over a dozen missions behind them, C for Cecilia's crew graduated from being freshmen to something closer to veterans. They had made their mark on the squadron of twenty Wellingtons and were thought to be as reliable and solid a crew as any.

That spring a film documentary crew descended upon East Wretham. They were there to shoot a morale-boosting film showing how Bomber Command was taking the fight to the German enemy — a message that everyone in Great Britain was desperate to hear. For too long the Allies had been on the back foot, as the Germans' seemingly invincible war machine had stamped its jackboot across much of Europe. The film, entitled *Target for Tonight,* was to tell a very different story — that night after night the crews of Bomber Command were flying into the teeth of the German guns, striking at the heart of the enemy.

Recognizing that Antis was an integral part of 311 Squadron — he wasn't just its mascot; he was a working part of what made it whole — Squadron Leader Pickard decided the dog was going to have to play his part. Pick had a real soft spot for Antis. As Great Britain had struggled to feed her own people under the German sea and air assault, many pets — beloved dogs included — had been ordered to be put down (as many as one hundred thousand in the war). As a result, Antis was something of a rarity, and Pickard well appreciated the morale-boosting effect of putting a brave and handsome dog on the screen.

Pickard was to star in the film as the pilot of "F for Freddie," and he decided Antis should figure as the dog that led the aircrew from their briefing in the crew room to the aircraft as they prepared to get airborne. Strictly speaking, the aircrew didn't run to their aircraft. The distance was too far, and they'd go by crew bus. But Pickard wasn't averse to a bit of poetic license, and neither was the British Ministry of Information film crew; nor, as it turned out, was Antis, who seemed to love the rehearsals and the filming that followed.

Pickard had made it clear to Robert that if the unfortunate happened and C for Cecilia did ever fail to return from a mission, then he would love to take the dog as his own. Robert had thanked him for the offer, but made it clear that he had no intention of ever failing to return. In any case, Pick would have to join the line of would-be owners.

Little did Robert appreciate then what a debt he'd owe to Pickard and his love of dogs, for there would come a time in the near future when the squadron leader would be called upon to save Antis's life, and from a threat very much closer to home than that posed by the German enemy. But for now, there were missions to fly and a war to be fought. And there was the trauma of the death of close colleagues to be borne by the men, seemingly on a daily basis.

Shortly after the filming of *Target for To-*

night was complete, there was news of further tragedy. Of the three crews that had joined 311 Squadron on New Year's Day — Robert's and two others — one had already been shot down over France. Now came worse news: the second crew had failed to return from a night raid. Their Wellington had been seen going down in flames over the German city of Düsseldorf, and it was presumed that all were lost. One of those was Stetka — the larger-than-life beer-swilling airman they had first met at RAF Speke, and a man to whom both Robert and his dog had grown close.

In the few short months that they had been based at East Wretham, Stetka had gotten to know every pub and bar in the vicinity. He was always broke, always borrowing money from his pals, and always spending it on beer. Three days before his final, deathly sortie, Stetka had approached Robert in an uncharacteristically somber mood. He'd asked him for a private word, and Robert presumed that his friend was seeking yet another loan, something that he had never once refused him.

"Robert, can you help me?" Stetka had asked.

"Of course. How much is it this time?"

Stetka had shaken his head vigorously.

255

"No, no, I'm not after a loan. In fact, I want you to make me a solemn promise you will never lend me any money again. I owe seven and six to Josef, fifteen bob to you, and eight to Ludva. Tomorrow is payday, and I can settle my debts with three pounds left over."

Robert hadn't known what to say. Why was Stetka in such a strange mood, and why on earth was he so determined to pay off his beer debts? And what would he do for money to finance his happy habit once the three pounds was exhausted? Robert had agreed to Stetka's request, though it had all seemed very odd.

Two days later his good friend was dead, and had gone to his grave owing no money to any of his friends. Robert could only presume that Stetka had had a premonition of his own death. Nothing else made any sense. And being the thoroughly decent fellow that he was, he'd decided to pay off all his loans before the Grim Reaper claimed him.

The morning after Stetka's death, Robert and Ludva were awakened by the noise of RAF orderlies clearing out his room, which was adjacent to their own. They were packing up the airman's few possessions, most likely so a replacement could have his room.

"Why the hell can't they at least wait until we've gone on a mission or something?" Robert demanded angrily. "Why do it now, when we're still here?"

"Steady, Robert, steady," Ludva replied. "He was my friend too, you know. It's best not to think about it. After all, it will come to most of us sooner or later, you know."

"Thanks!" Robert snorted. "That's really cheered me up."

"Well, I tell you one thing," Ludva continued, "when my time comes they'll have no problem sorting my gear." He jerked a thumb at the end of his bed. "It's all there, neatly piled, with a list drawn up of everything and who it's to go to." He paused. "You know, I wanted to get married someday, but I've a hunch that I won't make it."

Robert stared at Ludva in alarm. His roommate was normally as high-spirited and upbeat as the beery Stetka had been. "What the devil do you mean?"

"Well, someone has to get lucky, just as others don't," Ludva replied casually. "I've a strong feeling you'll be all right. You'll make it through. As for me, well, let's just say I wouldn't place a bet on myself . . ."

Before Robert could think of a suitable reply, Ludva rolled over and sighed heavily, then seemingly went back to sleep. Robert lay awake pondering what his close friend had said. Was it really coming to them all? The odds would suggest so: since Robert had joined 311 Squadron they'd lost two-thirds of the aircrew, and that in a few short months.

Should he too make a list of his possessions? Robert wondered. But the more he thought about it the more he realized he only really had one thing that he valued, and that was Antis. The only "possession" he'd bother putting on any list was his dog — and Antis was already promised to his brother airmen, if ever he didn't make it back again. He dropped his hand over the side of the bed and felt for his dog. He ruffled the thick hair a few times, and heard Antis give a little snort of satisfaction — an acknowledgment in his sleep that he'd felt his master's touch and was comforted by it.

Antis would wake in a few hours' time and discover that another of his two-legged brothers was gone — Stetka, the bighearted one who was always trying to get the squadron mascot to drink his fair share of beer. It was another loss that the poor dog would have to come to terms with.

In light of Ludva's morbid remarks, Robert made a mental note to move Wing Commander Ocelka to the top of the list. At the rate they were losing regular aircrew, none might be left by the time someone was needed to adopt Antis. Being the squadron's commanding officer, Ocelka flew fewer sorties than the others, and by rights his chances of survival should be greater. Robert then decided he would tell Ocelka that he was the chosen one, and with that thought he rolled over and went back to sleep.

He was shaken awake sometime later by the duty officer, who was standing between Robert's and Ludva's beds with a clipboard in his hand.

"How many crews on the list tonight, sir?" Robert asked sleepily.

"Eight. And both you and Ludva are on it."

That evening Robert and his fellow airmen set off for the crew room to collect their parachutes, leaving Antis to make his own way to his regular nightly position on the dispersal area. Antis had had his paws trodden on one too many times in the crew bus, and preferred to make his way to the airstrip on foot. At the entrance to the runway stood a guard in the dark blue uniform of the Air Ministry Constabulary. Unbeknownst to Antis, this hard-faced military policeman had taken a dislike to 311 Squadron's mascot. In his mind the squadron's business was flying missions against the enemy, not keeping pets.

Seeing Antis trotting along the roadway toward the main gate, this man decided he'd had enough of the dog's damned impertinence. It was high time he exerted his authority. He dragged his bicycle across the road so as to block the dog's path. He yelled at Antis, telling him to clear off. Amazed, the dog stopped dead in his tracks. He'd rarely if ever been the object of such behavior and couldn't for the life of him understand what was happening.

He tried to skirt around the irate policeman, but each time the man wheeled his bike one way or the other to block the dog's way. Antis had never faced such naked human aggression. More importantly, he'd never had a human try to keep him from his master. Deciding that the policeman was best avoided, Antis opted to jump the ditch and fence that bordered the gate. But the policeman, realizing what he was up to, jammed his bike into the dog's way. Antis jumped, failed to clear the bike, and crashed into it painfully.

Suddenly, Antis's mood flipped. He'd realized by now this man was intent on keep-

ing him from his master, and no one —
nobody — ever got away with that. His eyes
flashing fire, Antis wheeled around, growling menacingly at his oppressor. This sudden change of demeanor had the gallant
policeman on the defensive. With the bike
held protectively before him as a shield, he
backed toward the safety of his tiny little
wooden hut that lay to one side of the gate.

Antis advanced as the policeman retreated, determined to get through the gate
and on his way to dispersal. But as the
policeman backed away he caught his heel
on the grass verge, tumbled backward, and
with the bicycle on top of him, fell into a
muddy ditch. Completely ignoring the
policeman's curses, Antis continued to go
about his business. At that moment three
other airmen — who had seen the confrontation unfolding — came rushing up to lend
what help they could.

Their concern was all for the squadron's
dog. Throwing a few choice insults at the
stocky policeman, who was still struggling
to get out of the ditch, they grabbed Antis
by the collar and moved off toward the
airfield. Antis knew that he'd lost precious
time during the confrontation, and that C
for Cecilia might already be getting airborne. Head down and legs pumping, he

raced for the dispersal area, resisting the temptation to take a shortcut across the runway.

He got there just in time, and was able to nuzzle a wet nose into Robert's hand as he listened to the final briefing prior to takeoff.

"What kept you, boy?" Robert whispered. "You're late!"

There was no way that Antis could relate what had just happened. It was good enough for him that he'd made it to his position to see his master into the air on another mission. The target tonight was Osnabrück — one of the first German cities to have been bombed by the Allies during the war. It lay in the direct flight path of Bomber Command squadrons heading for Berlin and central Germany's industrial heartland, so it was a stepping-stone in the process of familiarizing aircrew with that route.

Tonight's raid was to be one of the first flown by the crew of C for Cecilia into Germany itself. With their radar-controlled searchlights and integrated air defense systems, the defenders of most German cities were able to vector both ground fire and fighter planes onto Allied aircraft far more effectively than their counterparts in the rest of occupied Europe — hence bombing missions flown into Germany itself were rightly seen as being by far the more risk-laden. Antis had been right to insist on getting to the airfield in time to see his master off, for there was every chance of losses on tonight's mission.

As matters transpired, the enemy fire over Osnabrück was less fierce than expected. C for Cecilia was able to drop her bombs and return to base well before dawn, as were the rest of that night's aircrew. Antis met the returning aircraft with his now-familiar war dance for joy, and after a quick breakfast man and dog retired to Manor Farm for a much-needed sleep. It wasn't to prove very restful, however.

Robert hadn't long been asleep when he was shaken awake. "Sergeant Bozdech, you're to report to the adjutant's office," the orderly sergeant told him.

"What, now? I'm off duty. I was on operations last night."

"The adjutant wants to see you at eleven sharp." The man glanced at his watch. "It's five past ten now. You'd better get a move on."

Hurriedly, Robert shaved and dressed himself. It wasn't usual to deprive an aircrewman of much-needed sleep after a night operation, especially as he might be needed to fly again that evening. But the sun was out and Robert was feeling remarkably contented as he cycled into the base with Antis trotting beside him. He reached the main gate and called out a cheery "good morning" to the policeman on duty. All he got in return was a sneer, plus a scowl for his dog.

He headed for the main building, made his way down the polished corridor, and knocked on the adjutant's door. It was five minutes to eleven, so he had actually arrived early. He was called in and came to attention. The adjutant was sitting bolt upright in his chair, arms folded, an expression like thunder on his features.

"You sent for me, sir?"

"I did." He threw a glance at Antis, who was standing obediently at Robert's heel. "That dog of yours — he has to go."

"Sorry, sir? Dog? My dog has to go? Go where, sir?"

"He must be removed from the camp forthwith!" the adjutant snapped.

"But he's the squadron mascot, sir. Why would he have to go?"

"It's simple. It's come to my attention you have no official permit to keep a dog on this camp. Ergo, the dog has to go."

"Group Captain Pickard never asked for one, sir. He knew the dog was here and was happy . . ."

"Group Captain Pickard is no longer the station commander," the adjutant cut in. He was right. Pickard had been promoted and moved on to other duties.

"But Wing Commander Ocelka is equally —"

"Wing Commander Ocelka is away at present. That leaves my good self having to deal with a very unfortunate matter that has arisen." The adjutant picked up a sheet of paper lying on his desk. "I have before me a report from the Air Ministry warden on the gate that your dog tried to savage him last night. The report outlines the laws that exist in this country to deal with vicious dogs."

"It's the first I've heard of any of this. Antis would never go for anyone —"

"Are you accusing a British policeman of making an unfounded allegation?"

"No, sir. But it doesn't make any sense. Antis isn't a vicious dog, or savage. Can I speak to the wing commander about this?"

"As I said, he is presently away on a visit to the Air Ministry, but I am certain he will back my decision. You are to report to the station warrant officer, who has an official letter for you, outlining what you must do. You are to read and sign that letter, then continue as instructed. That is all."

Robert made his way to the SWO's office, his mind a whirl of thoughts. He didn't believe for one moment that Antis had attacked anyone. Even if he had, there had to be a reason, and there was no way that Robert was going to take this lying down. It was all very convenient that this had blown up just when Ocelka — a man who had formally accepted Robert's request that he adopt his dog should Robert be lost in combat — happened to be away from the base.

Robert smelled a rat. His fears were more than justified when he collected the letter. It gave him forty-eight hours in which to find an alternative home for his dog. If he wasn't off the base by then, Antis was to be "destroyed."

The letter was penned by the adjutant, and it was almost as if he had signed Antis's death warrant.

FOURTEEN

Robert stared at the letter with unseeing eyes. It was as if his mind was incapable of processing the words he had just read. One thing stood out to him above all else, though: it was the adjutant's signature at the bottom of the page. Robert returned to the man's office in one more effort to make him see sense.

"Sir, if I might have a word, please?"

The adjutant barely glanced up from his desk. "Not now, Sergeant. Can't you see I'm busy? Anyhow, you have your written orders. See that they are carried out."

For a long moment Robert stared at the balding head of his tormentor. The man was a coward. He was a desk-bound pen pusher, a man who never once had flown into danger as had Robert and his fellow airmen. His lack of backbone was typified in his decision to let the station SWO deliver the letter to Robert, instead of having the guts to face him. Robert despised the man.

"Sir, now see this," Robert announced.

As the adjutant glanced up in surprise, Robert began to slowly and methodically tear up the letter in front of his face. He took a step forward and placed the shredded remains on the adjutant's desk.

"I've never known such insubordination!" the adjutant exploded. His eyes were bulging out of their sockets as he stared at Robert's handiwork. "You know the consequences of what you've just done, don't you, Sergeant?"

"Yes, sir."

His actions had been incendiary, but also very deliberate. Nothing was more likely to see him go before the CO than what he had just done — tearing up his orders. Come what may, he'd get to say his piece before Ocelka.

"I should by rights put you under arrest. But you are operating tonight, so I shall desist from doing so. But, and mark my words, when the wing commander gets back I shall ensure he deals with you. In the meantime, you know my orders concerning your dog, even though you have had the temerity to tear them to pieces. Make sure those orders are carried out. Now, get on your way."

With Antis at his heel, Robert made his sorry way to the mess. By now word of the adjutant's orders had spread around the base, and he was greeted by a posse of airmen whose anger and indignation were clear for all to see.

"We'll form a delegation and put it to that bloody despot," Uncle Vlasta exclaimed. The father of the Original Eight was never one to lose his cool, but the adjutant's orders had really stirred his ire. "The CO's away and this happens — it's a bloody frame-up!"

"Vlasta's right," added Cupak, who served as Ocelka's rear gunner. "It would never have happened were the 'old man' here!"

"Antis is one of us," Ludva added, "and if anything should happen to him . . ."

All present knew what Ludva was driving at. Like airmen everywhere they were a superstitious lot, and each carried with him some form of lucky charm or talisman to keep him safe in the air. Capka, the pilot of C for Cecilia, had his unwashed maroon underpants that were first issued to him in the French Foreign Legion. Gustav had a set of miniature ivory elephants without which he would never fly. And Antis was the squadron mascot, the lucky charm that arguably kept them all safe in the air. For many it went even deeper than that. For the surviving members of the Original Eight — and for many others who'd listened to their stories — Antis was the miracle dog who'd gotten them out of war-torn France alive. It was unthinkable that some puffed-up outsider like the adjutant might have the power of life and death over such a dog.

"Come on!" exclaimed Ludva. "What are we waiting for? Let's go! All for one, and one for all! Antis is one of us, and no one's getting rid of our dog!"

Glancing around the sea of flushed faces, Robert could well imagine what was going to happen if they went en masse to confront the adjutant. His fellow Czechs were by nature a solid and mellow bunch, but only until their ire was roused, whereupon they'd fight like the best of them. The situation was heated enough already and he could easily see it coming to blows. It was bad enough having one of them — himself — facing a court-martial, let alone the entire squadron.

Robert quieted the men down. "We'll find another way. All we need to do is hold out long enough for the CO to return, and then Antis will get his reprieve." He checked his watch. "Come on, there's an air test scheduled shortly. Let's get it done, then work on our battle plan."

The route to the airfield took them through the gate manned by the policeman who was the cause of all the present trouble. As the group of airmen approached with Antis trotting happily in their midst, the blue-uniformed symbol of authority stepped out of his little hut and stood blocking their way.

"Do you have a permit to keep that dog on Air Ministry property?" he demanded. "If so, I need to see it."

"You know I haven't!" Robert retorted as he clenched his fists with anger.

"Take it easy, Robert," Uncle Vlasta warned. "He's only trying to provoke you."

The policeman held out his stubby fingers. "The permit, if you please? Otherwise he cannot pass."

"You listen to me," Robert rasped. "You may think you are a very fine policeman, but you are actually a complete fool. We are airmen on duty, flying missions against the enemy, and all the while you remain here in your cozy little hut. You'd best get out of our way and stay out of our way, if you know what's good for you!"

"You're headed for that ditch a second time," Ludva added, "only now it'll be head bloody first!"

"Come on," urged Capka, "on we go. Don't take any notice of him."

They hustled past the red-faced policeman, Antis growling at him from their midst.

"There's going to be hell to pay," muttered Josef as they headed for their aircraft.

"Maybe. Maybe not," replied Robert grimly, the germ of an idea forming in his mind.

How many times now had he been all but forced to abandon his dog? There was the time at the French farmhouse in no-man's-land, when Robert had slipped the tiny puppy inside his flying jacket instead. There was the time at the quayside in Gibraltar, when a trick with a bucket on a rope had reunited them. There was the time when a dog hidden in a mountain of luggage had evaded British customs. Then there was the confrontation at RAF Honington with a SWO who was an unredeemable hater of dogs.

Together, he and Antis had survived it all, and Robert had a good idea how they might do so again.

Once they were back at Manor Farm, Robert went and sought out Colly, an old man who lived in a nearby farm cottage. Over the months Robert had struck up a friendship with him. He was a natural-born rebel, as well as a dyed-in-the-wool country-man. Robert had gotten into the habit of bringing him an ounce of tobacco, for he didn't have much, and listening to his stories of the "olden days." Colly had been an arch poacher in his youth, and Robert loved the tales he told of midnight fistfights with gamekeepers and subsequent escapes across moonlit fields.

Colly was also an ardent admirer of Robert's dog, and he felt certain the old boy would have an answer to the adjutant's cruel diktat. He found him digging potatoes in his back garden.

"Do away with your dog!" Colly exclaimed, once Robert had explained things. "That's criminal, that is. Bloody mindless authority. We'll soon see to a way to fix 'em."

Colly thrilled to the idea of sticking it to the adjutant, not to mention the policeman. Authority was there to be resisted, in the old boy's view. He showed Robert to a set of steps at the rear of his cottage that led into an old cellar. It was half hidden with brambles and it looked as if it hadn't been used for many a year.

"Still dry she is," Colly told him as he lifted the ring set into the trapdoor. "Many a crop of 'taties we've had stored in there.

We'll clean her out a bit, and your Antis'll be quite safe in there. I'll take him food and water when he needs, and let him out at night for a minute to see to his needs. And none of them fools will ever think of looking in there."

Robert helped Colly clear one end of the cellar, which seemed to run the entire length of the cottage. Then, with the help of his brother airmen, he carried whatever they felt Antis might need down there, including some of Robert's things, in an effort to make him feel more at home. That done, Robert went and fetched his dog. He led him down to his new home, settled him on his blanket, and spent a good deal of time talking to him, explaining that they were in real trouble and that Antis needed to stay hidden here until it all blew over.

Everything depended on the hiding place remaining undetected, Robert explained. Antis seemed at last to understand. When Robert went to leave, his dog didn't try to follow, but instead settled down on his blanket, throwing a trusting look at his master as he climbed the rough wooden steps and disappeared.

Two days passed with Antis remaining secreted in his subterranean hideout. On returning from night operations, Robert was able to take him out for a short walk, with Capka, Josef, Uncle Vlasta, and Ludva positioned as lookouts keeping watch for the enemy — the adjutant, or the Air Ministry police. That Friday, with C for Cecilia's crew relieved of flying duties for the weekend, Robert moved into the cellar alongside his dog. The adjutant's forty-eight-hour deadline was all but expired, but by Monday Ocelka, the squadron CO, was expected back at the base.

That Saturday afternoon Robert and friends got a tip-off that the adjutant was on his way. Robert, Vlasta, Josef, and Ludva were sitting on the farmyard wall as the adjutant, escorted by his orderly sergeant and a corporal, strode into the farm. The Czech airmen could hear the search going on inside their quarters as the three men rattled windows, lifted beds, and slammed cupboard doors. They could see the adjutant's ramrod-straight figure striding angrily from room to room, searching for Robert's renegade dog.

Ten minutes later he was back in the farmyard, his face crimson with rage. For a moment he stood resolute on the porch, as if torn as to his next course of action. And then, without a word to the Czech airmen — Robert included — he stomped out the gate and took the road leading back to the airbase, his minions trailing in his wake. Barely ten minutes later the corporal was back again.

"Sergeant Bozdech to report to the station adjutant's office immediately!" he announced.

Robert slid off the wall. "Lead on, Corporal."

The corporal paused for a moment, glancing all around to check that he wasn't about to be overheard. "They've all come forward," he hissed. "All four of 'em."

"All four of whom?" Robert queried.

"The four crew who saw what the bleedin' copper did to your dog."

"So what did they say?"

"The truth. That your dog was provoked. That it was the copper's fault."

"My God, you're in the clear, Robert!" one of the others exclaimed. "That's what we've been waiting for!"

"That," said Robert, "remains to be seen. Knowing the adjutant . . ."

He left the last part of the sentence unsaid and made his way to the adjutant's office. The man's face when he entered was a darker shade of puce than Robert had ever imagined possible.

"Sir." He saluted. "You asked to see me."

"Where is that damn dog?" the adjutant barked.

"Hidden, sir."

For a long moment Robert feared the man was going to have a heart attack. "Hidden! What d'you mean, hidden? I ordered you to hand that dog over or have him destroyed!"

"Sorry, sir, that's an order I cannot carry out."

The adjutant's fist slammed onto his desk. "Do you have any idea what you are saying! I will have you court-martialed for disobeying an officer!"

"If that's what you feel you have to do, sir, so be it. But I could never obey such an order, especially in the knowledge that my commanding officer wouldn't approve it."

"That's quite enough! Get out!"

Robert stood his ground. "Look, sir, if you'd known all the facts I'm sure you'd never have drafted that order in the first place. Four witnesses have come forward —"

"Oh yes, I know all about your witnesses!" the adjutant cut him off. "I daresay the entire base would back you and that hound of yours, he's oh-so-popular. If you imagine for one moment I'll risk losing the co-operation of the police over a dog — well, you're sorely mistaken. Now, as I said, get out of my office!"

As Robert had suspected, the adjutant was far from done. Knowing that he was scheduled to fly a mission starting at nine o'clock that evening, the adjutant put a call through to the local civilian police force. He reported that a savage dog was loose somewhere on the base, and asked that they mount a search starting at precisely fifteen minutes past nine, when the dog was likely to be out and about and could be apprehended.

As C for Cecilia taxied toward the runway Antis must have heard her familiar engine noise from his hiding place. He let out an excited bark, and those acting as his chaperones during Robert's absence had to try to calm him before his yelping gave them away. The candle in the cellar was kicked out, and in the darkness they waited for the crunch of boot on gravel that might signal their discovery.

That night Robert was set to fly a sortie over the German port city of Hamburg, bombing the docks. But all through that mission half his mind was back at Manor Farm, in a darkened cellar. The police who had been called out soon learned the nature of the supposedly savage dog for whom they'd been tasked to search: it was Antis. Everyone in the East Wretham area knew the dog well, and they didn't believe for one minute that he was capable of savaging anyone. After a perfunctory search of the base, the policemen were soon home and tucked up in their beds.

At midday on Monday Wing Commander Ocelka returned to East Wretham. News reached Robert almost immediately that the CO was back. Pausing only briefly to reassure Antis that his imprisonment would soon be over, Robert cycled over to the base at top speed. He made straight for the adjutant's office.

Robert lifted a salute to the man he had learned to hate. "Permission to see the CO, sir."

"Refused," the adjutant shot back at him, his eyes hard and cold as ice. "He's only just back and is far too busy —"

"Is that bloody Bozdech?" a friendly voice called out from the CO's office. His door was half open. "And if it is, where's my best friend, Antis? I've got something for him."

"Yes, it is, sir, it's me," Robert replied.

"Well, come on in, and bring your dog with you," the CO called.

"Thank God you're back, sir," Robert blurted out, saluting smartly. "I'm in bad trouble."

"Nothing new." The CO smiled. "More

importantly, where's the dog? I've got him a new collar."

"In hiding, sir."

Ocelka glanced up at him sharply. "What d'you mean, in hiding?" He was twirling a shiny new collar between thumb and forefinger. "How can I give him this if you've hidden him?"

"I'm sorry, but I had to hide him, sir . . ."

A stiff figure appeared at Robert's shoulder. "Let me explain, sir. You need to hear this, anyway. While you were away this man's dog attacked an Air Ministry policeman . . ."

Ocelka shook his head. "Impossible. Antis wouldn't hurt a fly, let alone a fellow human being. Well, not that he's human, of course, but he practically is, squadron mascot and all that."

"I'm afraid the policeman's report is very clear," the adjutant continued stiffly. " 'Savaged by a ferocious Alsatian' is how he describes it. I had no option but to order the dog to be removed from the base, or if not, destroyed. Sergeant Bozdech has unfortunately done nothing to comply with my order. In fact, he ripped up my letter of orders and —"

The CO waved the adjutant into silence. "Yes, yes, that's as may be, but it isn't my chief concern. My chief concern is this: I have spoken to you every day while I have been away, by phone, so why didn't you tell me what was happening?"

The adjutant bristled. "It's a straight-forward case, sir. Sergeant Bozdech has no permit to keep the dog on camp. I didn't think you'd want to be bothered by such a minor —"

"You're my adjutant," the CO cut in. "Anything concerning the personnel who serve in my squadron concerns me, and it's your duty to report it to me." He turned to Robert. "Now, let's hear it from your side, Sergeant, and hold nothing back."

As Robert related the story he could see the CO's demeanor getting darker and darker. It was only his presence that was preventing Ocelka from unloading with both barrels on the adjutant. It was clear as day that the man had seized the chance when the CO was away to try to get rid of the squadron's mascot. For a man like Ocelka — both a dog lover and a gentleman — it was unforgivable.

Once Robert had finished speaking, Ocelka called for a file copy of the adjutant's letter. When he read the order for the forty-eight-hour deadline, after which the mascot of 311 Squadron was to be destroyed, he couldn't contain himself any longer. He turned and dictated a short letter to his typist, to be rendered both in English and Czech.

It read: "Permit for German Shepherd Antis, 311 Squadron's mascot, to remain at RAF East Wretham Airbase. Access: unlimited. Time limit: none. The dog is of a friendly nature and it is considered unnecessary to keep him on a lead."

"And that," announced Ocelka, "is that." He turned to the adjutant. "Good day, Adjutant. Sergeant Bozdech, if you'll stay behind so we can have a few words."

Robert and Ocelka chatted for a while as the Czech airman brought the CO up to speed on all the squadron's news. Then Robert was dismissed, and he pedaled back to Manor Farm at top speed, a copy of the precious "dog permit" jammed in his pocket. The first thing he did when he got home was release Antis from the cellar, and thank old Colly profusely. Antis bounded up the steps, took one sniff of the afternoon air, and did a quickstep version of his war dance for joy.

A few days after Antis had gained the formal permit giving him the freedom of RAF East Wretham, the war in Europe shifted seismically. On June 22, 1941, Adolf Hitler launched 187 divisions of the Wehrmacht against Germany's eastern neighbor Russia, and so opened a new front in the war to establish the thousand-year Reich.

In the 311 Squadron briefing room the mood was electric, just as soon as news of the invasion had filtered through to them. Russia lay directly to the east of the Czech airmen's homeland, and with war opening in that direction Germany was now fighting on two major fronts, west and east — as long as the bombers from 311 Squadron and the other RAF aircrew could keep up the pressure of their nightly raids.

In answer to the new German aggression, 311 Squadron was tasked to bomb the railway yard in Hamm, in the west of Germany. Winston Churchill was eager to aid Britain's new ally in the war by whatever means possible, and vast quantities of rolling stock were known to be passing through the terminus at Hamm, en route to the newly opened Eastern Front.

It was not the best of nights for such a mission. An impenetrable bank of clouds lay low over the base, and even at ground level visibility was poor. Regardless, the trusty Wellingtons — C for Cecilia included — were bombed up in preparation for the coming sortie. As dusk fell the aircraft trundled along the perimeter track, each waiting for clearance from the control tower to get airborne. As C for Cecilia followed the string of aircraft climbing into the low clouds, little did a German shepherd waiting on the dispersal area know what lay ahead of him.

"He'll be back soon enough, old boy." Adamek comforted the dog as he gazed into the now-empty sky. "Come on, into the shelter, and not to worry, eh?"

Antis trotted after Adamek and flopped down in the entrance to their tent. Now and again as the men played cards he wandered out into the open, his ears tuned to the night noises all around him. He'd gotten into the habit of chasing rabbits, to make the long hours of his vigil pass more quickly, but tonight nothing seemed able to tempt him from his watch.

It was approaching one o'clock, and the Wellingtons would be well on their way home, when Antis awoke from a long doze as if with a sudden shock. With head raised he moved outside the tent and stood, limbs quivering and muzzle thrust toward the south, the direction from which the squadron was expected to return.

"What's up with him?" Kubicek, one of

the ground crew, asked nervously. "Is Jerry paying us a visit, d'you think?"

Adamek moved over to the dog, who was standing statuelike in the same pose. He crouched down beside him. "What's up, boy? What's troubling you?"

In answer, the dog neither stirred nor growled, but remained stock-still and one hundred percent focused on the distant horizon.

Adamek turned to the others. "That's not the way he warns of Jerry, and it's too early for Cecilia to be back. I wonder what it is?"

"Well, come on in," one of the others replied. "It's your deal."

Adamek shook his head. "You play on without me. There's something up." He tried to get the dog's attention, but Antis seemed unreachable. "I tell you, boy, it's too early yet. Too early. Come back inside and get warm."

As Adamek watched him worriedly, he noticed Antis had begun to shiver. It was a June night and it wasn't overly cold. Adamek knew instinctively that the dog was shivering out of fear. Then quite suddenly the big German shepherd threw his head back at the dark heavens and began to howl. It was a sound that the men had never heard him make before: it was hollow, full of loss, spine-chilling.

Instinctively, Adamek understood. "Cecilia's in trouble!" he called to the others. "Antis can sense it! God knows how, but he can."

There was a battered old alarm clock hanging in the tent. Its hands pointed exactly to one o'clock in the morning.

FIFTEEN

Antis took up the same position during each and every sortie that his master flew, faithfully awaiting his return. No matter what, he would not be moved.

For tonight's raid over Hamm, Robert had taken a turn as C for Cecilia's rear gunner. As the hands of his watch crept toward one in the morning, he had felt a slash of blinding light burn into his eyes as a searchlight swept across their aircraft. They were returning from bombing the target, and were passing over the Dutch coast where the Germans had some of their most fearsome defenses. Cecilia was trapped in a cone of blazing light, and Robert could sense the flak creeping ever closer.

Some two thousand feet below he could see a pair of Wellingtons likewise caught in the deadly glare. Dark puffs of smoke erupted all around them as the flak gunners zeroed in on the warplanes, and he watched in morbid fascination as fingers of glowing tracer groped toward the bellies of the aircraft. An instant later one of the Wellingtons began to glow an eerie golden red as fire bloomed all along her fuselage.

Within seconds the warplane had started to fall to pieces, blazing fragments spinning toward the ground. Moments later the second aircraft seemed to disintegrate before his eyes as a blaze of fiery wreckage tumbled toward earth. Robert tried not to think of the twelve airmen who had just lost their lives — snuffed out in an instant — and very likely from his own squadron.

C for Cecilia was flying an unvarying course dead straight ahead, which could only mean one thing: they must have been hit, and the Wellington's controls were partially damaged. Capka, their ace pilot, would have been trying to shake off the searchlights otherwise, throwing the heavy bomber into any number of twists and turns. But as the Wellington droned onward neither the pitch of its engines nor its course altered a fraction, and Robert began to wonder just how bad the damage might be.

Capka would only warn them if they were in danger of going down. He was as cool as a cucumber, and as a rule he kept flight chatter to a minimum.

The violent blasts in the sky to left and right crept closer. With each it felt as if a massive fist were punching into one or the other flank of the warplane. Every now and then Robert could hear the horrible sound of burning-hot shards of metal tearing into the Wellington's fuselage. He tensed his shoulders over his twin Brownings, fearing the shrapnel would bite into him.

A shell burst blindingly close — seemingly right beside the tail of the aircraft — and milliseconds later a shard of metal punched through the Plexiglas gun turret, shattering it, and buried itself in Robert's forehead. A hot, sticky wetness seeped into his eyes, blinding him to the skies all around him.

He felt a surge of panic grip his guts. *I can't see! I can't see!* And if he couldn't see he couldn't use his guns to defend the war- plane.

He scrunched his knuckles into his eyes, trying to rub away the worst of the cloying wetness. They came away smeared in blood, but at least he could see better now. He scanned the skies from his lonely position at the rear of Cecilia, adrenaline blinding his mind to the pain of the injury. His watch lay on his bloodied wrist, but he only had eyes for the enemy now, and the time of his wounding — one o'clock precisely — went unremarked.

Yet, two hundred miles to the northwest of their position, a dog had felt that wound just as powerfully as if he had been injured himself, Antis throwing his muzzle to the night and howling out his pain and his distress.

Cecilia was losing height now. Any lower, and she'd be a target going begging for the gunners below. Robert had lost a lot of blood and was on the verge of falling unconscious. As the aircraft nosed through the night sky, scattered tufts of cumulus cloud drifted across its path. Sensing cover, Capka banked the aircraft gently to the left and a thicker mass of clouds loomed before them.

As the vicious flak tried to snatch them from the sky, the warplane lumbered into the clouds, the glare of the searchlights dissipating in the heavy, moisture-laden air, before losing them completely. Minutes later Cecilia dropped out of the clouds and Capka found himself over the North Sea. *Not far now.*

The crippled bomber droned onward, but with every turn of her tired propellers the Wellington seemed to sink a few feet toward the waves. As the coast of England loomed before her — a dark line on the blacked-out horizon — Capka found that he was so low as to be beneath the line of the cliffs.

He needed a miracle burst of life from Cecilia, or they were going to crash into them.

At East Wretham, S for Sylvia was the first of the returning aircraft to light up the horizon, blinking on her identification lamps so she could land without being mistaken for an enemy warplane. Further aircraft followed, the last being M for Marie, Wing Commander Ocelka's Wellington. Three of those that had set out on the raid over Hamm had failed to return. One of the missing was C for Cecilia.

At the tent beside the dispersal area Adamek stared into the east, where the skies were showing the first hints of dawn. "We'll give it another fifteen minutes," he muttered, glancing worriedly at Robert's dog.

Antis was sitting on his haunches perfectly motionless, his gaze fixed on the eastern horizon. Every now and again he raised one of his paws, seemingly to point toward the stretch of sky where Cecilia should appear, then lowered it, whimpering softly. Adamek tried placing a comforting hand on the dog's shoulder, but all it did was make him start. Antis glanced at the Czech for a second, then looked away, eyes flicking back to the patch of light above the trees where the sun would rise, and where Cecilia should by rights reappear.

By now the ground crew had packed up their few things and were readying themselves for breakfast. They tried to retain a cheerful spirit in the face of losing possibly three aircraft — and their aircrew — in the one sortie. But as much as Adamek tried to coax Antis to leave the dispersal area, he was immovable. He had settled down to keep watch, ears straining for the sound he hoped beyond hope to hear.

Presently, Ocelka drove up in his car. The wing commander was still dressed in flying jacket and boots. He pulled to a halt beside Antis, the car bumping across the summer grass. He held open the door for the dog.

"Come on, old boy," he called. "Into the car with you. You can't do any good here."

Normally, Antis loved his rides around the base in Ocelka's vehicle. Not today. He flicked a swift glance of concern at the wing commander, and then his eyes were back on the horizon once more.

"Any news of Cecilia?" asked Adamek.

Ocelka shook his head. "We'll hear soon enough." For once the strain of the night's mission was showing, not to mention the trauma of the potential loss of three Wellingtons and their crews.

"There's still a chance they lobbed down somewhere else, isn't there, sir?" Adamek asked.

"That's the hope. But come on, no sense in waiting here any longer. Clear off for breakfast and try to relax a bit. As soon as we hear I'll let you know." He fixed Antis with a look of real concern. "You too, boy. Into the car now." He'd said it like an order, but the dog barely flicked an ear in response.

Ocelka got down from the vehicle and went over to him. He petted Antis for a good while, before trying to move him. "Come on, old boy," he coaxed as he put his hands on the base of the dog's back and tried to give him a push. All Antis did was stiffen his limbs and dig in with his paws.

Ocelka straightened up. "All right, have it your way . . . I've always dreaded this moment. We'll just have to leave him alone and hope he changes his mind when he gets hungry."

At that moment Ludva appeared. Other than his master, perhaps no one was closer to Antis than Ludva, but even he couldn't get the dog to move. Whining miserably, Antis resisted all efforts the Czech airman — one of the Original Eight — made to shift him.

"Damn it, I can't stand this," Ludva muttered. "He knows more than we do. I always said it would be me first, and not Robert. Damn this bloody war!"

As the airmen and ground crew drifted away, Antis alone was left on the side of the airfield. It began to rain. One of the ground crew hurried back to throw a ground sheet over the dog. Then Antis began to howl. It was an eerie and dreadful sound, echoing back and forth between the tethered warplanes, and every man on the base who heard it could sense the dog's terrible pain and distress, not to mention his fear of what he had lost.

Throughout that dark day airmen and ground crew paid frequent visits to the dog, but still he would not be moved. His coat was sodden wet from the rain and he was visibly shivering, though more from the shock than from the cold. Around midday Adamek and some of the others decided to construct a shelter around him, to keep the rain off. Using wood and several ground sheets, they built a makeshift tent, but the dog seemed to resent it and moved out into the cold and wet once more.

"I reckon it's so he can hear better," Adamek muttered. "He doesn't want anything to get in the way of his sight or his hearing."

A plate of roast liver — the dog's favorite dish — was procured from the kitchens. But when it was laid on the ground beside him, Antis left it ignored.

Late that afternoon there was some positive news for the men at East Wretham. C for Cecilia had landed all but intact. Apparently, Capka had coaxed enough power from her engines to get her over the English cliffs, whereupon the port engine had spluttered and died. They'd made an emergency landing at the nearest airfield, which happened to be RAF Coltishall. No sooner was the stricken aircraft down than Robert was loaded into an ambulance and rushed to the nearest hospital.

It was welcome news for all, but no one could think how to pass on the glad tidings to Robert's dog. All through that night Antis kept his lonely vigil. Come the witching hour, the dog seemed to perk up a little. With dawn would come that special time when aircraft returned to base, and the dog had to be reasoning that Cecilia might be among them. But the squadron had been stood down for the night, and not a single Wellington loomed out of the skies.

An hour after first light Antis began to howl once more. It was a terrible sound to hear, and especially heartbreaking for Ludva, who brought Antis his first meal of the day. It was another plate of roast liver, but as with the first it went untouched. Ludva tried everything he could think of to let the dog know that his master was safe and well, if suffering a head injury, and that he was being treated at Norfolk Hospital.

Turning his gaze on Ludva, the dog made real contact with a human being for perhaps the first time since C for Cecilia had failed to return. His eyelashes were bejeweled in dew, his coat was slick with the soft rain that was still falling, and he was a picture of misery. But his tail attempted a few feeble

296

thumps on the ground as he tried to show his gratitude for the man's care. It was torturing Ludva — the man who, after Robert, loved the dog more than just about any other, and who had been through so much with him — to see Antis so forlorn and hopeless, and without need, for his master had returned, just to a different destination.

He knelt down beside Antis in the wet grass. "Come on, boy. Let me take you in. Let's go find Robert. Let's go find him."

The dog's ears perked up at the mention of his master's name, but when there was still no sign of him his focus returned to his resolute vigil. Ludva tried to move him, but a low growl from Antis said it all. *Thanks for the comfort, friend, but I will not be moved.*

Wing Commander Ocelka seemed as tortured as was Ludva at the dog's stubborn loyalty. He drove around the perimeter track that afternoon, determined to make a concerted effort to move the dog. He roared to a stop beside Antis, and next to him in the vehicle he had the base chaplain.

"Will you look at that!" Ocelka exclaimed angrily. "Why the devil hasn't someone moved him? Men on operations should never have pets. You can see the misery it causes when the master doesn't return."

Ocelka's angry outburst masked the pain

he was feeling at the dog's awful predicament. The chaplain placed a calming hand on the wing commander's arm.

"Sure, sir, but isn't it an example to Christianity, such devotion. No man could wish for a more faithful companion and many of us could profit from this lesson."

"Ludva, get the blanket from my car," the CO ordered, pretty much ignoring the chaplain's words. "Cover Antis with it and keep him warm. I'm clearing you of all duties. You're to get Antis back to your and Robert's room, and stay with him until he's fully recovered. And make —"

"It'd break the dog's heart to move him," the chaplain interjected. "And besides, he'll howl like the devil and keep awake all those crews trying to sleep."

"Well, what do you suggest?" Ocelka snapped.

It was all very fine talking about Christian examples and the like, but Robert was likely to be in the hospital for several days, and Cecilia was likewise grounded for repairs. If the dog refused to eat or take shelter for all that time, he'd very likely die.

"I think with God's grace I may have the germ of an idea, sir," the chaplain replied, with a twinkle in his eye. "You told me Robert is in pretty good shape considering. Why not ring the hospital, and persuade them to let him out for a few hours, so he can come in person and fetch his dog in?"

"Damn and blast it! That's the answer! Why the devil didn't I think of that?"

The chaplain shrugged. "The Lord works in mysterious ways . . ."

"D'you think the hospital will allow it, though?"

As it happened, the hospital matron was happy to let Robert out for a few short hours, but only when he was deemed fit enough to travel. They'd have to wait another twenty-four hours before that would be possible. Once more Antis settled in for a long night's vigil. Once more his friends tried to erect some form of shelter for the dog. But once it was finished he crawled out on legs stiff and cramped with the cold so he could keep his uninterrupted view of the skies.

Antis flopped down, weakened by lack of food and sleep, plus the chill, and he set his eyes toward the horizon. Troubled though they all were, there was nothing more that his friends could do for him.

At dawn the following morning Ocelka's car once again raced around the perimeter track. With a lack of available ambulances, the chaplain had cooked up a plan with

Ocelka to go and fetch Robert themselves. He'd driven all through the night in the wing commander's vehicle, and now here they were, with a bandaged, stiff, and bruised Czech airman riding in the car's rear.

In the silence after the driver cut the engine, you could almost hear those gathered around Antis holding their breath. The car door opened and Robert stepped down, supported by the ever-resourceful chaplain. At the sight of Antis he almost ran the short distance toward him. He sank to the ground beside his dog.

"Antis, you fool, why didn't you go inside?" His eyes were blinded by tears as he spoke. "Why didn't you let your friends take you in?"

The dog swung his gaze toward the voice, his exhausted, traumatized eyes trying to focus on whoever it was had come to speak to him. While the voice of this visitor seemed familiar, the smell was strange — a mixture of disinfectants and hospital wards, not to mention overcooked hospital food. Robert spoke again, whispering reassurances in the dog's ear.

"Antis, my boy, it's me. It's me. It's Robert. I've come to get you."

For a long moment the glazed eyes stared

at the strange-smelling figure beside him, with its head swathed in bandages and features half obscured. *Is it really you, Dad? Is it really you?*

"It's me, boy, it's me."

The voice finally seemed to do the trick. A tongue flicked out and licked his master's face, tentatively. Through the lint and the iodine Antis could just detect that familiar taste and smell — his master. It was true then. Robert had returned. The master he had presumed was gone had returned from the dead to claim him. Antis tried to climb into Robert's arms, but he was too exhausted to manage it.

Instead, the wounded airman picked up his dog, and cradling him in his arms, he carried him to the waiting car.

SIXTEEN

The chaplain drove Robert back to Nor-
wich Hospital, where both man and dog
mended remarkably quickly. C for Cecilia
took longer to put back together again. The
only sign of Robert's injury was a pink scar
on his forehead, but Cecilia, it seemed, had
suffered more long-term damage. From
now on the aircraft's heater would cut out
above ten thousand feet. High-altitude
bombing runs were to prove more than a
little chilly in the future.

It was late June by the time C for Cecilia
was scheduled to fly her first mission after
her forced landing at RAF Coltishall. The
aircraft had been grounded for several days,
and the crew was itching to get airborne
again. The target for that night was a crucial
one — Bremen, a city in the northwest of
Germany with a key industrial and port
complex on the River Weser. The port — lying some thirty-seven miles inland — har-

bored hardened U-boat shelters, a Focke-Wulf aircraft factory, plus the AG Weser and Bremer Vulkan shipyards.

This was to be no ordinary sortie. Using every warplane available to Bomber Command, a thousand-aircraft raid was planned, employing Halifax, Stirling, Lancaster, Blenheim, Whitley, and Mosquito bombers. But by far the largest component of the aerial armada would be made up of Wellingtons — some 470 of them, of which 311 Squadron was to contribute all twenty of her aircraft from East Wretham.

But unbeknownst to all, one dog was also going to be flying on that thousand-aircraft raid. As soon as Antis saw the bomb trailers being rolled out and C for Cecilia being bombed up for the coming mission, he sensed that something was afoot. Having suffered acute — some would argue life-threatening — separation anxiety as a result of Cecilia's last, all but abortive mission, the dog of war was determined not to be left behind again, to wait and suffer alone.

At seventeen minutes past eleven C for Cecilia took to the skies, but none of the crew were any the wiser that they had a stowaway aboard. The massive formation of aircraft formed up over the Channel and set a course for the target. But no sooner had

Cecilia climbed above ten thousand feet than her heating system failed. Seated in the forward gun turret, Robert chewed on handfuls of raisins, to keep his blood sugar up and to help ward off the freezing air that began to seep into the warplane.

In any case, Robert had bigger worries on his mind than the cold. For the first time ever Antis had been nowhere to be seen as they had completed their preflight checks and taken to the air. Capka had commented on his absence, and Robert had sent Adamek to search for the dog, but he was nowhere to be found. He'd been there with Robert at their room in Manor Farm as he'd collected his flight gear. He'd accompanied his master to the aircrew roll call that preceded every operation. But somewhere between there and takeoff Antis had gone to ground.

Robert tried to shrug it off. Maybe it was to be expected, after his dog's long and traumatic vigil during the previous mission. Antis had doubtless had a bellyful of it all. Still, his dog was if nothing else an animal of habit. It was odd — and somewhat disconcerting — not to have seen him in his regular place by Adamek's tent waiting for Cecilia to get airborne and for the aircraft's much-longed-for return. There was nothing to be done about it now, Robert reasoned. He was sure to get his answer when they touched down at the end of tonight's mission.

Robert focused his mind on the dark skies to their front. They would soon be over the German coast and danger beckoned. Feeling a touch on his elbow, he turned, expecting it to be the navigator with some comment or other, but he could see the man bent over his charts. Puzzled, Robert gazed into the darkened belly of the aircraft, and in the dim glow cast by the orange light next to him he caught sight of a familiar shape — a German shepherd lying prone on the floor.

He shook his head and looked again. Surely it couldn't be. It had to be the effects of the altitude playing tricks on him. And yet there he was. Antis must have somehow crept aboard their aircraft and stowed away, being careful to remain hidden until C for Cecilia was almost over her target. Recovering from the shock, Robert tried to take in all that he was seeing. His dog's flanks were heaving, his lungs desperate for breath, which was very likely why he'd alerted Robert to his presence. They were climbing to sixteen thousand feet and Antis was having increasing trouble breathing in the thin, oxygen-starved atmosphere.

Taking a massive gasp himself, Robert unstrapped the oxygen mask from his face, bent, and pressed it firmly over his dog's muzzle. He watched anxiously as the dog took a few deep breaths of the life-giving oxygen, before eventually his breathing seemed to settle down to something like normal. Feeling his strength returning, the stowaway dog clearly figured some kind of apology was in order. He raised himself unsteadily and offered one of his paws for Robert to shake.

Ignoring it, Robert pointed sternly at the floor. "Get down and stay down, boy, I've got work to do."

Robert grabbed his spare radio headset so he could keep in touch with the rest of the crew while Antis breathed from the oxygen mask. The mask contained his main radio pickup, and he could only imagine that he and his dog were going to have to share oxygen for the remainder of the flight. A few moments later he heard a squelch of static in his earpiece, signifying that someone was coming up on the air.

"Robert, have you gone to sleep down there?" Capka, their pilot, queried.

"No. Why?" Robert replied.

"Sounds like you're snoring your head off.

What's going on if you're not snoozing?"

Robert suddenly realized what Capka had to be referring to. Antis's labored breathing sounded something like a man asleep on duty, and it was being broadcast live via the oxygen mask's microphone!

"Well, as it happens we have an unexpected passenger. A four-legged one at that —"

"What the hell? Who? Don't tell me it's Antis? That's why we couldn't see him back at base . . ."

Where 311 Squadron's mascot was concerned, there was little that could surprise the crew of C for Cecilia anymore. It seemed as if they had an extra — and somewhat illegal — crew member aboard. So be it. For the raid over Bremen at least, Antis had become the seventh member of 1958-C's aircrew.

"Keep him close by your legs," Capka warned Robert. "We're almost over Bremen and the ack-ack's getting worse. I'll need to fly evasive action, so we'll be thrown around a little."

They began their bombing run at fifteen thousand feet, an altitude where the dog needed the oxygen. Robert had no option but to continue operating without it, for he couldn't keep switching the mask with his dog. He needed his hands free to operate the guns. At first he seemed able to cope just fine, but then his heart started to race and beads of sweat were breaking out on his forehead.

He was reaching down to grab the mask for a few desperate breaths, when a series of explosions burst in the night sky just beneath the aircraft. Cecilia reared and shuddered as the blast waves pounded into her underside. Searchlights swept the heavens, combining with the moonlight to turn night into an otherworldly blue-white glow. Below, the Bremen docks were a mass of flame, testament to those aircraft that had dropped their bombs before them.

Between the aircraft and the target lay a series of cleverly camouflaged barrage balloons. They were tethered to the earth in the hope that the warplanes might stumble into their cables or the balloons themselves, with catastrophic consequences. But the sky over Bremen tonight was awash with light, and the barrage balloons were clear for all to see, as was their target. With bomb doors open, Cecilia released her payload over the Bremen oil refinery and turned for home. Lightened of her 4,500 pounds of bombs, the Wellington seemed to leap forward and become more responsive and eager to Capka's touch.

But still the flak tore up the air all around them as the German gunners threw everything they had at the mighty air armada. Cecilia shuddered and slewed about as Capka tried to steer the safest course through the bomb bursts. With Antis gripped firmly between his knees, Robert kept his eyes on the heavens, searching for the enemy's nightfighters that he knew must be lurking out there somewhere.

Antis's face was lit a harsh white as a searchlight flicked across their path, but his eyes fixed upon his master's face appeared remarkably cool and untroubled. As long as his master remained calm, the dog took his lead from him. As for Robert, he found himself drawing extra strength and resolve from the brave German shepherd grasped between his knees.

Suddenly, the stark silhouette of a twin-engine Messerschmitt Bf 110 *Zerstörer* — Destroyer — rolled out of the heavens, its guns sparking white-hot as it opened fire. Robert recognized the warplane instantly, for it was the Luftwaffe's foremost night fighter and a formidable adversary. But he was equally quick, his hyped-up senses enabling him to swing the guns around and meet fire with fire. The twin streams of bloodred tracer from his Brownings rocketed across the intervening space as the *Zerstörer* hammered fire into the Wellington from its 20mm cannons.

For an instant C for Cecilia rocked under the impact of the heavy rounds, but Robert held his aim and kept firing, and moments later the Messerschmitt rolled gracefully and vanished into the darkness. Keeping his eyes glued to the skies in case it should return, Robert reached a reassuring hand for his dog. Antis responded instantly, moving closer to his master and resting his warm muzzle on his knee.

Having survived the night fighters, ground fire, and the threat of barrage balloons — not to mention a stowaway — C for Cecilia made it safely back to No. 311 Squadron's East Wretham airbase. Just as the first rays of dawn broke over the flat expanse of the runway, the Wellington put down with a hard bang, bounced a couple of times on the uneven grass, then trundled to a stop on one side of the runway.

There waiting at the dispersal area was chief ground crew Adamek, who'd spent a very worried night wondering what he was going to tell Robert about the whereabouts of the squadron's much-loved dog. Never before had Antis missed C for Cecilia's takeoff and landing, and Adamek and his men had spent most of the night searching for him. They were convinced something terrible must have happened to 311 Squadron's impetuous mascot.

Before the Wellington's engines had come to a full stop, the side door swung open, and the first thing to appear was the furry streak of a four-legged creature. Antis leaped out, touched down, got blown off his feet by the back blast from the Wellington's twin propellers, regained his feet, and practically jumped into Adamek's arms. Bouncing and prancing about, Antis went through an extra-ebullient and noisy war dance for joy, completing several wild circuits around the aircraft — only this time he had been truly a part of C for Cecilia's crew.

As Robert and his fellow airmen descended the ladder they couldn't help but laugh at their dog's crazed antics. Antis whirled around on the spot like a dervish, rolled onto his back and wriggled like a snake, then set off again for another whistle-stop circuit, grass flying from his paws and forming a haze in the crisp early-morning light. No doubt about it, this had been an extra-special homecoming — and for no one more than Antis, who had practically suffocated to death up there on the roof of the world.

Antis knew from Robert's laughter that he had been forgiven his temerity in sneaking onto the aircraft and stowing away, but had Adamek forgiven him for going missing during that long night's operation? The stocky little Czech corporal stomped over and grabbed Robert's arm.

"So that's where the little devil was!" he exclaimed. "You had him hidden in the Wellington all along! We've been up half the night searching high and low for the little so-and-so."

Robert shrugged. "We were none the wiser, not until he needed some of my oxygen and came out of hiding!"

Antis could tell from Adamek's tone of voice that he was more relieved than angry. The dog sprang toward the stocky Czech, getting up on his hindquarters so he could give Adamek a good lick around the face. In return Adamek grabbed the big, powerful dog in a massive bear hug so as to welcome him home.

"You miserable little sod," he remarked. "I've been looking for you everywhere I could bloody think." He glanced at Robert. "So how did he do up there?"

Robert shrugged. "Fine for a dog. But he

half suffocated at altitude and I was forced to share my oxygen, which meant I half suffocated too . . ." Robert broke off. He could see Wing Commander Ocelka's car driving along the airfield toward them. "Don't look now," Robert muttered, "but I reckon I'm for the bloody high jump good and proper. What with the RAF and all their rules . . ."

As everyone knew, it was strictly against Britain's Air Ministry regulations to take an animal into the air, and especially when flying on a combat sortie over enemy territory. The car drew to a halt and Ocelka got out. Antis bounded over and flung himself at the wing commander, who he seemed to know by now was one of his greatest fans on the airbase. Ocelka glanced at the dog, rolled his eyes in amazement at his miraculous reappearance, then cast a look at Robert.

"Antis's back on form, I see," he called over. "No guessing where he's spent the night, then."

Robert figured he detected an ominous tone to the wing commander's voice. He might have proven to be Antis's foremost protector at East Wretham, but there were surely limits that even Ocelka wouldn't cross. He was a fantastic leader, and he would often make a personal call to returning aircrew, just to hear how the sortie had gone and to boost their morale. But Robert suspected he was here for a different reason now — namely to investigate how Antis had gone missing overnight, only to become their *flying* dog of war.

Ocelka turned to the pilot, Capka. "So, how did it go?"

"All good, sir," Capka replied. "We had a *Zerstörer* on our tail for a while, but he veered off after Robert gave him a few nasty bursts."

Ocelka eyed Robert. "Did you hit him?"

"Not a hope, sir," Robert replied honestly.

Ocelka arched one eyebrow. "Too worried about that dog at your feet, no doubt." He patted Antis on the head, before turning to Josef, the other gunner. "What about you, eh? I don't suppose you were so easily sidetracked? Maybe you got to hit the 110 for me?"

Before Josef could answer, Robert intervened. "Sir, please, let me explain. None of us knew that Antis —"

The wing commander threw up a hand to silence him. "There's a very good English expression. It goes like this: *What the eye doesn't see the heart doesn't grieve over.* I believe it's more often used in connection to matters amorous, but it does just fine for last night's little escapade."

"Sir, rest assured it won't happen again —"

Ocelka threw up his hand for silence again. Bending down so he was eye to eye with Antis, he gripped the dog's head in both his hands and wrestled it playfully from side to side. Antis made a play-growl in return, nipping at the wing commander's wrists.

"You know something, Antis, sometimes you have a fool for a master," Ocelka mused. "He talks too much when he should stay silent. I've got enough on my hands with two-legged troubles to be bothered about four-legged ones. What the eye doesn't see the heart doesn't grieve over, eh, boy?"

Antis gave a short bark of agreement. Ocelka laughed. "That's my boy!" He raised his eyes to Capka. "Walk me back to the car and tell me again about that new belt of mobile flak you encountered over the Dutch coast."

The two men wandered off with Antis keeping them company.

"You're dead lucky we've got such an easygoing wing commander," Lancik, the navigator, remarked, when Ocelka was out of earshot. "We're all of us damned lucky to have got off so lightly."

315

Robert nodded. "We are. But there's more to what he said than just that. *What the eye doesn't see the heart doesn't grieve over.* I reckon he was giving us the nod that he's happy for Antis to fly with us. What do you reckon?"

"So Antis gets to be a permanent member of the crew?" Lancik shrugged. "Let's see what the skipper has to say."

It was more than just sentimentality or their attachment to their dog that lay behind all of this. Like all aircrew, that of C for Cecilia was always on the lookout for some special talisman. Some aircrew flew with a silk stocking wound around their necks like a scarf, courtesy of a sweetheart back home. Others flew with photographs or crucifixes or lucky shamrocks, and they would each swear blind that it was their own particular talisman that kept them safe in the air.

After last night's death-defying sortie, the crew of C for Cecilia was beginning to feel the same about their dog.

SEVENTEEN

When Robert suffered injury on a sortie and was hospitalized, Antis waited for days in the cold and rain beside the runway for his master's return.

After a long talk with the wing commander, Capka rejoined Robert and the rest. They put the question that was on all of their minds: did Ocelka mean they were clear to fly with Antis whenever they wanted?

"Lady Luck was certainly with us tonight," Capka told them, "and very likely in the form of one very handsome and brave dog. And yes, Ocelka will turn a blind eye. He figures Antis has been bloodied now and can take it. But, Robert, you're to get him to the workshop and get him an oxygen mask made up. Ocelka can't have one of his turret gunners fainting for want of oxygen, and all because he's sharing his mask with a dog that shouldn't even be there!"

Two nights later C for Cecilia was given her next combat mission, for the murderous pace of operations had yet to falter. The threat of an invasion by Germany might have receded, but the power of the Nazis was still in the ascendancy, and the Wellingtons could ill afford to remain on the ground for long. By now Antis had been fitted with his own oxygen mask, one made up for him by the East Wretham fitters. It consisted of a standard pilot's mask, cut and modified to suit a German shepherd's long and slender snout, as opposed to the flatter, boxier face of a human.

The mask attached to his head with a special set of straps that ran around the back of his thick and powerful neck, with extra fastenings latching on to his collar. Antis didn't particularly like the thing, but he proved happy enough to wear it so long as Robert was wearing his. This was crucial. If Robert and Antis were to be able to fly further sorties together, Antis would have to behave himself impeccably when in the air and under attack — conditions that could melt the composure of many a man, if not break him. Antis needed to prove that his innate fear would be trumped by his attachment to his master, even in the most extreme circumstances.

Their target for tonight was Hanover, one of the most dangerous of them all. At first Antis couldn't quite believe it when his master called for him to jump up the ladder and take up his position in the aircraft. But once he realized this was for real, he offered his paw to shake to Adamek and the other ground crew, climbed the ladder leading into the aircraft's nose, and took up his place in the gun turret at his master's feet. As C for Cecilia took to the air there wasn't a happier dog in all of England.

The sortie over Hanover proved largely

uneventful, although it did serve to prove how suited Antis was to combat flying. He wore his oxygen mask whenever Robert did, snoozed at his master's feet for most of the long flight, and only seemed to become disturbed when a bursting shell from the savage flak tossed the aircraft around more violently than usual. But one look at Robert and he took his cue from his master's apparently confident and unconcerned manner: *If he can do it, so can I.*

If he can do it, so can I. The feeling was in many ways mutual. Not only Robert but all the crew got an added sense of peace from having their dog flying into the heart of death with them. It was almost as if they were more worried for Antis's welfare than their own, and that took much of their anxiety away. That night's sortie was C for Cecilia's thirty-second, which signified that sometime soon their first tour of duty would be drawing to a close. But in the coming days and weeks they would need their lucky-charm dog more than any of them had ever imagined.

The very next sortie flown by Robert was a vital one. Once again 311 Squadron had been tasked to hit the German battle cruiser *Prinz Eugen* — the warship that had so narrowly escaped their previous attempt to sink her. Sadly for Antis, he was forced to sit this one out, for C for Cecilia had developed engine trouble. Robert joined the crew of Wellington No. 3221-O instead, and it wasn't every pilot who was happy to bend the rules and have a large shaggy dog as a member of his crew.

The flight of eight Wellingtons reached Brest on the westernmost tip of France after a quiet passage over a dark but peaceful sea. The port lay perfectly quiet and largely without illumination as they came over target. Only as the lead aircraft began its bombing run did the searchlights come to life, probing the night sky, and the antiaircraft batteries started throwing up their vicious fire.

The nineteen-thousand-ton battle cruiser lay to the east side of the jetty, on Dock 8. The Brest smoke screen had been activated by now, a defense designed to blanket the dock in thick smoke so as to obscure any targets. But the wind was in the wrong direction, and it blew the smoke inland, leaving the docks and the battle cruiser in stark relief. The *Prinz Eugen* was totally blacked out and all but invisible against the dark waters, yet the crews of the Wellingtons knew exactly where she was moored due to their pre-mission briefings.

The flight of Wellingtons approached along the waterfront, with terrifying volcanoes of flak erupting all around them. They held steady to their course, and Robert saw the first bombs fall from flight leader 1015-L. A string of 1,500-pounders straddled the position of the warship. The first bomb scored a direct hit on the jetty, and further bombs landed all around the battle cruiser where it lay at anchor, the oily flare of the explosions lighting up the inky darkness.

Robert's aircraft followed suit, her string of bombs pummeling the location of the German warship, one of the finest in the enemy fleet. Robert felt the thrill he always did when hitting back at the enemy, and he only wished he could have had his war dog there at his feet to share it with him. All eight aircraft made it safely back to East Wretham, and subsequent reports from the French resistance suggested that the battle cruiser had indeed been hit during the raid.

The first days of July proved hugely demanding for 311 Squadron. Robert — and Antis — found themselves flying raids every second night. Essen, Münster, Cologne, Bremen, Hanover, Hamburg, Mannheim, and Brest — C for Cecilia was in action above them all, and such an intensity of operations took a heavy toll. When Robert had first arrived at East Wretham he'd noticed how tired and gray the veteran aircrew looked. Now he understood why.

The need to be constantly alert during the long night missions, coupled with the fear and the overbearing tension, was hugely stressful and draining. Near misses and lucky escapes — hits from machinegun fire and shrapnel that didn't bring down an aircraft or wound or kill — these had become the "new normal" for the aircrews of 311 Squadron. They barely warranted a mention in the mess as crews chatted over a beer and decompressed after their missions.

In a sense the enemy fighters that pounced on the lumbering Wellingtons were the lesser of the evils they faced. What ensued was a duel to the death between each bomber and the enemy fighter's guns, one that the best man would win. It was the searchlights and the flak that were the most terrifying, for there was little the pilot or crew could do to avoid those. Survival was largely down to luck and not being in the wrong place at the wrong time. With luck playing such a pivotal role, C for Cecilia's lucky talisman — their flying dog of war — was an invaluable morale boost, but Antis's composure in the air and his bond with his master were about to be tested to the very limits.

C for Cecilia's next raid was to be over Hanover again. As the aircrew notched up combat missions, so the tension mounted that sooner or later their good fortune was going to run out. But Antis seemed to remain sublimely unaware of both the risks and the dangers, and his joy at every takeoff put added steel in the souls of C for Cecilia's crew.

Once again the battle-scarred Wellington climbed for altitude over the English Channel. Just prior to topping ten thousand feet — the altitude at which most aircrew found themselves struggling for breath — Robert took his eyes away from the skies momentarily, reached forward, and strapped the oxygen mask to his dog. It had become a strict routine for him and Antis: the dog's mask went on first and came off last, just in case Robert became unconscious before strapping his dog in, leaving Antis to die of asphyxiation.

C for Cecilia reached her cruise altitude of 15,500 feet and set a course for the German city that was such a vital strategic target for the Allies. With its road junction, railhead, and factories, Hanover was a pivotal link in the supply chain for men and matériel heading to the Eastern Front. Disrupting those facilities was the chief aim of tonight's mission, as Churchill sought to show solidarity with Britain's new allies in the east. Hitler's lightning advance had bludgeoned aside any Russian resistance, and the rate at which the Russians were in retreat did not bode well. They were clearly in need of all the help they could get.

Tonight's target was the tank factory M.N.H. Maschinenfabrik Niedersachsen, one of Germany's most important plants making tracked armored vehicles, including the fearsome Panther medium main battle tank, and the *Jagdpanther* — hunting panther — tank killer. Using the River Leine as a visual marker, the flight of Wellingtons thundered in toward the city's industrial district, but the flak that blossomed ahead of them was the most fearsome yet. It appeared as a towering inferno thrown before the aircraft, the black bursts of the explosions lit here and there a fiery orange by detonating shells and bursts of tracer fire.

As with the aircraft ahead of him, C for Cecilia's pilot, Capka, was forced to fly evasive action, throwing the heavily laden aircraft into a series of turns as he tried to thread a course through a seemingly impenetrable wall of explosions and arrive over the target. As the Wellington lurched this way and that, Robert reached down to caress the ears of his dog in an effort to comfort him. He had his eyes glued to the heavens above, in case an enemy fighter might dive to attack, but few German pilots were likely to risk doing so when the flak was so thick.

Robert himself had no idea how they made it through the flak unharmed. Their bombs released, Capka banked away from the monstrous storm of high explosives and jagged shrapnel that rent the skies all around them. But C for Cecilia had been driven off course as a result of all the twists and turns she'd been forced to make, and the needles of the fuel gauges showed the juice was running low. In level, straight flight and at normal cruise speed the Wellington's fuel consumption was manageable, but flying such maneuvers as Capka had been forced to make, and at close to their top speed, he had burned up the gas.

C for Cecilia crossed the British coastline three-quarters of an hour behind their flight schedule, testament in itself to how far they'd erred from their intended course. Every turn of the aircraft's twin radial engines brought her nearer to their base, but at the same time sucked up the remaining fuel. Capka had to land the warplane at their East Wretham base by the most direct and quickest route possible. There was one major problem: as he pushed northward, the entire expanse of East Anglia turned out to be blanketed in thick fog.

As the first rays of dawn flared over the pencil-thin horizon, the aircrew gazed down upon a scene that under different circumstances would have appeared quite magical. Golden rays of sunlight lit up the rolling cotton wool of the fog bank in a thousand shades of pink and orange. But few of the crew had eyes or thoughts for how beautiful the summer mist might look: the fog lay to a height of six hundred feet above ground level, and it spread to the far horizon in every direction. There was no way they could land at RAF East Wretham — or any other base within their sight — and the fuel gauge was flickering on zero.

Capka's voice echoed over the aircraft's intercom as he calmly informed the crew of their predicament. It had been fairly obvious to all, even without their captain laying it out for them. Robert glanced at the dog sleeping peacefully at his feet. As was Antis's wont on such sorties, once their aircraft had turned for home — bombs gone — he seemed to sense that the worst of the night's adventures were over, and went to sleep.

"I'll fly a holding pattern and keep trying to speak to control," Capka informed them. "Stand by."

Robert felt the Wellington shift course imperceptibly, and he sensed Capka had put her into a graceful turn. For twenty minutes the aircraft circled the airbase as Capka kept radioing East Wretham. For all he knew, the fog might be clearing at ground level as the dawn rays burned it off, and a landing might just be possible. Trouble was, he couldn't seem to raise anyone. Dawn and dusk were never the best times to try to make radio contact, due to the fast-changing atmospheric conditions at those times of day, which tended to interfere with radio communications.

When Capka finally managed to get through, he was told the Met forecast was for no change, at least not for the next hour or so. The Watch Office at East Wretham had been firing Very lights at regular intervals, and if none had been spotted by C for Cecilia's crew, that proved how thick and impenetrable the fog must be. Unfortunately, conditions were equally bad at neighboring airfields.

As all the crew were plugged into the

aircraft's intercom, they'd all heard the bad news. They also heard the final order given to Capka.

"Climb to ten thousand, set a course for the coast, and abandon your aircraft. Good luck."

The logic behind the order was simple. Ten thousand feet was the optimum height at which to abandon an aircraft: it would give the Wellington plenty of glide altitude, more than enough to ensure it was over the waters of the North Sea before it crashed. It was also about the maximum altitude the crew could parachute from without needing breathing equipment. If they bailed out, the aircrew would most likely live, but they'd sacrifice their aircraft. New Wellingtons were churning off the production lines daily: it was finding crews to fly them that was the real challenge, especially with the attrition rates suffered by squadrons like their own.

All of that made perfect sense apart from one thing: they had a canine crew member, and no one had thought to make a parachute for their dog.

EIGHTEEN

Finally, Antis refused to remain behind when his master flew into war and stowed away on his aircraft — facing bailing out, crash landings, and worse.

None of the crew of C for Cecilia had ever bailed out. It wasn't Air Ministry policy to give the crews of Bomber Command more than a basic grounding in the theory of parachuting. Robert had gotten East Wretham's tailor to make some further adaptions to his dog's oxygen mask, so it fitted as snugly as a sock now, but he was beginning to wonder if he shouldn't have asked the parachute section to make Antis a doggie parachute.

Whatever, it was too late to worry about it now, and there was no way that Robert was about to bail out without his dog. If he went they both went, and he could only imagine he'd have to jump with a terrified dog clutched in his arms — though how he'd be able to pull his chute and steer it while holding on to his dog he didn't have a clue.

Robert had never felt so anxious in all his hours of flying. As for Antis, he dozed on, oblivious to the danger, his head resting on his forepaws on the cold metal floor.

"Starting to climb to ten thousand," Capka reported to control. "I'm heading due east for the coast, fuel gauge on the absolute minimum reading possible."

In reply, a new voice came up on the radio net. "Not to worry, Jo," their squadron leader intoned. Bearing in mind the circumstances, Wing Commander Ocelka seemed as cool as a cat. It was heartening. "If your indicator's at zero you've still got some twenty gallons in the tanks. Should be enough to get you near the coast and up to ten thousand. There's no point trying a landing in the thick muck that's down here, so you're better off bailing."

"I could try to put down," Capka suggested.

"It's your call," Ocelka replied, "but I don't advise it."

The radio traffic went dead for a second as Capka eased the bomber into a shallow climb. In the blinding dawn light Robert spotted the glint of an aircraft away to their right. For a moment he tensed his shoulders and prepared to swing his guns around to face the threat, before recognizing the four-engine aircraft for what it was — a Stirling heavy bomber. As he watched, the first of a series of seven parachutes bloomed beneath the aircraft as the Stirling's crew did what C for Cecilia's aircrew were about to attempt. The Stirling, set on automatic control, continued on its steady course flying eastward out to sea.

Josef's voice came up on the intercom. "There's a Stirling to starboard and they've all jumped."

"Must have got similar orders to us," Capka remarked calmly. "I've set a course east and we're climbing, but what d'you all want to do?"

Several voices — Robert's first and foremost — responded with the same answer.

"Try for a crash landing, skipper."

They knew their pilot well, and other than "old man" Ocelka himself he was the best in the squadron. If anyone could get them down in one piece, Capka could. They were also loath to abandon C for Cecilia, the trusty Wellington having brought them home from so many sorties when by rights she should have been a goner.

"Mr. Karel?" Capka queried. "D'you think we can make it?"

Capka, a sergeant, always called their navigator, Karel Lancik, "Mr.," in deference to his officer status, three officers and three sergeants making up the Wellington's crew.

"Try for a crash landing at Honington," Karel replied calmly. "It's only five miles away, so we should make it. Glide the last bit if you have to. You know Honington like the back of your hand, and maybe she'll be a little more fog-free."

"Sounds like a plan to me," Capka remarked. "What's the heading, Mr. Karel?"

As Karel worked out the bearing for RAF Honington, Robert reflected upon the elephant in the room, as it were, which was Antis. No one had said as much, but all six of the aircrew knew that if they bailed, Robert and his dog would have to jump together, and if Antis panicked both of them stood next to no chance of making it. Like the rest of them, Robert had never even done a practice jump, let alone rehearsed for doing one with the flying dog of war grasped in his arms.

"Warning light's on for zero fuel," Capka intoned. "You have that bearing?"

"Zero eight seven degrees," came Karel's reply.

"Zero eight seven," Capka confirmed. "Everyone, brace for a rough landing, and Robert, get that dog in your lap and hold on tight. Once we're down, all out as fast as we can, dog included —"

"I can't raise Honington," the copilot's voice cut in. "Try reaching them via East Wretham."

"I'm trying for a landing at Honington," Capka radioed Ocelka. "Can you radio through a warning —"

"Got it," Ocelka cut in. "I'll deal with it. You concentrate on getting down in one piece, dog and all! Stand by."

The seconds ticked by in a tense silence. Robert could feel the Wellington coming around onto its new bearing, and he sensed the aircraft losing height. He doubted whether they had enough fuel in the tanks to fill a cigarette lighter, but from this altitude they should be able to glide the five miles in, as Karel had suggested. The problem with doing a glide approach was that it left zero room for maneuver, which was bad enough in full visibility. It was close to suicidal when going in completely blind.

Robert reached for his dog, grabbed his thick metal collar, and gave his head a good shake. "Antis! Antis! Wake up!"

Antis opened one sleepy eye, heard the reassuring drone of the twin engines, and tried to settle back down to sleep again.

"Wake up!" Robert shook him some more. He leaned back from his guns and presented his lap. "Hup! Hup! Hup!"

For a second Antis eyed him in confusion. He knew the rules: flying was a deadly serious business and the last thing he or his master ever did was fool around — yet here he was being invited onto his master's lap! Maybe Robert was about to teach him to use those long, noisy pointy things, the ones that his master used to scare off the enemy? Either way Antis was being ordered to get up, and get up he would. He took a leap, landed in Robert's lap, and sat there half smothering him.

"Honington's unusable." Ocelka's voice

came back on the air. "Fog's down like pea soup. But if you want to give it a try they'll do what they can. Watch out for a red at the beginning of the only runway they think you might get down on. Good luck."

"Roger," Capka confirmed. "We'll try for the landing." He switched to the intercom. "As you heard, we're going down. Brace yourselves, and hold tight to that dog!"

Moments later the air around the Wellington grew dark as she plummeted into the fog. Robert's gun turret was surrounded by a soggy gray-whiteness, like a fishbowl packed around with cotton. He hugged his dog closer, bracing for the impact that would tear Antis from his arms and throw him forward into the guns or the turret if he wasn't careful. That was another thing they needed for their flying dog, Robert reflected ruefully — a flying harness, so they could strap him in properly.

Robert felt Capka begin his last turn, which would line the Wellington up with the runway itself — the maneuver known as "the final." Right now it was *beyond final* — for they had zero fuel left in their tanks. To his left one of the engines began to cough and splutter as it sipped on fumes. Robert saw a faint red glow within the fog to his left, lighting it up an eerie pink. Moments later the squat form of a hangar roof loomed out of the fog, and as Robert gripped his dog in a crushing hold the ground rushed up to meet them.

There was a thump and a screech of tires hitting solid ground, and moments later the Wellington was thundering along the runway of RAF Honington. Capka held tight to the controls as the aircraft rolled to a halt, still on the runway and still intact. Their pilot had made a perfect landing with zero fuel, only one working engine, and next to zero visibility — he had been flying on instruments only.

C for Cecilia was towed by a waiting tractor to a position adjacent to the hangars. Once there, Capka had no need to shut down the engines, for both had died due to lack of fuel. In no time the aircraft had been surrounded by a crowd of admiring onlookers.

"Nice work," one of the officers remarked as Capka rolled aside the cockpit window. "You're the first to land here today. How the devil did you manage it?"

"Well, sir, there was nothing to it, really," Capka replied, with a sheepish grin. "You see, as soon as I spotted your lights I just eased the stick back a little, closed my eyes, and started to pray!"

"What's with the dog?" the officer asked, nodding at the head of a German shepherd that the crew had painted in silhouette on C for Cecilia's flank.

Capka laughed. "Oh, that . . . That's our lucky charm. Every crew's got to have one . . ."

"So does the dog really exist? He looks like a handsome brute . . . We've heard talk of this flying dog, but no one's ever seen him."

Capka figured there was little point in trying to hide Antis, for they'd have to disembark sooner or later and everyone here at Honington seemed to know. Very soon, Antis was being petted and feted by all at the airbase for having survived a mission that had so nearly ended in disaster.

The story of the flying dog of war and the Wellington's miraculous fogbound landing quickly made the rounds. Somehow, it leaked out to a reporter with a national newspaper. The British press was hungry for positive stories about the war effort that would lift the nation's morale, and this was without doubt a doozy. Before C for Cecilia could be refueled or return to her base, a press photographer and reporter materialized at RAF Honington, seeking out the RAF mascot that had flown into combat over Germany.

It was one thing for the squadron commander to turn a blind eye to Antis's presence on such combat sorties. It was quite another to have such blatant rule breaking splashed all over the nation's newspapers. The reporter wanted a photo of C for Cecilia's crew — dog included — scrambling for a sortie and making a run for their aircraft, with Antis in the lead. But, inexplicably, an hour before the photographs were due to be taken, Antis mysteriously vanished. A good search didn't uncover the dog, and the press photographer had to be content with a few pictures of the human aircrew and the warplane.

Throughout all the fuss being made around the Wellington, Antis had remained secreted in his usual place in the aircraft's dark interior. In a rerun of the days he'd spent hidden in a cellar from a dog-hating adjutant and several bemused policemen, Antis remained perfectly still and quiet, as Robert had ordered him to. He was puzzled to have been ordered into Cecilia so long before takeoff, but as ever with his master, his was not to reason why.

The article that hit the press duly showed the crew of C for Cecilia posing by the warplane, the veteran of so many missions, in the gathering dusk, as they "prepared for another daring raid against the enemy." Predictably, the elusive animal that reputedly flew with the Wellington's crew was described as the ever-faithful and indestructible "dog of war."

So far, incredible good luck and the friendly hand of fate had kept the crew of C for Cecilia largely out of harm's way in the air. But it couldn't last. On July 10, 1958-C was allocated a mission over Cologne, Germany's fourth largest city and one of the Allies' key targets in the war. Set in the west of the German landmass, Cologne was a major Military Area Command Headquarters, being home to the 211th Infantry Regiment and the 26th Artillery Regiment.

It was mid-August when 311 Squadron took to the skies to bomb the city, some dozen Wellingtons forming up with their fighter escort. The flak over Cologne was so fierce that several times Robert felt and heard the harsh clatter of shrapnel tearing into the Wellington's underside and flanks. Each time he braced himself for injury, or for the aircraft to suffer serious damage. But the Wellington's unique geodesic airframe design, devised by the air engineer Barnes Wallis, meant the aircraft was able to take incredible punishment and remain flight-worthy.

The Wellington's fuselage was formed of Irish linen stretched over a latticework of aluminum crossbeams and interlaced with wooden struts. When the linen was treated with several layers of dope, this formed a taut outer skin. Whole sections of the framework could be blown off, punctured, or burned away, and yet the aircraft could still remain airborne and limp home to base.

Over the months the aircrew of C for Cecilia had grown used to the odd, popping sound that hot shrapnel made as it tore through the taut linen, and unless any crucial human or mechanical item was hit, they paid it little heed. During tonight's raid the bombs were released over target and the Wellington turned for home with a good few holes in her fuselage, but nothing that Adamek and his ground crew couldn't easily fix. It was only after the aircraft had rolled to a halt, and Antis bounded down to start his war dance for joy, that Robert noticed that his dog seemed to be lame.

"Come here, boy," he called. "What's the matter with your leg? Have you hurt it?"

Antis lifted his left forepaw so Robert could inspect it. He noticed a nasty cut in the foot, one that had the clean but ragged signature of a shrapnel wound. It had stopped bleeding by now, but Antis would need it cleaned and bandaged in the sick bay if it were to heal properly — the pads on a dog's feet being one of the most sensitive parts of its body. Robert bent to check his dog more thoroughly, and as he ran his hands over Antis's handsome head he felt him flinch. There was a similar-size hole torn in Antis's left ear, and a shallow but bloody furrow scored across his muzzle.

How many chunks of shrapnel had hit his dog Robert wasn't certain. It looked like two at least, one to the foot and one to the head. But either way the brave and stoical dog had let out not the slightest whimper or complaint for the whole of the flight, and Robert would scarcely have known he was injured had it not been for the slight limp.

"You've got your first war wound, my boy," he told him as he gazed into the dog's eyes. "I guess it was only a matter of time, eh?"

In answer, Antis flicked out his tongue and gave his master an almighty slurp. Robert thought back over all the lives that Antis had saved: their own, certainly, during the escape from France; several more, very likely, when acting as an air-raid early-warning system; and those that he'd dug out from the bombed terrace in Liverpool. Now, on top of being a lifesaver, Antis had proven himself to be an incredibly hardy and tough warrior of the air.

"It's the sick bay for you, my lad, at least until they've given you a good once-over. We've got to get you fit and well for Cecilia's next sortie against the Hun . . . We can't be going up without you, can we?"

As they set off for the sick bay, Robert noticed something was lodged in his flying boot. He stopped, bent down, and pulled out a razor-edged lump of shrapnel.

He held it out to Antis. "Is this what did it, boy? Is this what cut you? We'll keep it as a souvenir of your first wound in action, shall we?"

Robert Bozdech's dog was at the peak of physical condition and he recovered swiftly. But in years to come his injured left ear would start to droop, hanging down that side of his head much lower than the other ear. And now, news of such injuries suffered in the course of flying combat sorties against the enemy brought more media attention for the RAF's flying war dog.

On August 21, the BBC paid a visit to the base to do some radio interviews, followed shortly by British Movietone News shooting film for newsreel. And then, in a rare

treat for those at RAF East Wretham —
whose lives seemed to have been reduced to
an endless round of deadly missions flown
into the teeth of enemy fire — there was a
very special film screening in the NAAFI
(Navy, Army, and Air Force Institutes). It
wasn't any old movie that was being shown:
it was the film in which the 311 Squadron
aircrew played star parts.

Target for Tonight was a gritty and realistic
portrayal of Squadron Leader Pickard's
aircraft — F for Freddie — flying night
bombing missions over Germany. It had
proven hugely popular with the British
public, showing as it did the RAF taking
the fight to the enemy. The film proved how
Britain — aided by brave aircrews from
countries like Czechoslovakia — was striking at the heart of the German war machine.

But that gritty spirit of resistance, coupled
with the relentless pace of operations, was
about to cost one aircrew and their dog
dearly.

NINETEEN

Hit repeatedly by German fire, C for Cecilia, their rugged Wellington bomber, refused to go down, as Robert and Antis manned the rear gun turret.

A few days after seeing their exploits immortalized on film, the crew of C for Cecilia was back in action. The target was Mannheim, a city in the southwest of Germany that lies at the confluence of the Rhine and Neckar rivers. Though a small city compared to Hanover or Cologne, Mannheim was a crucial industrial center for Nazi Germany, and its size belied both its importance to the war effort and the lengths the Germans had gone to in order to arm the city against attack from the air — as C for Cecilia was about to learn to her cost.

The battle-scarred Wellington had unleashed her bombs — 4,500 pounds of high-explosive ordnance — but they fell to the south of Mannheim's industrial complex, so missing their intended target. It was hardly surprising that on this night their navigator and bomb aimer had given the call to release wide of the mark: the aircraft had been flying through a storm of flak, the Wellington being tossed about violently as the blasts pummeled her from every side.

Then, as the aircraft lurched ahead with bombs gone and began her ponderous turn for home, disaster struck. As she banked around, a shell exploded right underneath her belly, the force of the blast almost flipping the aircraft over and causing her to "turn turtle" (go upside down) in midair. At the same instant a whirlwind of blasted steel fragments raked the aircraft's underside, tearing through the thin linen fuselage and slicing into the Wellington's interior.

The veteran lady of the air shuddered and heaved as Capka fought to right her and keep control. For a long and terrible moment the stricken warplane seemed to stagger and stumble, as if she were about to fall from the skies. Capka struggled desperately with the damaged controls, with the rest of the crew horribly aware that one wrong move by their pilot would spell disaster. As Cecilia seemed to hang motionless and mortally wounded above the city, more flak exploded all around her. One more hit like the last and they were done for.

Gently, but with a firm and sensitive touch, Capka eased the wounded bomber back onto a level flight path. He held her there, nursing her around until he could set a course for home. But he was painfully aware, as were all the crew, that no evasive action would now be possible. Cecilia was badly injured and barely airworthy. Only the reassuring roar of the twin engines gave the pilot and crew any hope that they might make it. The controls remained stiff and unresponsive, and there could be no attempt to fly around or avoid enemy fire.

In the rear turret Robert fixed his eyes on the skies behind them. It was all up to the gunners now.

"Keep your eyes peeled for Jerry," he muttered at his dog, who lay curled up at his feet. "Keep 'em peeled."

Antis seemed remarkably calm and sanguine after what they had just been through, and not for the first time Robert marveled at the courage and fortitude of his dog.

"Everyone okay?" Capka's voice came through on the intercom.

There were a series of affirmatives.

The whirlwind of shrapnel that had raked the Wellington seemed to have left the crew unscathed. Or had it? Robert could feel Antis gazing up at him, but he didn't have a second to tear his eyes away from the threatening skies. Had he been able to return that look, he would have noticed an expression on his dog's face that he had never seen before. In Antis's eyes, in the tautness of his features, and in his shivering, he would have read real shock and pain.

But Robert's attention was focused on the darkness to their rear as the firestorm over Mannheim faded into the moonlit distance like a nightmare. Damn the moon, Robert told himself. It would make it so much easier for marauding German fighters to find them. He reached down and patted his dog's powerful head, without taking his gaze away from the heavens.

"Good boy," he comforted Antis. "Keep your eyes out for the Hun. Good boy."

No doubt about it, having Antis there for company made this kind of mission far more bearable. The rear gunner's position was the loneliest, for he was separated from the main body of the crew by some sixty feet of fuselage. It was also the point from which the enemy was most likely to try a surprise attack. Robert crouched over his twin Browning .303 machine guns and waited.

Moments later he found himself dazzled and blinded. A powerful glare had flicked across the aircraft as a German searchlight swept the sky. It flicked back onto them again as the searchlight's operators brought it onto the target. The Germans were operating radar-controlled searchlights — ones that could be vectored onto an aircraft's flight path by radar signature alone. As the blue-white light pinned them in its burning glare, Robert cursed. They were lit up like a beacon now, presenting a perfect target for any German fighters.

A dozen or more searchlights converged on the stricken warplane. She was caught in a concentrated cone of light, yet Capka had no choice but to plow resolutely onward. If he tried to weave or dodge in an effort to lose the deadly light, he might lose control of his aircraft and she might plummet out of the skies. Robert redoubled his watch as one formation of searchlights after another took over the task of illuminating the Wellington. The aircraft was a sitting duck, and no one doubted that the enemy's warplanes were coming.

Robert stared out of his gun turret, trying to shade his eyes from the blinding dazzle and see the enemy coming. Flak still burst around their aircraft, and few German fighters would want to brave all of that. He figured the enemy warplanes were a few minutes out. Then the bursting of shells ceased quite suddenly. In its place there was an ominous silence. Where the hell were the enemy fighters? he wondered.

There was only quiet now, plus the eerie inrush of the wind through the aircraft's punctured fuselage. The silence was broken by a terrifying sound: the staccato, punching beat of heavy cannon fire. Robert felt Cecilia shudder violently as the shells tore into her. But the skies to his rear were devoid of enemy fighters, and he could only presume they were being attacked from the front or the flanks. He swung the twin Brownings around, scanning for the enemy, finger itching to unleash fire, but not a sign of a German fighter could he see.

Up front, smoke and the sickly firework smell of cordite filled the cockpit. A gout of hot oil splashed across the windshield, half blinding Capka and his copilot. Cold air gushed in through the hole in the floor between them — the one that allowed them to communicate with their front turret gunner and their navigator/bomb aimer. It made an eerie whistling sound — proof positive if they needed it how extensively their aircraft had been holed. But at least the inrush of air cleared the cockpit of the smoke and choking fumes. While Capka fought to keep the stricken aircraft airborne, the others struggled to stem the flow of escaping oil.

A further burst of rounds tore into the side of the aircraft, yet just when Capka had decided she could take no more and they were going down, the firing ceased. For no discernible reason — perhaps they were out of ammo? — the German fighters were gone. Still coned in the blinding light, Cecilia plowed stubbornly onward. The crew braced themselves for the next onslaught, the one that would surely finish her. Robert's mind flipped to thoughts of his dog, and how on earth the two of them were going to manage to bail out together — just as it had when fog lay thick over their East Wretham airfield, preventing a landing.

Well, come what may, he was determined to take Antis with him. If they survived the jump and were captured, Robert would probably face a firing squad, as would the rest of the Czech crew. But he had to presume that because a dog has no nationality the Germans might take pity on Antis, though how he would survive without his master Robert dreaded to think. He reached down and ruffled his dog's hair. It struck him as odd that Antis could remain so still and so quiet in the midst of so much murderous fire and carnage.

"Get ready to make the jump, boy," he murmured. " 'Cause if Jerry comes back for another go, I reckon we're all getting out of here. You and me together to the end, eh, boy?"

Once again Robert felt his dog's searching gaze upon him, but he was unable to take his eyes from the night sky. He could sense the enemy out there poised to attack. He needed to be ready.

Up ahead Capka spotted the promise of relief: a thick bank of clouds. He eased the wounded aircraft around, hoping and praying that her injuries wouldn't prove mortal.

The Wellington rattled and thundered her way onward, and for now at least she seemed to be stubbornly refusing to give up the ghost. The cloudbank drew inexorably closer. Holding their breath and praying that they would make it, the crew of C for Cecilia counted down the seconds. Then the first wisps of sullen gray flashed past the aircraft's windows, and the Wellington churned her way into the blanket of water vapor.

The bomber shook and rattled all the more as the turbulence within the cloud mass threw her about, but to the crew of C for Cecilia it was a very welcome rough ride. Almost the instant she had hit the cloud the searchlights lost her, and for now at least she was safe from enemy warplanes. Cecilia droned onward. Her engines seemed to have found their rhythm again. Every now and then there was a worrying cough and a splutter, but otherwise the cloudbank threw back only a comforting drone to the six men who were longing to reach home.

In the rear turret Robert allowed himself a moment's relaxation. There would be no spotting enemy aircraft while they thundered onward through this cloud.

He let go of the gun's grips. "How you feeling, boy?" he murmured. He reached down for an instant to commune with his dog. "We did a fine job of weathering the storm, eh, and as long as we get home in one —"

Robert's words froze in midsentence. For the first time since they had been raked by that burst of flak above Mannheim, he had been able to take a good look at his dog. Antis was gazing back at him with his head held at an odd angle, and there was a distinctly glazed look in his eyes. It wasn't the look of sleep; and anyway, even Antis couldn't have managed to doze through the last hour or so.

With a growing sense of panic Robert flicked on the shaded light that lay to one side of his turret. The sight that met his eyes was a sickening one. His dog was lying in a slick of blood. With shaking fingers he unhooked the straps that held the mask to the dog's face. He held Antis's head in both his hands, gently stroking him. He was lost for words, and he could feel hot tears pricking at his eyes. He had no idea how badly wounded his dog was, and they were still a good forty minutes out from RAF East Wretham.

Unhooking his own mask and flight harness, Robert bent to inspect his dog. He had to know how serious his injuries were:

was it a shrapnel wound, or had Antis been shot? He felt around until he found the cause of the bleeding. Antis had a deep gash in his chest, one that looked as if it had been caused by a large chunk of shrapnel. But at least as far as Robert could tell, the dog hadn't been hit by an enemy bullet, so hopefully none of his internal organs had been damaged.

Either way he seemed to have lost one hell of a lot of blood. They needed to land their damaged aircraft and get their dog into the sick bay, and quickly. As far as Robert was concerned, nothing else mattered now but saving their dog of war — for if Antis died, their talisman would have died. And as legend had it, any aircrew that lost their talisman was surely doomed.

If, as seemed likely, Antis had been wounded by flak when they were over Mannheim, he had lain there for hours in a pool of his own blood, suffering intense pain. Yet never once had he cried out or whimpered, or tried to distract Robert from his task — that of defending their aircraft. He had borne his injuries with a fortitude that would challenge the bravest of men, but heaven forbid that the end result would be the loss of their dog of war.

Robert lifted his eyes from his stricken

dog, only to realize that they'd left the cloud behind. Cecilia had lost altitude and they were coming in across the English country-side, with dawn reddening the skies to their east. It looked as if the battle-worn Welling-ton was going to make it home in one piece; whether their canine crew member did as well was still to be determined.

Capka's voice came over the intercom. "Can't get the wheels down. Brace for a crash landing. As soon as we stop rolling get out fast, and be ready for a fire."

For a moment Robert wondered whether he should warn everyone that they had an injured crew member. There didn't seem to be much point. Capka had enough to deal with landing the stricken aircraft, after which every man's responsibility was to get out fast, before the Wellington caught fire or exploded.

As they came in toward East Wretham the copilot fired off a red Very light from the cockpit — the recognized warning signal for a crash landing. With Antis clamped be-tween his knees, Robert strapped himself in and braced for what was coming. The last thing he did was throw a protective arm around Antis's head as he heard Capka cut the engines. To left and right the propellers spluttered to a stop, and in the last few eerie moments before impact the only noise was the rush of the wind through the torn and shredded flanks of the warplane.

She hit with a deafening crunch, the belly of the Wellington tearing into the soft grass of the runway. With a horrible shrieking of tortured metal, the wounded beast of the air skidded and juddered for several seconds, before finally coming to a halt. Firemen and an ambulance speeded out to intercept her.

The rear turret was resting on the ground, and Robert was able to kick open the emergency exit door. He jumped down, leaned back inside, and levered up his injured dog, lifting him out. With the heavy animal held in his arms he ran for the ambulance. As far as Robert knew, Antis was Cecilia's only injured crew member, so he felt perfectly justified in claiming pole position in the waiting vehicle.

Seeing the state of their dog, 311 Squadron's mascot — hair soaked in blood, head hanging limply — the ambulance crew needed no urging. They set off, the speeding vehicle taking their wounded crew member to the station sick bay. From the ambulance he was rushed directly to the operating table. As a male nurse held Antis's paws, keeping his legs out of the way, the doctor inspected the chest wound. Robert couldn't bear to look. A lump of shrapnel had torn a three-inch-long gash deep into Antis's chest, and the doctor wasn't sure if the jagged piece of metal still lay inside.

"He's lucky it missed his heart," the doctor remarked as he reached for his surgical instruments. "Hold him and comfort him, Sergeant Bozdech, for I'll not be able to use any anesthetic on a dog."

As the doctor cleaned, probed, and sutured the wound, Robert held Antis's head in his hands, and talked to him constantly. His dog must have sensed that, in spite of the pain, all those around him were trying to help, and that whatever process he was undergoing here, it was critical to his life. An hour later the operation was all but done. The doctor raised his eyes from his task and fixed Robert with a look.

"I'd like to give him blood, of course, but we have none for dogs. Even so, he should make it through okay. He's a strong dog and in perfect condition." The doctor paused. "But make no mistake, Robert, he needs to be grounded for some time to come now. No more flying combat missions for Antis. He needs time to rest and recuperate, and in any case his wound might burst open under the pressure of flying at any altitude."

Robert told the doctor that he understood. For now at least, the flying dog of war was very much grounded.

As luck would have it, Ludva — the redheaded, fiery-tempered member of the Original Eight — was fresh out of the sick bay himself, having been wounded on a recent mission over Germany. So at least Antis had one of the all-for-one-and-one-for-allers to keep him company as he convalesced back at their digs in Manor Farm. Antis clearly hated being grounded. He disliked even more being banned from the airfield, but Robert felt he had no choice but to keep him away, for fear he might sneak onto C for Cecilia and stow away once more.

Each time Robert and crew left their digs to prepare for a mission, Antis would wag his tail and whine entreaties, lobbying hard to be allowed to go. Each time he had to be refused. To the flying dog of war this was anathema. It was also inexplicable. He was one of C for Cecilia's regular crew; he had never comported himself with anything but the utmost professionalism when in the air; and he was the only crew member to have been badly injured — yet this was his reward, to be left behind.

It didn't sit easy with the dog.

He started refusing to eat in mute protest at the way in which he was being treated. Robert spoke softly and patiently to Antis, for he recognized the seeming injustice of the present situation.

"Listen, boy, it's for your own good. We don't want to leave you behind: none of us do. But you've got to have the time to heal — doctor's orders. Be patient. Get well. You'll see — you'll be back with us in no time."

At least the torture of not being allowed to accompany his team was lessened a little by the fact that Antis couldn't actually hear C for Cecilia getting airborne. The Wellington was so badly damaged from the mission over Mannheim and the crash landing that had followed that she was out of service for nine consecutive days. As a result, Robert, Capka, and crew were forced to fly a sister Wellington, U for Ursula, which meant that Antis couldn't detect the engine noise of his beloved Cecilia taking to the skies.

He was saved that particular torture, and in the meantime Robert found Antis a mission all of his very own, one designed to further take his mind off being grounded: Operation Jacqueline. Jacqueline was a pretty four-year-old girl who lived in the end cottage at Manor Farm. Her father had been killed during the evacuation of Dunkirk, at a similar time to when the Original Eight — Robert and Antis included — had themselves been trying to escape from war-torn France. Jacqueline's grandmother ran the grocery shop at the far end of the village. She had been nicknamed "Mother" by the Czech airmen, for she had gone out of her way to make them feel at home in their adopted country.

Jacqueline's mother was busy working on the farm, and her grandma was likewise busy with her shop. Robert set Antis the task of being the little girl's babysitter, chaperone, and protector. Very quickly there developed an unspoken understanding between dog and child. Antis seemed to be able to read her mind, and he would rise early to meet her as they headed off together on whatever adventures she had planned. With her tiny fingers hooked in his collar, Antis would lead her through the village to Grandma's shop, or to the nearby fields to play. He was a couple of inches taller than she, and his thick, dark hair set off her wild blond curls admirably.

When Antis was with Jacqueline all knew that no harm would come to her. A photo of the two of them appeared in the local newspaper, under the caption "Little Red

Riding Hood." The story that accompanied the photo spoke of their unique friendship. The veteran dog of war, wounded twice in action, had proven to have a heart of gold.

Their favorite place was a water meadow near the farmhouse. Antis would lie on his belly as Jacqueline made daisy chains to string around his powerful neck. Robert had warned Antis never to let the little girl near the stream that ran through the meadow. If ever she strayed too close to it in search of flowers to string together, he'd take the hem of her skirt in his teeth and draw her gently away.

Returning from the meadow after a morning's play, Antis would pause at the roadside, Jacqueline's fingers knotted in his hair. He'd stand stock-still, his acute hearing checking for the approach of any vehicle in either direction. Once he'd decided the road was clear, he'd allow Jacqueline to cross. With her great protector by her side, the little girl was quite safe, and her mother soon learned to entrust her to the dog's care completely. As for Antis, Jacqueline's company was a welcome distraction, for by now he could hear again the engine note of his aircraft — C for Cecilia — taking to the skies.

It wasn't until late August that C for Cecilia had been deemed airworthy again. But on her first mission and three subsequent ones she developed serious engine trouble. On one sortie it was so bad that the crew had to jettison her bombs early, in the English Channel, in an effort to get the ailing bomber back to base.

All being well, Robert's first combat tour of duty would finish sometime in early September, when they would top two hundred hours of flight time. But the last few combat missions were always the most dreaded. It was a case of so near and yet so far. Many a crew had lost their lives during their final few days of operations, when exhaustion levels were at their peak and dark superstitions had it that they were most vulnerable. Indeed, any number of crew had fallen at the eleventh hour of duty, failing to return from their very last flight over enemy territory.

As they faced those fateful last few combat sorties, Robert and the rest of the crew of C for Cecilia were conflicted. On the one hand, they desperately wanted their lucky talisman with them in the aircraft. On the other, Robert was adamant that Antis, the flying dog of war, should not take to the air. His war wound was the perfect excuse to keep his four paws on the ground. At least that way, Antis would not lose his life if C for Cecilia were to be shot down.

On September 1, Robert Bozdech was promoted to flight sergeant. On that very night he and his crew were in action again, but once more they were flying 8784-U — U for Ursula — Cecilia suffering from ongoing mechanical problems. Their target was Cologne. Two nights later they were sent out to hit the port of Brest once again, this time targeting the mighty German battle cruisers, the *Gneisenau* and *Scharnhorst.*

East Wretham was again fogbound when their aircraft returned from the Brest raid. U for Ursula was diverted to the airfield at RAF Wittering, so it was doubly fortunate that Antis was banned from the airfield. The last thing the recently injured dog needed was a long sojourn on the flight line over cold September nights.

In the second week of September, Robert, Capka, and the crew were to fly their final mission of the tour, with Antis remaining safely on the ground. C for Cecilia took to the skies for — as fate would have it — one of the last missions she was ever to fly. Their target was a fitting one for their final combat sortie: the German capital, Berlin. But, as was now her wont, Cecilia developed engine trouble and Capka was forced to turn for home early. They opted to release their bombs over a target of opportunity — the German port city of Kiel — bombing the docks.

A little over an hour later Cecilia touched down at East Wretham, although once again gaping holes had been torn in her fuselage from enemy fire. At least they had made it back to base in one piece and their tour was finally over. It was a historic one for many reasons, but most notably — and tragically — because they were the first Czech aircrew to complete an entire tour without losing any members. Robert had completed 206 operational flying hours, many of which he had shared with his dog, and both he and Antis had been wounded in action.

The losses among the men of 311 Squadron were legion. Robert felt a mixture of incredible relief and regret when Cecilia touched down at the end of that final flight. He was relieved to have survived; but he was full of regret that he would be leaving — at least temporarily — others of his Czech comrades to continue the fight. 311 (Czech) Squadron had suffered enormous losses, and they had fallen upon a group of men who invariably knew each other well. Almost every death meant the loss of a close personal friend.

A day after that final mission Robert and Antis caught the bus to the local railway station so they could go on leave. Ludva went with them — he who had kept Antis company at the Manor while both were recuperating from their war wounds. Ludva it was who had half strangled to death the guard outside the collaborators' party in France, when they had so desperately needed to steal a vehicle. After all they had been through together, he, Robert, and Antis were the closest of friends.

Needless to say, the two men and one dog said a poignant farewell, their forced and cheerful smiles hiding their real feelings. Little did Robert or Antis know that this was the last time they would ever see Ludva alive.

But before that loss could hit them, there was more and worse to come.

TWENTY

Operation Jacqueline. Seriously wounded by shrapnel during a sortie over Mannheim, Antis was grounded and given the duty of looking after a local widow's daughter.

There was only one place for Robert and Antis to head for their leave: Wolverhampton, a town within easy striking distance of

RAF Cosford, and Pamela. For fourteen blissful days Robert and Pam renewed their romance, and Antis and Pam their delicious friendship. Emotions were quickened by how close man and dog had come to death during their tour, and thoughts of the long years of perilous struggle that lay ahead before the enemy might be vanquished.

But for those two magical weeks, Robert and Pamela strolled through the autumn countryside, talked of the future and of peace and of love, and dreamed impossible dreams. As for Antis, he was in rabbit-chasing heaven once again, and even his recent injury didn't seem to have slowed him down.

Man and dog came back to reality with a bump. Robert and Antis returned to East Wretham to say their farewells to their fellow aircrew. Robert had received his orders, and after a short Christmas break he was being posted to a gunnery training school, at RAF Evanton, in the Scottish Highlands. It was the last thing he wanted: in spite of the palpable dangers, he longed to remain with his brother airmen, taking the fight to the enemy. But someone had to train a new generation of bomber crews, and for whatever reason Robert had been chosen. Orders were orders and he was leaving 311 Squadron, possibly for good.

It was a late October morning when Robert packed his meager possessions in preparation for their departure. By the time Antis had seen the blanket on which he slept, plus his dog bowl and his lead being packed away, he knew this could be no normal parting. He lay in the doorway to their room, ears pricked forward and watching his master's every move.

Robert glanced over at him. "Sorry, lad, none of us wants this . . . But I'm afraid we've got our orders and we're to go."

Antis banged his tail on the floor in a couple of desultory thumps, as if to say: *Why would anyone want to leave this place?* Robert glanced around their room at Manor Farm and out the window at the autumn countryside. The wind was gusting, blowing clouds of leaves from the trees, and he could sense winter only just around the corner. With roaring fires lit, the Manor would be a fine place to last out the cold and bitter months, and there was no better company than his fellow Czech airmen with whom to do so. But it was not to be.

Robert and Antis made their way to the airbase so they could bid their farewells to Capka, Ludva, Adamek, and the others. But there was shocking news awaiting them.

Their cherished Wellington bomber had failed to return from her last mission. On just her second flight with her new crew, C for Cecilia had been shot down during a bombing raid over Berlin. Fellow aircrew had seen the venerable old lady fall from the sky in flames, and she was most definitely lost. As for those who had been flying her, all six were feared killed in action.

It was a deeply sobering moment for Robert. From Antis's hangdog expression he reckoned his dog also knew that some dark calamity had befallen C for Cecilia, and that his chariot of the air was no more. Robert had completed forty-odd sorties in the battle-scarred Wellington; by contrast, her new crew had failed to last even two. It was a chilling reminder of the transient nature of life, especially for those tasked to fly missions in the teeth of enemy fire.

Having said a somber goodbye to the remaining aircrew — and vowing to meet as promised for Christmas in London — Robert went to see Wing Commander Ocelka. He found him in his office, but before he could even begin to thank him for all that he had done, Ocelka waved Robert into silence.

"So, I hear you're on your way out of here," Ocelka remarked, speaking as much to Antis as to Robert. The dog had bounded over, and Ocelka was giving him a good rub around the ears. He fixed Robert with a piercing gaze. "Tell me, how d'you feel about being sent away for a bit of a rest?"

"To tell you the truth, sir, I'd far rather be staying."

Ocelka nodded. "We're sad to see you go, the both of you. What's 311 going to do without its mascot, eh, Antis? Any suggestions, Bozdech?"

Robert shrugged. "Not a clue, sir."

"You're damn right. How could we ever replace Antis?" He glanced at Robert thoughtfully. "Seriously, though, we'd like to keep you, but this is just the way it is. Air Ministry knows best and all that." He paused, and threw a play punch at the dog at his feet. "No chance of you leaving Antis with me, is there?"

Robert laughed. "Not a chance, sir."

"Bloody typical. Well, all that's left is for me to wish you good luck. Where will you be spending Christmas?"

"With Pamela is the plan, sir. Maybe a quick trip to London as well, to catch up with the boys."

Ocelka laughed. "You've got one hell of a girl, you've got the dog to die for, plus a fine bunch of friends. And you're off to a training squadron . . . There's not a lot you're going to miss about East Wretham, is there? Well, anyway, get away with you, Sergeant."

As Robert turned to leave, whistling for Antis to follow him, he reflected on Ocelka's question. The answer was simple. The one thing that he would really miss was the most important of all to him — the fellowship and the shared struggles of his brother warriors of the air.

As things transpired, Robert's plans to spend Christmas with Pamela didn't quite work out. For some reason — maybe the shock of the loss of C for Cecilia; maybe that, coupled with being sent away from his squadron — Robert felt restless and illtempered, as if something vital were missing from his life. For the first time he and Pamela quarreled. Sensing that their Christmas wasn't quite shaping up right, Robert decided to split. He took Antis and they caught a train to London.

Robert booked a room in a hotel close to the Czech National House, which had been opened a few months earlier by the Czech president in exile, Dr. Beneš. Sure enough, he ran into some of his old comrades carousing at the bar. There were Uncle Vlasta, Jicha, and many more of the old stalwarts. For a while Robert seemed unable to get his mind off the girl he'd left behind, but as brandy followed brandy he found himself being swept up in the party mood.

By the time Robert had started to sing, Antis was getting seriously worried about him. He'd witnessed many a rowdy evening at the local pubs around East Wretham, and he knew that when his master started to croon in his cups he was seriously well oiled.

Antis curled up on a chair in one corner, watching closely. It was well past midnight by the time the party broke up. Still singing away, Robert decided to escort his friends to the nearby subway station. By the time he'd seen them off he'd forgotten both the name of the street on which he and Antis were staying and that of the hotel itself. Still, with a confidence born of inebriation, he set off in the general direction, with Antis trotting happily by his side.

For an hour they wandered through streets thronged with partygoers. Finally, the crisp December air began to clear Robert's head a little. He'd realized by now that they were lost, but he didn't want to admit as much to his dog. Antis had been throwing his master suspicious looks, for they'd passed the same London landmarks several times now. Robert knew that Antis knew they were lost, but he wasn't about to own up to anything.

Robert had a stubborn streak — the same that had led him to desert Pamela at Christmas, as opposed to making up with her — and his stubbornness even extended to his dog. It was only when they were halfway down the same street for the third time that he finally gave in. Antis had an almost sardonically triumphant look on his face as Robert slumped onto a wall in defeat.

"All right, damn it, I'm beaten," Robert remarked. "But let's see if you can do any better."

In reply, Antis gave a smug toss of his thick, glossy mane, as if to say, *Just watch me, Buster, just watch me.*

Antis knew right away what Robert wanted of him, and it was truly amazing how completely man and dog understood each other. Yet to them their instinctive communication had become like second nature, and it warranted little if any special notice.

During their wanderings across half of Europe, not to mention their frequent deployments to different airbases, Antis had learned to always take careful note of his surroundings. And while the city environment was somewhat alien to him, he still retained a scent map in his head, a plot of those smells that were familiar to him no matter where he might be — for instance, his own odor and that of his master.

With his head down, sniffing up the scent like a vacuum cleaner, Antis began to move. He led Robert across the street and began to retrace the route they had just taken. Within five minutes, he stopped in front of a large Edwardian property — one in a row of almost identical buildings. He stood gazing up at it, his head cocked to one side and his tail wagging fiercely.

Here we are then, his expression seemed to say. *That wasn't so difficult, was it?*

The city streets were totally blacked out, and Robert could barely see a thing. He struck a match and gazed doubtfully at the building's brass nameplate.

"Well, I'm damned!" he finally exclaimed. "St. Margaret's Hotel . . . It's all coming back to me." He turned and patted Antis's head, a little sheepishly. "All right, old boy, you win. Thank goodness one of us is sober, anyway."

A few days later they left London, but before man and dog could head for their Scottish training base, Robert had to train to be a trainer. He was assigned to RAF St. Athan, in south Wales, one of the RAF's largest bases in Britain. At St. Athan he roomed with Vladimir Cupak, a fellow Czech airman who knew both Robert and Antis from the time he had served at 311 Squadron. All was going well until Robert was sent to attend a gunnery leaders' course at RAF Chelveston.

Because the people at Training Command were known to be sticklers about rules, especially with regard to instructors keeping pets, Robert asked Vladimir if he would look after Antis for the next few days. On arrival at Chelveston he'd apply for a permit for Antis to join him, after which they could travel on together to RAF Evanton, their permanent assignment. Robert figured it would take him only a few days to get the permit, so theirs would be a brief parting.

He said his farewells to both Antis and Vladimir that Sunday at the nearby station. Sure enough, a couple of days after reaching Chelveston, Robert had secured his permit. He put a call through to Vladimir, to tell him he'd be back to collect Antis during the weekend.

"Hold on," Vladimir interrupted, just as soon as Robert had begun to talk, "we're in trouble, bad trouble. Antis's chased a sheep and he's been shot."

For a moment Robert felt as if his heart had stopped. "What d'you mean he's been shot? Is he dead?"

"No, he's injured, but recovering. That's not the main problem. Antis has been locked up by the police and he's going to be put on trial."

"What d'you mean, put on trial? Antis is in prison?"

"No, no, he's in the guardroom at the base, but things are still pretty bad . . ."

Robert asked for the story from the beginning.

"I took Antis for a walk this morning and he wanted a run," Vladimir began. "He's been acting odd since you left, but I figured a good blast might do him some good. I let him off his lead and it was then he spotted some sheep —"

"So what if he saw some sheep," Robert interrupted. "He's seen hundreds. He's never gone chasing any before."

"Well, like I said, he's been acting strangely since you left. Anyhow, he dashed off after them and refused to be called back. He went around a hedge and I heard a shot. Antis seemed to stagger back toward me, and then there was another shot and he fell. He picked himself right back up again, but then I saw the farmer on his tail. He came right up to me as livid as can be. Claimed Antis had killed three of his sheep in the past few weeks. He's demanding compensation and that Antis be put down . . ."

"How on earth can Antis have killed any of his blasted sheep?" Robert raged. "He's never been out of our sight to do so."

"I know. But the farmer went right to the police and the CO's ordered Antis to be locked up until he can go before the local magistrate."

"So he is going to be put on trial!"

"He is, which is why I said we're in trouble."

"So how is he now?"

"Not so bad. They took thirty-six lead pellets out of his hide. There are quite a lot left, though. I'm putting poultices on his injured eye every two hours, and I'm allowed to take him for a walk twice a day. Otherwise, he's locked in the guardroom."

"But he must be hating it!" Robert paused. "So when does his case come up?"

"No one seems to know, but it'll be heard here, at Cowbridge. D'you think you can make it back? The CO's flat out to help, but he's in a bit of a bind because the farmer, Mr. Williams, is out for blood."

"Damn Mr. Williams! I'll do everything I

can to make it."

That night Robert couldn't sleep. He'd asked for leave that very day, but it had been refused, largely because he'd only just started the course. He was at his wits' end. After all they had been through, and after their countless near misses at the hands of the enemy, was Antis finally to lose his life courtesy of an angry Welsh sheep farmer? Not if Robert had anything to do with it he wasn't.

As dawn broke across the winter sky Robert sensed a ray of hope piercing his despair. Both Wing Commander Ocelka and his former boss, Group Captain Pickard, had promised help if ever Robert or Antis were in trouble. Well, now was most certainly his time of greatest need. Pickard's name in particular might carry some weight and help sway the judge, for he was a war hero of some standing.

Robert penned a letter to both, outlining Antis's predicament and asking for their help. He sent them express and waited on tenterhooks for some kind of response.

The following afternoon Robert received a telegram. "Will see what I can do. Good luck. Pickard."

Ocelka replied in a similar vein and Robert felt his spirits rise a little. Days passed.

He could only imagine Antis's state of mind, locked in the guardroom and bereft of his master, and largely cut off from any of his friends. His dog would be going out of his mind.

On the day of the court hearing, Robert had to force himself to sit in a lecture on gunnery skills, pretending to pay attention, when his mind was one-hundred percent focused on a trial taking place in rural Cowbridge, one that would decide the fate of his beloved dog.

He got the phone call just after midday.

"It's good news!" Vladimir exclaimed. "Antis has been pardoned. We have to pay costs, compensate the farmer, and sign a pledge to keep him under proper control. But other than that, he's free!"

Robert was lost for words. Once again, Antis had evaded being taken by the Grim Reaper, who seemed so determined to claim him. Luckily, the letters written by Wing Commander Ocelka and Group Captain Pickard had been read out at the start of the court case. Pickard's letter pointed out that Antis had flown dozens of daring sorties with the RAF over Germany, and that his airman owner wanted him back as soon as possible, so as to "recommence operational flights once again." Ocelka's letter praised the bulldog spirit of 311 Squadron's official mascot, who was needed back on duty.

Those letters played a key part in swaying the judge. By the end of the court hearing the local police had lost the argument that the dog should be put down. The magistrate gave a firm ruling against ending the life of such a veteran war hero. The court reporter duly picked up on this amazing story. In spite of the RAF's stonewalling, the British press finally had proof — in sworn court documents — that the flying dog of war existed, and it lapped up the story.

The newspaper reports hailed Antis's reprieve: "The Dog That Flies Over Germany — His Life Saved For More Sorties." All they needed now was the name of the dog and that of his airman master — which had so far been withheld — and the pair's renown and their fame as great British war heroes would be complete. Robert's birth name was Václav Bozdech, but ever since arriving in Britain, he had adopted the name Robert. Yet none of newspapers had yet been able to get either his or Antis's name.

With the court case won, Antis's trials and tribulations were far from over. The dog was sick from his wounds and lovesick for his master. Vladimir had given a solemn promise to the court that Antis would be kept under firm control. But in Antis's mind there was only one thought now: if his master couldn't come to him, he would go to his master.

The first morning that Vladimir was reunited with Antis, he left him asleep on his blanket, with Robert's possessions scattered all around him for company. Vladimir headed to the mess for breakfast, but en route back to his hut he was accosted by the base CO, Wing Commander Shepherd.

"Sergeant, where did you leave your dog?" he demanded angrily.

"In my room, sir."

"Are you sure?"

"Quite sure, sir. I left him there when I went for breakfast."

"Then how do you explain that I found him near the railway station in the village?"

"It can't be Antis," Vladimir objected. "With your permission, sir, I'll fetch him from my room."

The CO snorted. "Don't bother. Just come with me."

Wing Commander Shepherd marched Vladimir to his office. He threw open the door, and there was Antis tethered firmly to his desk by a gas-mask strap. The dog had a guilty-as-sin expression on his face, and it wasn't helped by the way the CO proceeded to tear into Vladimir.

"You do realize you gave a promise to the magistrate that you'd keep this dog under proper control? And this is how you keep your word! Just one more episode like this and the dog will be shot. I'm willing to try to help, but not if you fail to keep your word. Now get out, and see that there's no more trouble of this nature!"

Vladimir couldn't understand it. He'd left Antis locked in his room, so how the devil had he escaped? He discovered the answer just as soon as they were back: he'd left the key in the lock. At East Wretham, Antis had been taught to open doors by twisting the handle with his jaws, so he could come and go at night when he needed to pee. He'd clearly adapted such skills to turning a key and unlocking a door!

Vladimir swore to himself that he'd take no more chances. Robert was due back that Saturday — in four days' time — and he was determined to keep Antis out of trouble until then. That Friday evening Vladimir decided to take in a movie. He left Antis triply secured. He was tied to his master's bed with a strong strap, the window and door were latched and locked, and the key was safely in Vladimir's pocket.

After his friend's departure, Antis must have lain in the darkness for a long time, puzzling out his predicament. He could smell his master's things in the room, so he clearly hadn't abandoned him for good. But where was he? He'd been gone for weeks now, and man and dog had never before been parted for more than a few days — and that due to injury and their aircraft having been shot up. Antis felt certain something dreadful must have happened to his master, and he was determined to go to his aid.

Whining from the pain of his recent injuries, he tried to bite and chew his way through the strap that constrained him. But the thick leather defeated his efforts. Now and again he could hear the hollow thump of boots as the camp guards made the rounds of the base perimeter. When all was quiet he went back to his task, using his powerful jaws to work on the strap. Finally, with a twang, it parted.

Antis jumped onto his master's bed, from where he could reach the window. He began to worry at the latch. The catch was not the strongest ever made, and after several powerful bites it buckled, and Antis was able to nose up the window. He poked his muzzle out, sniffing carefully at the air. Were any guards in the vicinity? Judging that the coast was clear, he jumped out of the window, trotted across the grass, and disappeared into the shadows.

He made his way across open fields to the village. He was headed for the railway station, the place where he had last seen his master and where they had said their goodbyes. It was the only place at which he could think of restarting his search. Darting from bush to bush, he approached his target. Reaching it, he lurked in a patch of darkness for the train he knew must come. In Antis's mind one of those puffing steam engines had carried away his master, so if he followed in his footsteps he would most likely find him.

His patience was rewarded. A train came to a squealing halt at the station, the doors opening to disgorge a few passengers. Like a streak of gray lightning Antis dashed across the platform and darted inside. His journey to find his master had begun. Now all he had to do was pick up his scent among all the other human smells on the train, and track him to wherever he might be.

■ ■ ■ ■

When Vladimir returned from the movie he could barely believe his eyes. He organized all the men he could find into search parties. While some pedaled off on bicycles for the railway station, others went to scour the nearby fields, especially those with flocks of sheep. As sunrise neared, Vladimir was dreading the new day. He would have no choice but to go and report that his dog was missing, at which point the CO would more than likely order him to be shot.

At dawn, groups of airmen returned to the camp from their various searches. All were empty-handed. All hope seemed to have been lost. There was no sign of the errant dog, and Antis might be just about anywhere by now. Vladimir and a friend were the last to return to the base, having made one final abortive tour of the nearby fields.

They dragged their tired limbs along the road leading to RAF St. Athan, with Vladimir dreading what was coming.

TWENTY-ONE

By the time C for Cecilia, the veteran Wellington bomber, was shot down over Berlin, man and dog had been deployed to a training squadron near Inverness.

As the two men neared the main gate, a bus pulled up to allow several servicemen to alight. Vladimir had his head down and shoulders hunched in despair, and his friend was the one who spotted it. One of the passengers was holding a frayed lead, on the end of which was a fine-looking German shepherd.

"Look! There's the lovely little bastard!" he cried. "That's Antis, isn't it? I told you we'd find him!"

"Thank Christ for that!" Vladimir exclaimed. He couldn't believe it. Where on earth had the dog appeared from now?

It was a fellow Czech airman, Sergeant Lazar, who had hold of Antis's broken lead, and Vladimir knew that Lazar had just come back from leave.

They rushed over. "Where the hell did you find him?" Vladimir asked. "We've been up all night searching for the beast! Where was he?"

Lazar couldn't help laughing. "You will never guess . . . I was at Cardiff station waiting for my train, when I spotted this dog nosing through the crowd and clearly searching for someone. The nearer he got the more I was certain it was Antis. I knew Robert was doing a course, so I went and grabbed him. As soon as I saw the broken lead I guessed what had happened. He didn't like it, of course, but I wasn't letting go and he knew he had to come . . ."

For the remainder of the day Vladimir kept Antis glued to his side. That afternoon Robert returned to base, and Vladimir was more than happy to hand over his charge to his rightful master. The reunion was a joyous one on both sides. For Antis it signaled that the lonely, torturous search was over. For Robert, it signaled that his wayward dog was safely back in his hands.

Robert didn't have it in him to punish Antis for what he had done. He knew why he had behaved in such an extraordinary fashion, and if anything, it only went to prove how utterly inseparable he was from his master. But there was one thing that did have to change. With the help of a friendly local farmer — not Mr. Williams — Robert was going to teach Antis to break his habit of chasing sheep.

He took his dog into a field of the farmer's finest ewes and told him to sit. He left the field, making sure the dog remained where he was. He repeated the process over and over, leaving his dog alone with the flock of sheep for longer and longer stretches of time. Over three days he trained Antis to stay among such animals and show them total respect. At the end of his training Antis would lie in the field for hours on end, surrounded by curious sheep nosing all around him. If ever he had been a sheep worrier he'd certainly been cured of it now.

In a way this was the worst kind of punishment Robert could have devised to deal with his dog's errant behavior. As the sheep gazed at Antis in insolent wonder — a dog that was separated from his controlling master, yet seemingly didn't have it in him to chase them — Antis's dignity was upset and his humiliation complete. To be mocked by *sheep* — animals of a tiny intellect compared to his own — was almost more than he could bear. But his master had his reasons, of that he was certain, and in any case his word was Antis's command.

At the end of the third day's training Robert strode into the field to fetch his dog. His smiles and his hugs were more than enough reward for the long-suffering animal.

"Come on," Robert announced, "the torture's over! I don't think you'll forget that in a hurry, will you, lad?"

Together they strolled back to base through the winter fields that had so nearly proved the death of Antis — more so in fact than the dog's sojourns over German territory on flying missions for Bomber Command. His injuries from the buckshot had yet to heal, and some of the lead pellets remained embedded in his body. The base doctor had assured Robert that they would work their way free in time. But what with his ear, nose, and chest wounds resulting from German fire, and having been riddled with shot by an irate Welsh farmer, the dog of war seemed beset by enemies on all sides.

The scenery at their new assignment, RAF Evanton, lifted Robert's spirits. The base was perched on the far northeastern shore of Scotland, surrounded by dramatic hills, deep lochs, and dark forests that reminded him very much of his native Bohemia, and once he'd gotten his dog settled he began to feel very much at home. As for Antis, he was in heaven. During breaks from the training lectures that Robert was tasked to give, his master took him hunting for wild mushrooms in the forests that surrounded the base. For the dog who'd survived a long separation and being shot, followed by the threat of execution, it was wonderful to be back together with his master.

With his extensive Bomber Command experience, Robert found that he was hugely respected and looked up to by the young trainee airmen at RAF Evanton. He was a decorated veteran of numerous sorties and the untested cadets held him in some awe.

They found it easier being intimate with Robert's hero of a dog, who quickly became everybody's favorite. Robert was happy to show off his dog's obedience and tricks. He had taught Antis to put out a cigarette with his paw without burning himself, and to open any kind of door with his teeth.

Life in the remote Scottish Highlands seemed far removed from the febrile wartime atmosphere that held the whole of England in its grip. The nearest city was Inverness, where the social scene was lively enough almost to allow Robert to forget there was a war on. The handsome foreign airman was both exotic and heroic in stature, and with his veteran war dog at his side Robert became hugely popular.

Man and dog won a prize at a dog show in the nearby town of Dingwall, which raised their profile considerably. It was reported in the local press: "Prizewinning Dog Flew with RAF on Raids." For the first time the article identified both man and dog by name. The story was picked up by the national papers — first the *Sunday Mail* and then scores of rival newspapers. None of the press seemed to realize it was strictly against regulations to take a dog on RAF missions, and the coverage was overwhelmingly positive.

But during the guilt-ridden yet euphoric weeks after their release from flying combat missions, Robert found himself missing Pamela hugely. In an effort to fill that void he started to court the local Scottish lasses. Many a night out at dances led to him and Antis spending numerous evenings apart. Antis was proving so popular on the base that he was starting to become everyone's dog, and that in effect meant that he was no one man's responsibility.

One night Robert decided that an evening at the Inverness movie theater was in order. He set out on the bus, leaving Antis in the care of some of his cadets. But as he walked through the streets to the Empire Theatre, he was shocked to hear the familiar *scratch-scratch* of paws following behind him. Antis had evaded the cadets, escaped from the camp, boarded a bus behind Robert's, tracked him through the streets, and finally caught up with him.

Robert couldn't exactly admonish him there and then. Not wanting to miss the movie, he persuaded the theater's cashier to let his dog sit in the office while Robert settled down in the darkened theater to enjoy the show. But it hadn't long begun when there was a startled scream from a lady seated below him. She'd felt something cold and damp snuffling at her legs, and in the ensuing panic someone trod on a mystery animal that had sneaked its way into the theater.

Antis let out a pained howl, and Robert knew for sure that it was his dog that was the cause of all the chaos. He jumped out of his seat in the circle, dashed below, and in the light of the flashlights being shined around the place he found the offender. Red-faced with embarrassment, he grabbed Antis's collar and dragged him outside, where the doorman and the manager were waiting for him.

Robert gave a hurried explanation as to what had happened, aided by the cashier, who'd come to join them. Antis had sneaked out of the office when her back was turned, the cashier explained, and he must have gone searching for Robert. The theater manager was obviously a dog lover, for he seemed to take Antis's side in all of this.

"Well, you can't blame the dog," he remonstrated. "He obviously felt lost and lonely left in a strange place, so he came looking for you. My dog would have done the same."

"It was really my fault," the cashier interjected. "I should have kept a closer eye."

"Not at all," the manager objected. He

fixed Robert with a look. "The dog needs to be properly looked after. What's his name?"

"Antis," Robert replied. "And he's not usually this disobedient."

The manager seemed to be searching his mind for something, and then a smile lit up his face. "I thought I recognized him! Isn't this the dog that appeared in the newsreel and in the papers? The one who flies?"

"It is," Robert confirmed. "He was with me at 311 Squadron."

Antis had been watching the exchange of words, sensing the tension in the air and knowing that he was the cause of all the trouble. At the mention of his flying adventures and his fame, the movie-theater manager seemed to have become far more conciliatory. Seizing the moment, Antis offered his paw for the man to shake.

The manager grinned. "Well, it's not every day that I get to shake hands with a celebrity. Does he often go to the cinema?"

It was Robert's turn to smile. "Not at all. This is his first and very likely his last visit!"

"Well, why not let him stay and watch, now that he's here," the manager suggested. "As long as you keep him under control we should be all right."

There were two seats on the end of an aisle normally reserved for usherettes.

Seated beside Robert, Antis leaned his body against that of his master as the film played. With ears pricked forward and eyes glued to the screen, he seemed almost hypnotized. At one point he stirred and growled protectively as a man carried a crying child across the screen. A few minutes later a forest fire crackled and burned, and Antis pressed closer to Robert, shaking and whining at what he was seeing.

But the final straw was when a herd of frightened animals came charging out of the forest fire right through the screen toward him. Fearful that he was about to be trampled in the stampede, Antis tensed his muscles to jump, and Robert had to slip a reassuring arm around his dog to keep him in his seat. Just as quickly as it had appeared, the scene was replaced by peaceful countryside views, and Antis was able to settle down once more.

Though it had started out badly, their trip to the movies had been redeemed by the good fortune that the Empire Theatre's manager was a dog lover, but it might not have gone so well. Antis's wandering ways needed to be curtailed, but the trouble was their present assignment. At their previous base there had been the all-consuming rigor of a war to fight, plus the matchless company of fellow warriors of the air in which to share the evenings. Here at Evanton there was neither, and both man and dog were increasingly unsettled.

Released from the intensity of flying death-defying missions, and deprived of the kind of brotherhood they had found within 311 Squadron, both Robert and Antis felt strangely lost. They had undertaken their epic escapes — first Robert from Czechoslovakia, then both of them from no-man's-land, and finally from war-torn France — for one reason only: so they could take the fight to the German enemy. Training others to do so — while undeniably worthwhile — just didn't satisfy that burning need.

While Robert spent his days lecturing trainees on gunnery skills, he knew that his Czech, British, and other colleagues were daily risking their lives in the air fighting the good fight for real. He hungered to get back into action alongside them. As for Antis, he could sense Robert's disquiet and it unsettled him. There was trouble brewing for both the flying dog of war and his master.

A few weeks after the incident at the movie theater, Robert was determined to go to a dance at nearby Dingwall, the place where

Antis had won the dog show. At the show Robert had met a local girl, Betty, and he had a date to join her at the dance. Frustrated by the lack of any chance to go into action against the enemy, and missing Pamela, Robert decided to risk an evening away from his dog.

He headed to the railway station, leaving Antis stretched out in the sun with seemingly not a worry in the world, and in the care of the cadets. But no sooner had his master disappeared from view than Antis went into action. He slipped away as if going for a pee in the nearby forest, then cut back through the base. He picked up Robert's scent and tracked him to the station, where he was just in time to see a train pull up and his master climb aboard.

This time Antis's dash for the nearest railcar was thwarted by a hyperalert porter. The man seized Antis by the collar and held him back until the train had pulled away. Thinking the dog would now have no choice but to return to base, the porter released him, but Antis wasn't to be so easily thwarted. He leaped onto the track and started to run after the train. In spite of all the injuries he'd suffered Antis was in the peak of physical condition, and he was soon able to catch the train.

It was seven miles to Dingwall, and as the train puffed into the station, so did Antis, barely a few yards behind the rear coach. He was swiftly up on the platform, sniffing out his master among the sea of air-force blue uniforms, and moments later he was on Robert's tail. He threaded through the streets of Dingwall, and by the time he'd caught up with the young Czech airman he was strolling arm in arm with his date. Antis knew better than to intervene when his master was courting. He held back, tracked them from a distance, and bided his time.

At first glance the pale-skinned Betty didn't seem to hold a candle to Pamela, but his master was sure to have his reasons. In any case, Pamela seemed to have disappeared from their lives completely, which pained Antis, for Pam had fallen as much for the dog as she had for his master. The dance was being held in Dingwall Town Hall, the same venue where Antis had won the dog show. As a result he knew the place passably well. But he missed one of the turns that his master had taken and ended up losing himself in the maze of corridors.

Letting his ears lead him toward the sound of music and laughter, he nosed carefully through a thick maroon curtain. Beyond him a strange and somewhat alarming sight met his eyes. He was at the rear of the stage on which a band was playing. As the music swelled in volume, he was about to back off the stage in alarm, when he caught sight of what was beyond — a crowd of people milling about and apparently fighting with each other on a wide floor.

Antis could see scores of men in the familiar RAF uniform, each of whom seemed to be wrestling with an opponent who was wearing a dress of many assorted colors. As with his experience at the movie, he'd never seen anything like it before. He stood rooted to the spot, the music blaring in his ears and his mind a mass of confused thoughts and fears. Most worryingly of all he had not the slightest idea where his master was. And then he saw him. There in the thick of battle was Robert, apparently being throttled in a close embrace.

Believing his master to be in mortal danger, Antis went into action. With a deep growl he dived off the platform into the seething throng. Hackles raised, he thrust men and girls aside as he powered across toward his master and his attacker. Before the startled Robert could stop him, Antis sprang at Betty. In his attempt to push her away from Robert, his claws caught in the material of her dress, and an instant later he'd torn it from her shoulders.

Betty was left shocked and stunned, her dress lying in a heap at her feet and her nakedness only shielded by her underclothes. Robert sprang into action. He whipped his tunic from his shoulders and used it to cover the girl. At the same moment he grabbed Antis and held him back from any more such mischief that he might have in mind. But the damage was done. Betty's mother came storming over, steam coming out of her ears, and with a look that could kill she led the mortified girl from the dance floor.

For Robert and Betty their short romance was over. Neither mother nor daughter would ever speak to Robert again, and Dingwall became one of the few places in the area that Robert was loath to visit. His and Antis's relationship also suffered. Robert had been an animal lover practically since birth. He had an innate empathy for all things wild, and for those that had come from the wild. He understood the instincts that drove animals like Antis, who for all his apparent domesticity was not so far removed from his lupine ancestors — wolves. He had never once raised a hand to Antis, yet at the same time he needed to demonstrate to his dog that he had done wrong.

The discipline Robert needed from Antis he'd won through patience, firmness, and love. Accordingly, he chose now the most effective form of punishment he knew, short of physical chastisement. For a whole week he didn't speak a word to his dog or take him on his daily walks. Antis was mortified. All he'd sought to do was to protect and safeguard his master, and this was his reward. If there was one moment more than any other when the dog wished that he could speak to his master and explain things, this was it.

But at the same time he knew he had disobeyed his master. He'd been told to stay at the camp, but he'd chosen to ignore that instruction and follow. At the end of the day his motive may have been the right one, but he had still done wrong. As he watched his master reading in his bunk, or moving around the hut, with neither a word nor a glance to acknowledge his presence, Antis was distraught.

He was torn between his conflicting needs to obey his master and to safeguard him, and that was what had gotten him into such trouble.

Twenty-Two

Tall, dashing, and a decorated war veteran, Robert knew that with his fine-looking and famous flying dog of war at his side he was a catch for the ladies.

In September 1942, Robert received his commission as an officer in the RAF. His work at the Air Gunnery School continued as before, and the only noticeable change in life was his and Antis's move into the officers' mess. While Robert lectured by day, his dog was free to roam the outskirts of the base, set as it was in wild countryside. Occasionally, he'd pop his head around the door of the lecture hall to check on his master, before wandering off to enjoy himself once more.

Antis's favorite spot by far was the bank of an icy brook that tumbled from the nearby hill and gurgled beside the accommodation huts. The trees of a dark forest — the Darreuch Wood — swept down to the opposite bank, and above the forbidding woodland rose the wild and inhospitable folds of Cnoc-Fyrish, the hills all but bare of vegetation on their heights. Antis would spend hours lying by the water, watching the antics of a wild duck and her seven offspring as they took their daily swimming lessons.

At first the mother duck had been hugely alarmed at the appearance of this large and powerful-looking stranger. But over the weeks she seemed to relax, and at last she sensed that he meant them no harm. Soon the tiny ducklings could swim right up to the dog's nose, and he'd do little more than twitch his muzzle in amusement as he watched over them benevolently, with mother duck rounding up the stragglers at the rear.

Antis's behavior with those wild ducks typified the nature of the dog. He could chase rabbits with a hunter's instinct and a burning desire to catch and to kill. He seemed to sense that was fair game, for rarely did he actually overrun one and the rabbits stood a sporting chance. But with anything like those ducklings — the helpless, the vulnerable, or the very young — his protective instincts came to the fore, and he wouldn't dream of harming one.

Christmas 1942 came and went, ushering in a bitterly cold and frosty January. An icy wind blew off the rolling heights of Cnoc-Fyrish, bringing with it the first gusts of snow. It lay across RAF Evanton, deep and crisp and even, and brought all training flights to a temporary halt. The snowbound huts of the officers' mess were double-skinned and had proper heating, and Robert was more than a little thankful for it now.

One early January evening he settled down in the room that he shared with his dog, a book in one hand and Antis sound asleep at his feet. The snow was falling, deadening any sound from outside, and the wind had dropped to a whisper. It was wonderfully still. Apart from the odd snuffle or shiver from his dog as he chased rabbits in his dreams, all was quiet. They had been together for three years now, and in spite of their recent misadventures Robert felt closer to his dog than ever before.

Eventually the book fell from his hands as Robert dozed off. He woke with a start, and with no idea how long he had been asleep. A distant sound had torn him out of his slumber. He strained his ears and there it was again. Somewhere out there in the icy wilds a dog was howling. Antis had pricked up his ears. He'd heard it too.

Without a word or a look to his master, the dog was suddenly on his feet. He crossed to the door and stood with ears thrown forward, head erect and body tense, facing the direction of that ghostly sound. Thinking he must need a pee, Robert got out of the chair and unlatched the door. It opened onto a corridor, with a door at the far end leading outside.

Normally, Antis would trot down its length and wait for Robert to open the far door, if he couldn't manage it himself. But now he had stopped dead on the threshold of their room. The door at the far end lay partially open, a shaft of moonlight thrown across the floor, the snow outside glistening an unearthly blue-white in the light.

Antis gazed at the open door, the moonlight glinting in his eyes.

Then he raised his head and answered the call from the wild with a howl of his own.

It was deafening, especially in that confined space. Several doors flew open as fellow officers tried to ascertain the source of the racket. But before anyone could say anything, Antis was off. He flew down the length of the corridor, bounded into the snow, and was gone. Robert followed, reached the doorway, and gazed outside. He felt a strange sense of urgency bordering on panic, as if he knew already all was not right with his dog — or at least, not as Robert understood things should be.

Antis stood rigid, a coal-black silhouette against the crystalline mass of white, his body taut like a statue and his muzzle raised toward the nearby hill. He was barely twenty yards away, but Robert could sense how distant his dog's mind was from him right then, and how great was the danger that he was about to lose him.

"Antis, come here, boy," he tried. "Come here."

He saw the ears flick back a second as his dog registered the sound of his master's voice, but the head didn't move a fraction of an inch. It remained glued to the distant hillside.

Robert called again, an edge of insistency creeping into his voice. "Antis, come here! Now, boy!"

In answer the big, powerful animal kicked out with his hind legs and raced away, his paws flicking up puffs of snow as he thundered into the trees, his thick tail streaming out behind him. Away high on Cnoc-Fyrish a bitch was calling for a mate and Antis had seen fit to answer the call.

For all of the following day Antis remained missing. Countless cadets offered to walk the slopes of Cnoc-Fyrish, once a thorough search of the base and surroundings had turned up not a sign. Robert himself had traced Antis's paw prints as far as he could, before a fresh fall of snow had obliterated his dog's passing. But the direction of travel had been quite clear: from what Robert had seen, Antis was headed for the bleak and snow-swept high ground.

Another day passed, and still no sign of Antis. When he wasn't busy lecturing or out searching the snowfields, Robert made desperate inquiries as to where his dog might be. Could the mystery howl have come from a bitch on some neighboring property? Might Antis be ensconced there even now, lovesick but at least safe from harm?

His heart sank when he learned who the most likely culprit — indeed, the only one — might be. Several years back a German shepherd bitch had gone wild, and she'd lived in the wilderness of nearby Darreuch Wood. The bitch had been shot by a game-keeper, but at the time she had a litter of pups who were some four months old. One had survived, and she still roamed those woods, hunting to survive. If Antis had answered the call of any female of the breed, it would be hers.

In a sense, who was Robert to complain if his dog chose a female companion over his master? Hadn't Robert favored Pamela, briefly Ann, and then Betty and one or two others over his dog? And how many times when his faithful companion had come after him had Robert scolded and punished him for imposing his protective instincts on his master's amorous adventures?

If Antis was gone for good — choosing a bitch over Robert's love and human companionship — so be it. That wasn't the worst of it. What tortured Robert more than anything was the thought of what Antis's fate would likely be, out there in the harsh snowbound wilderness. Antis knew how to chase rabbits and to watch over ducklings. He was far from being a dog that lived by his killer hunting instincts. What were his chances of being able to last the bitter winter in the wild?

More to the point, Antis had teamed up with a wild dog — one born to the wild — but he himself was an irredeemably people-friendly animal. There was no way that Antis would keep his distance from any human who might venture into their domain. The first gamekeeper that laid eyes on him would very likely shoot him, and unlike farmer Williams protecting his sheep, any gamekeeper would likely shoot to kill.

As Robert knew well, he didn't own his dog's soul. At the end of the day he was a free agent, and if he chose another, so be it. But he feared that Antis's amorous liaison could well prove the death of him, and he was beside himself with worry.

By the evening of the fifth day he was beginning to give up hope of ever seeing his dog again. He went to bed that night alone in his room, with Antis's blanket folded neatly beside him. For a second time in their years together he reached out in the night, fingers hoping beyond hope to make contact with a warm flank of hair. But Antis was gone, and the little sleep that Robert got was plagued by dark dreams.

The following day a group of cadets was returning from their lunch when they spotted a four-legged form moving down the lane toward them. There wasn't a man at RAF Evanton who hadn't heard of the famous dog's disappearance, and they realized in an instant that it was Antis. They'd spent long hours with Robert searching for the dog and they could barely believe that it was him. But the thrill of the wild was still in Antis's blood, and as the cadets rushed forward to grab him he made a leap over a nearby fence to escape.

Weakened from his days in the wilderness, Antis mistimed the jump. He landed belly first on the iron railings and ended up impaled on the sharp spikes. As gently as they could, the cadets lifted him free and rushed him to the sick bay, one of them setting off at a tangent to summon Robert. By the time Robert reached the sick bay, Antis was already on the operating table being examined by RAF Evanton's medical officer.

The MO shook his head worriedly. "I'm sorry, Robert, but this is beyond me. I can give you the name of a good vet in Inverness, but I've got to warn you . . ." He threw a pained look at Robert. "I don't give a great deal for your dog's chances."

One of the spikes had penetrated the dog's stomach, the MO explained, and it needed a veterinarian's expertise. Robert couldn't believe what had happened. His dog — faithful to the last — had come back to him, only to suffer an apparently life-threatening injury on a row of fencing that bordered their very base. It was the bitterest and most heartbreaking of ironies.

With the injured Antis cradled in his lap, Robert commandeered a friend's car and they drove hell-for-leather to Inverness. The vet turned out to be a gray-haired and kindly looking fellow, but even he doubted whether he had the skills to save the dog.

"I'll do all I can, of course," he told Robert, "but it'll be touch and go. His physical condition is in his favor. He's strong and fit and young. But I don't want to raise false hopes. Leave him with me and I'll be able to tell you more in the morning."

After a sleepless night Robert was back at the surgery early. But as soon as he laid eyes on Antis, he almost had a heart attack. He was a pitiful sight. Air had gotten into the dog's stomach through the holes the railings had made, and he was puffed up like a balloon. As Robert bent to caress the dog's head and whisper reassurances in his ear, he dreaded what the vet was going to tell him — but he needed to know.

"It's too early to say," the vet told Robert. "But don't give up hope just yet. He looks bad, but I've seen —"

"Please, I'd far rather know the worst," Robert cut in. "My dog means an awful lot to me, and I'd not like to be separated from him at the end, if this is the end."

The vet paused, considering carefully what exactly he was going to tell Robert. "As I've said, he's a healthy dog with a strong heart. At the very least I'd say he has a sporting chance. You can do no good by staying and I'll phone the camp if he worsens."

Robert had to settle for this, at least for now.

Two days later Robert got the call he'd been dying to hear. "You can come and get your dog," the vet told him. "He's weak and needs nursing, but he'll do."

Robert took Antis back to RAF Evanton, where a long convalescence ensued. With the help of the MO, Antis was gradually nursed back to full health. It was April by now and spring was in the air. Bit by bit Robert started to allow Antis on some of their favorite walks around the base. Gentle exercise and fresh air would be vital to ensuring a full recovery. Every so often Robert allowed his dog to lie on the riverbank across from Darreuch Wood and bask in the spring sunshine.

As far as Robert could tell, Antis had satisfied his call to the wild and had no desire to return to those ancient forests and hills. But one day in June Robert surprised his dog on the far side of the river, nosing excitedly in the undergrowth. By now the ducklings were almost fully grown, and Antis wasn't in the habit of crossing the water. He'd lie on the nearside, nose to the stream, and watch the birds dabbling about in the shallows.

Something must have drawn him across, Robert reasoned. He settled down to watch. Antis went down on his stomach at the fringe of the woodland, nose snuffling and rear haunches raised, as if to pounce. His ears were flicked forward, his head twisted slightly to one side, and his eyes fixed on a point just a few feet in front of his forepaws. Every now and then he'd shuffle forward on his belly, and Robert could only imagine he was trying to play with a hidden friend of some sort.

The question was, who or what? It could hardly be a duckling, in the dry brown bracken. It was unlikely to be a baby rabbit either. He tended to ignore the babies in his hunger to chase the adults. But every now and then Robert could see something rustling among the very fringes of the vegetation. It would almost poke through, Antis would make a play lunge, and it would dart back inside, only to emerge a little farther along. Antis was clearly playing with something, but what?

The dog repositioned himself and the mystery beast rustled the undergrowth, whereupon Antis let out an excited bark. Up and down the wall of bracken the game went, until Robert managed to get a better glimpse of just what was hiding in there. The tiny, moist black nose; the flopped-over V-shaped ears; the paws far too large for the chubby body; the tiny, stubby bare finger of a tail. It was a carbon copy of how Antis had looked when Robert had first stumbled upon him, back in a shell-blasted French farmhouse in no-man's-land.

Quietly and in wonder Robert watched the two at play. The dark streak along the puppy's back was unmistakable, and Robert had no doubt he was watching father and son. Robert whistled softly to Antis, in an effort to coax the little bundle of fur to follow his father out of the bushes. But the wild ancestry of his mother clearly held sway. The puppy would not be tempted, and as the late afternoon sun dipped below Cnoc-Fyrish he slid back into the woodland and was gone.

That evening Antis and Robert relaxed outside their hut, Robert mentally congratulating his dog on his fatherhood. Antis was now pushing into his thirties in terms of human years, and it was about the right time for him to have become a dad.

The following morning the puppy was back. Over several days Robert was able to woo him with gentle words and tidbits of food left on a saucer at the edge of Darreuch Wood. After a week of such enticements, the tiny pup was coaxed to the edge of the doorway leading into Robert and Antis's quarters, but he would come no farther. Antis stood there trying to urge his son to cross the threshold into his domain, but the wild within him wouldn't let him pass.

As for Robert, he was watching with bated breath. The education officer on the base had long admired Antis, and if he could just tame the pup enough he knew the man would jump at the chance of having him. Robert felt certain that between him and Antis they would in time manage to woo him.

But a couple of days later a group of youths came along the edge of the woodlands hunting rabbits with a slingshot. Spotting a flash of fur waiting patiently for his father, they unleashed several shots, and with an anguished yelp the puppy was gone. In one fell swoop the puppy's barely nascent faith in the human species was destroyed, and he fled deep into the sanctuary of the wild. Robert and his dog searched many a day for the puppy, but Antis's son was not to be found.

By autumn, Antis seemed to be one hundred percent recovered from his injuries. It was fortunate, for that October RAF Evanton was to close, and Robert and his dog were to leave the magical valley set at the foot of the wild hills. Their next destination was all that they had longed for. Robert — now a flight lieutenant — and Antis — still a dog fit to represent a fighting regiment — would be rejoining their original unit, 311 (Czech) Squadron.

Few of the Original Eight were left alive,

and none were still with the squadron. But at least one of Robert's old crew — those who had flown and cared for C for Cecilia so well — was around. Adamek, their chief ground crewman, was still with the squadron.

311 Squadron was now based at RAF Tain, to the north of the Moray Firth — just a few dozen miles farther up the coast from RAF Evanton. The squadron was no longer flying Wellingtons. Instead, they'd been equipped with the four-engine, long-range American heavy bombers, the aptly named Liberators. The squadron now formed part of RAF Coastal Command, and its mission was to fly out over the bleak expanse of the North Sea in search of enemy shipping, in particular the U-boats that menaced those waters.

Robert couldn't wait: finally he and his dog had gotten a second combat tour. Once again they would be flying into battle against the enemy.

TWENTY-THREE

Before being posted to RAF Tain, man and dog had to complete a training course, this one at the No. 1 Radio School in Cranwell, Lincolnshire. Flight Lieutenant Bozdech was scheduled to serve as a radio and radar operator on the Liberators, and he needed to be schooled in the use of such technology. Robert preferred the wild and knife-cut Scottish countryside to Cranwell's rolling hills and bucolic charm, but the fellow airmen he met at the Radio School — mostly combat veterans like himself — more than compensated, their fine company rekindling his sense of adventure and fun.

He and Antis shared a room with Simpson, a Canadian flight lieutenant only recently arrived in Britain. The two non-Brits bonded quickly, especially since Simpson was a hopeless dog lover, one who shared with Antis a refined sense of tomfoolery and of being the joker. Post-fatherhood,

419

Antis seemed to have gained in confidence and in his sense of mischief making — as if in siring his offspring on the Scottish hills he had somehow earned his spurs.

Simpson's ideas for finding fun became ever more inventive, but they were fired by one event more than any other. On a sunny afternoon two of the women on the base chose to hang out their washing just as Antis was passing. Seizing the opportunity, he grabbed an item of clothing from the basket and legged it. He dashed into the officers' quarters hotly pursued by the girls, and with a brassiere gripped in his jaws. Simpson took one look at what Antis was carrying and hustled him into a side room, where they hid until the coast was clear.

The ladies made for Robert's room, and failing to find the dog, they searched it high and low for the bra. Antis meanwhile was sent back by Simpson to pilfer yet more clothing from the basket. He returned triumphantly with a mouthful of assorted underwear, to hearty and enthusiastic praise from Simpson.

Two days later there was a party in the mess. Robert had invited a local girl for their first real date. She hailed from the nearby town of Sleaford, and Robert left around nine in the evening to pick her up at the railway station. Simpson offered to stay behind and babysit Antis, but his real intentions were very different. All was going well for Robert and his date when a fellow officer dragged the two of them outside.

"Come on, you two!" he exclaimed. "There's a show outside you really shouldn't miss."

At the entrance to the mess a large crowd had gathered. People were pointing and laughing uproariously. Pushing their way to the front, Robert and his lady friend saw the cause of all the merriment. Antis was holding a one-dog dress show. Sporting bright blue silk panties and two brassieres stuffed with cotton, he strutted to and fro. Robert glanced at his partner, fearing the worst, but luckily she was laughing along with all the rest.

With a barely audible whistle and a flick of the wrist, Robert got the attention of his dog. Using hand signals, he sent him off toward their quarters, where he hoped Simpson — who he felt certain was behind all this — might have the decency to undress him. That done, Robert grabbed his girl by the arm and steered her as rapidly as possible back toward the bar, before the comments from his fellow officers could become too ribald.

Fortunately, the girl didn't know that Antis was his dog, and for tonight at least he intended to keep it that way. However, some of the senior officers clearly intended otherwise. He was stopped at the entrance to the mess by the wing commander, a man whose attentions he really felt he couldn't afford to ignore.

"I must say, Flight Lieutenant, that was really quite a show," the wing commander enthused. "I haven't laughed so much in an age."

"Yes, sir." Robert muttered something under his breath and tried to move inside, but the wing commander held out a hand to stop him.

"Yes, indeed, a remarkably intelligent and witty animal, wouldn't you agree? But one thing puzzles me, Flight Lieutenant. I hope you don't mind me asking in front of this charming young lady, but where did you get those garments that your dog was wearing?"

As he'd made the remark, the wing commander had run an appraising eye over Robert's guest. A moment later the penny dropped, and the lady on Robert's arm went a beautiful shade of red.

She turned on Robert. "Do you mean to say that dog belongs to you?" she demanded.

Robert knew there was no point denying it. "That's right. I'm afraid he's mine. All mine. And don't think there isn't the odd occasion when I regret it."

With an angry glare at the two men, Robert's date made a beeline for the ladies' cloakroom, and he was never to see her again.

"I say, Flight Lieutenant, did I say the wrong thing?" the wing commander asked, trying desperately to contain his laughter. "I'm awfully sorry if I offended anyone."

"No harm done, sir," Robert replied. "But you had the wrong sense of things, for they certainly weren't hers . . ."

Later that night, back in his room, Robert tried to find it in himself to scold Antis, but it wasn't very easy. In spite of losing his date, Robert — like the wing commander and everyone else — had found Antis's show so damn funny. And where they were now heading — RAF Tain, to fly with Coastal Command in the teeth of a bitter Scottish winter — he and his dog were sure to need all their sense of fun if they were to keep their spirits up and make it through.

November on the Moray Firth proved a far cry from even the harshest months they had spent on active operations at East Wretham.

But there were compensating factors. After a long train ride the duo arrived at RAF Tain to the sight of tractors towing bomb trolleys, and ground crews loading up munitions onto the sleek, powerful-looking Liberators. Robert thrilled to the sight. These were state-of-the-art warplanes, and the sight of those munitions being loaded brought back all the old emotions.

He felt Antis stiffen at his side. For a long moment his dog held his head erect and watched. It was as if Antis appreciated that things had suddenly become serious again — returning perhaps to how they should be — one man and his dog preparing to wage deadly battle against the enemy. To Robert it felt as if a lighthearted interlude in their lives had come to an end — one that had been a diversion on the otherwise inescapable path of war.

He could feel Antis shivering with anticipation, as if all the old feelings associated with flying sorties in C for Cecilia had come back to him. Robert felt the same: a nervous thrill was knifing through his stomach, similar to that which he had felt when he'd first been deployed on active operations.

Robert was overjoyed to be reunited with Adamek. The bighearted Czech greeted Antis like a long-lost brother. He was also

424

pleased to see that one of his cadets from RAF Evanton, Arnost Polak, had been posted to Tain. But otherwise, there were few if any familiar faces. The losses suffered by 311 Squadron had been crippling. The squadron had taken part in some 145 bombing raids, but had lost 180 airmen and 20 aircraft in the process.

There were around twenty aircraft in 311 Squadron at any one time, and with six aircrew per warplane it meant an entire squadron had been wiped out in one year of operations. Averaged out, they had lost one airman every two days.

Operations at RAF Tain were to prove markedly different from those at East Wretham. It was the same squadron all right, but it was tasked with very different duties. The sorties flown in the Wellingtons from East Wretham had been against very specific targets — the mission being to fly to a destination, identify and bomb the target, and fly home. With Bomber Command the average duration of a flight was six hours: here at Tain with Coastal Command it was to be more like twelve.

The Liberators were designed as long-range bombers, and they were the most common heavy bombers built by the Americans during the war. But the RAF had found the Liberators unsuitable for combat over Europe, for their fuel tanks were nonself-sealing — crucial when flying missions into a storm of shrapnel. The Liberators were also deemed to have too few defensive guns to ward off enemy fighters in the battle-torn skies over Europe. But their ability to remain airborne for extended periods of time gave them great range, and that coupled with a heavy bombing capability made them ideal sea-patrol aircraft.

To Robert, the streamlined, four-engine aircraft with its twin vertical tail planes looked like a fantastic warplane to fly, after the redoubtable but outdated Wellingtons. More to the point, this was an aircraft well armed for its purpose. Their chief role being antisubmarine warfare, the Liberators had undergone extensive modifications so as to be able to hunt and kill their prey. This included fitting each with an Air-to-Surface Vessel radar (ASV), four forward-firing 20mm Hispano cannons slung under the bomb bay, plus eight sixty-pound rockets fitted on stub wings attached to the fuselage. The Liberators also carried good old dependable depth charges in their bomb bays.

The theory of U-boat hunting was fairly simple. The diesel-electric U-boat had to "snort" for long periods, cruising on or near the surface to suck in fresh air and to vent fumes from the interior of the submarine. Via the naked eye or the ASV radar, a U-boat would be detected by a patrolling Liberator. Of course, as soon as the U-boat had spotted the British aircraft she would attempt an emergency dive, so it was a race against time to try to sink her.

At range, the Liberator's rockets could engage the vessel. Closer in, the Hispano cannons could be used to rake her hull with armor-piercing rounds. If the U-boat survived both rocket and cannon attacks and managed to dive, the Liberator would thunder in over the spot where she had disappeared and drop depth charges, in an effort to finally sink her.

Mostly the missions flown from Tain involved spending long hours scouring a gray, sleet- and rain-swept sea for elusive enemy vessels. Patrols pushed far up into the arctic regions and could last for over thirteen hours. More often than not the weather at Tain itself — exposed as it was to bitter east winds blowing off the North Sea — was abysmal, making landing and takeoff a more than hazardous affair . . . as events were about to prove.

Shortly after Robert and Antis's arrival at Tain, Liberator Y-949 took off from the airfield at around ten o'clock for a night patrol. The aircraft flew north, but crashed some thirty minutes later at Rora Head, in Orkney, killing all of its crew. The weather was dreadful, and for long stretches at a time no flying was possible. At other times patrols would go out, only to be recalled due to deteriorating conditions.

But the work of 311 Squadron — frustrating and plagued by dangers though it was — was a vital part of the war effort. The U-boat threat to Great Britain was still one that might turn the fortunes of the war. After D-Day and the Allied breakout from the Normandy beachheads, the U-boats had lost their French coastal bases, from where they had plagued shipping in the Atlantic. Many had switched to Norway, using the deep fjords from which to prowl the sea. It was to counter this threat that the Liberator patrols were setting out from RAF Tain.

Robert understood well the dangers of what he was about to undertake: it didn't lessen his hunger to get into the air and into action. But for Antis there was to be no flying — at least for now. The former CO of 311 Squadron, Wing Commander Ocelka — the one man in the RAF who had done so much to safeguard the flying dog of war — had been lost in action, as had so many others. Under 311's new CO and under Coastal Command, rules were rigorously enforced. There would be no turning a blind eye to a dog joining a Liberator crew on an antisubmarine patrol.

In any case, Robert was no longer a gunner isolated in the rear turret of a Wellington — a position in which a dog crew member couldn't exactly get in anyone's way. As the radio and radar operator, Robert formed an integral part of the cockpit team, and there was simply no room for the big German shepherd, even if the rules could have been bent enough to allow him to fly. As Robert took to the skies again, Antis would have to sit out the sorties on the ground.

The first mission undertaken by Robert in his Liberator GR1 — the designation given to the antisubmarine version of the aircraft — would involve taking off and landing in the dark, for the hours of winter daylight were short this far north. As Robert loaded up in his cold weather kit and flying gear, it was clear that Antis expected to be accompanying him at least to the flight line, if not into the air. But it was a bitterly cold winter in the far north of Scotland, and the last thing Robert wanted was for his dog to spend a twelve-hour vigil in the freezing chill.

"Stay here, old boy," Robert tried to convince him, gesturing to the warm and snug room they shared. "It's too cold for you out on the airfield. Stay here."

Antis was clearly not amused. Whimpering softly, he gazed up at Robert with a clear message in his eyes. *If you're going, so am I — at least as far as they'll let me. We're partners, remember — on the ground and in the air.*

Shrugging in resignation, Robert grabbed Antis's blanket and they headed for the runway. He knew that if he locked Antis in the room, his howls would wake the entire barracks, and there were pilots to left and right sleeping off night patrols. Just as soon as Antis heard the Liberator take off he'd put two and two together and start crying for his master. There were no two ways about it: his dog would have to wait for his master on the flight line.

Robert comforted himself with the thought that he could trust Adamek absolutely to care for his dog, as he had at East Wretham. Here at Tain it was so bitterly cold that the ground crew was served hot meals out in the crew tents. Adamek could be trusted to ensure that Antis got his serving too. And as long as he waited out his vigil in the shelter of the crew tent, wrapped in his blanket, he should be okay.

That first sortie in the Liberator — as with many that followed — involved long periods spent scrutinizing a gray and empty sea. By the end of twelve hours staring out of the cockpit window — or in Robert's case, into the radar screen — the crew of the Liberator felt as if they were going stir-crazy. But there were matters that kept the mind occupied even on such a flight: as none of the engines consumed fuel at exactly the same rate, it had to be pumped from one tank to another to equalize the aircraft's weight, or she would become unbalanced. And if it was drama that Robert craved, he would get quite enough of that upon touching down at RAF Tain.

Antis was if nothing else a dog of unbreakable habit. Once Robert had taken to the skies in the sleek bomber painted the dark grays and greens of sea camouflage, his dog had assumed a position almost identical to the one he had adopted at East Wretham. In spite of Adamek's coaxing he refused to take shelter. Instead, he sat out in the dispersal area — the last point at which he had seen Robert climb into his aircraft and go. And that was where he had stayed for the twelve hours that his master was away.

To make matters worse, he had reverted to his old habit of refusing to eat when his master was airborne. Antis had had a hot meal with the aircrew, the one that they always ate directly after the final mission briefing, but during the twelve hours that followed he refused Adamek's every offer of food. It was as if he knew full well the danger his master was flying into, and his belly was so knotted with tension and worry that he couldn't stomach any food.

Such behavior might have been endurable in the sunnier climes of East Wretham, when his master was flying six-hour sorties over Europe. Here at Tain the ice-laden wind howled off the open expanse of the sea, blowing all the way from the frozen wastes of the Arctic. Yet Antis had had to last double the time — and many times the exposure — before his master returned.

By the time Robert touched down his dog was frozen stiff with the cold. So debilitating had Antis's long and lonely vigil proven that he found it all but impossible to do his traditional welcome home — his war dance for joy. It was immediately clear to Robert — as it was to Adamek — that Antis wouldn't last the long and punishing winter months ahead if he continued to keep his

432

lonely vigils.

He was no longer the one-year-old that had waited for his master at East Wretham. He was pushing four years old, and he'd survived more injuries in his few short years than most dogs would in a lifetime: he'd been wounded twice in action over Germany, shot by an irate Welsh farmer and peppered with lead, and he'd been impaled on metal railings at RAF Evanton, which had almost proved the death of him. There was only one thing to do: Robert would have to ban him from the flight line.

On his very next mission — a night patrol — Robert closed his mind and his ears to Antis's pleading and left him in the care of some fellow airmen. But all that long night Antis refused to be comforted. He howled and whined the entire time, and only regained his composure when Robert returned. The airmen who'd agreed to keep him had gotten barely a wink of sleep, and there was no way that this offered any kind of a solution.

The following day Robert took Antis to RAF Tain's tailors. He had a new idea how this problem might be solved. Once Robert had explained his predicament, the men seemed more than keen to help. They measured Antis up, and from some sheepskin they began to fashion for the dog a fleecy coat — one designed to keep out the very worst of the weather that northern Scotland could throw at man or dog.

The coat made a real hit with Antis. If nothing else, he loved the shared ritual. As Robert grabbed his flight gear in preparation for a patrol, so Antis was able to grab his sheepskin coat for his equally vital duty. He'd carry it over to Robert, as if to say, *Get this on me!* Once he was strapped into it, Antis would step toward the door as if to signal his readiness, and to emphasize that there was no excuse anymore for refusing him his role in the coming mission.

One biting January night, Robert's Liberator took off during the hours of darkness for a patrol that was scheduled to see them return to base just after dawn. The weather was fine and clear, if unbelievably cold. The moon was almost full and the conditions were excellent for spotting any U-boats that might be drifting through the seas, sucking in some much-needed fresh air.

But hours into the patrol, conditions worsened. A thick bank of freezing fog rolled in from the sea, blanking out the moon and stars. Antis remained seated in the dispersal area, patiently awaiting the Liberator's return. By now he knew the engine note of his particular warplane, and only when he detected that she was inbound did he start to relax a little, in anticipation of the reunion.

Though he was wrapped in his sheepskin coat, the freezing fog chilled him to the bone. Worse, his master's aircraft was just about to be diverted, even as a bitter storm blew in off the North Sea to engulf RAF Tain.

And Antis, the ever-faithful, immovable dog of war, was planted right in its path.

TWENTY-FOUR

Sleet began to spiral out of the fogbound darkness, growing thicker by the second. Adamek did all he could to persuade the dog to come in to the shelter of their tent, but Antis refused. At one point he tried tugging on the dog's thick collar, but Antis seemed to have turned himself into a statue. A low throaty growl warned the Czech ground crewman to stop his tugging and leave the dog to do his self-appointed duty.

A radio message came through from the Liberator that they were diverting to the Shetland Islands, the nearest airbase where there was good enough visibility to chance a landing. Everyone on the base who needed to know this was aware of it, apart from Antis, who refused absolutely to leave his station.

The driving sleet soaked into his heavy coat until it was wet through. As the cold worsened, the sleet turned to thick flurries of snow, and Antis's sodden coat became frozen to his body. Yet still he remained like a tree rooted to the earth, as the wind howled and the snow gusted all around him, isolated and alone on the edge of the frozen runway. Antis's whiskers stood out like icicles from his snow-flecked muzzle, but still he wouldn't abandon the wait — faithful, loyal, resolute — for his master's return.

Finally, with the dog sitting like a frozen statue in the midst of the snowstorm, Adamek decided that he had to force Antis to take shelter before he died of exposure. He recruited the help of two fellow airmen, both close friends of Robert's. Together they approached the dog with a blanket in which to wrap him and a jeep with which to speed him back to the warmth and shelter of his and Robert's room. They were only just in time. Frozen to the core and numbed to exhaustion, Antis was unable to put up any resistance.

Sensing perhaps how close he had come to death, Antis allowed them to load his frozen form onto the blanket, and using it like a stretcher they carried him to the waiting vehicle. In the warmth of the hut they stripped off the dog's coat and rubbed him all over with dry towels in an effort to thaw him out. Finally, he seemed to revive. But his terrible vigil had clearly taken everything out of him. He stretched out in front of the roaring stove in the room and fell fast asleep.

The following day the weather cleared enough for Robert's Liberator to fly in from Shetland and land. Robert's immediate thoughts were for his dog. He went and found Adamek and asked him what had happened.

"Flight Lieutenants Vaverka and Rybar took him away," Adamek explained. "He was in bad shape. I've never known anyone take him away from his vigil before . . . It was just like that time at East Wretham, when we all tried to move him. But this was worse, much worse. Back then it was summer in the south of England." Adamek swept a hand across the frozen wasteland of the airfield. "This is no place for a dog to wait in the open hour after hour . . ."

Robert shook his head worriedly. "God only knows what the end of all this will be," he muttered.

Thanking Adamek, he hurried to his barracks. He found Antis in their room, lying before the fire but strangely shivering, and with an odd, glassy look in his eyes. Robert tried to feed his dog, but he refused to eat. All he seemed to want to do was drink copious quantities of water. Robert took him outside for a pee, and he was shocked to discover that his dog was passing blood.

He was beside himself with worry now. His dog was definitely not his normal self. He didn't even acknowledge the friends whom they passed, and his nose seemed unnaturally dry and hot to the touch. Robert took him to the nearest vet, who gave Antis a thorough examination.

"There's no doubt about it," he said, once he was done. "Your dog's kidneys have been damaged in some way. Nothing else would explain all the symptoms. Have you any idea how it might have happened?"

In answer, Robert explained his dog's long vigils on the flight line, culminating in the frozen epic that had ensued when his aircraft was diverted to the Shetlands.

"Well, that explains it," the vet remarked. "That kind of cold can do irreversible damage."

"Is it serious?" Robert asked.

The vet tilted his head, until he could look directly at Robert over his glasses. "It's always serious when a dog's kidneys are affected. A dog needs them just as much as any human."

"So what are we to do?"

"Well, he's very, very sick. If his kidneys

fail completely it could prove fatal. But if he's properly looked after from now on — well, he might live for years. The trouble is he's clearly a very clean and obedient animal, and that's the greatest danger. If he's locked up for any period of time, and with his kidneys and bladder weakened, he'll try to hold it in so as not to mess his room — and that could kill him. Make no mistake — one more episode of extended exposure to the cold, and that will be his last."

Robert had heard the vet's warning and taken it very much to heart. He'd never wanted his dog to return to his lonely vigils, and certainly not here in the midst of a snow-lashed winter on the Moray Firth. But what was he to do? He'd tried locking his dog up, but to no avail. He'd had a thick fur coat made for him, but it clearly wasn't good enough. He sat in his room with Antis stretched listlessly before the fire, and he sank into a miserable mood. The last episode had very nearly killed his dog, but he could think of no alternative strategy that might break him of a habit that seemed destined to prove the death of him.

Then a thought struck Robert from out of the blue. It was so utterly unthinkable that it had never once even crossed his mind.

The dog was going to kill himself due to one thing only — devotion and love for his master. Therefore, the only way to save his life had to be to break the connection between man and dog — the very connection that Robert had always seen as unbreakable. For Antis's own sake and for the sake of his survival, Robert was going to have to do the unthinkable and betray him.

It was the hardest decision of his life, but once it was made, there was no going back. Robert called a council of war, for he could not do this on his own. He gathered Adamek, the two flight lieutenants who had rescued Antis from freezing to death, and one or two other friends. Robert opened the discussion by explaining what the vet had told him, and that there was no way Antis could survive another vigil on the flight line.

"Well, I don't see there's anything you can do," remarked Flight Lieutenant Rybar, one of those who'd rescued Antis.

He looked at the others for confirmation. Flight Lieutenants Vaverka — another of Antis's recent saviors — and Hering nodded their agreement.

"It's deadlock," said Vaverka. "You can't stop flying, obviously, and he won't be broken of his habit . . ."

"Which will be the damn death of him!" Robert exclaimed bitterly. "If he's not broken of the habit he's as good as dead, isn't he?"

It was not like Robert to show his emotions so openly, and his fellow airmen could see how the plight of his dog was torturing him. They glanced at each other. They knew the truth of what Robert was saying, but none wanted to be the one to say it.

"So what do you suggest?" Rybar countered, throwing the question back at Robert.

Robert paused, taking a long and lingering look at his dog. The subject of so much agonized discussion was stretched out by the fire, apparently oblivious to all the upset he was causing.

"If you can train a dog to do one thing," Robert remarked quietly, almost as if he were speaking to the dog in the room more than his fellow airmen, "you can train him to do another, surely."

"What do you have in mind?" the others prompted.

Robert raised his eyes to Rybar, Adamek, Vaverka, and Hering. "When I was at Evanton the cadets used to look after Antis in my absence, and I was away quite often. In fact, I left Antis alone far too much . . ."

"Scottish girls," Hering remarked.

"They nearly cost me my dog," Robert confirmed. "Eventually he went off to find his own mate, and I almost lost him. But the cadets did manage most times to care for him until my return . . ."

Rybar fixed Robert with a look. "So you're suggesting something similar, here and now? Like if you force Antis to spend time with others and to take orders from them, he might lose interest in you? If he gets handled and cared for by others, as Vaverka and I did the other night, he might begin to shift his allegiances, is that what you're thinking?"

Robert nodded. "I can't see any other way. His life's at stake, for God's sake, so it's got to be worth a try."

"It'll never work," said Rybar. "Without his love for you, he's finished anyway. He won't have a life."

"He's a dog," Vaverka declared, "not a human being. *We* might change allegiances like the wind, but not your dog."

"But if I get diverted again . . ." Robert rested his head in his hands. "It's the depths of winter and there's plenty more of this kind of weather to come. One more episode of cold, the vet said. One more will be the death of him. But if you'll help me, if you'll make a special fuss of him, take him for the walks he loves, and all while I ignore him — maybe it'll work?"

"When I was bad my father used to beat me with a stick," Rybar remarked. "He used to say it was for my own good, but boy, did my backside still hurt."

Robert looked at the others, the desperation he was feeling writ large across his features.

"I'll help," Adamek remarked quietly. "I don't think we'll manage it, but I'll help."

"Me too," volunteered Hering. "It's got to be worth a try."

"I'm in, then," said Vaverka, "but I still think we'll be wasting our time . . ."

Robert glanced at Rybar, who was the sharpest of the lot. "And you?"

Rybar shrugged. "Okay, in for a penny, in for a pound, as they say. I'll join you, but only under protest."

Vaverka reached out a hand and caressed Antis's ears. "You poor old sod," he muttered. "We're all in a conspiracy against you to make you break your heart . . ."

"Damn it, Vaverka, no one wants to do this, least of all me!" Robert exploded. "But he'll die otherwise."

"It won't work, Robert," Rybar repeated,

"but that doesn't mean we don't have to try."

"I wonder . . ." Vaverka added, speaking more to the dog at their feet than to any of the airmen in the room. "I wonder who will last the course . . ."

"What was that?" Robert demanded.

Seeing the deep distress on Robert's face, Vaverka decided there was only one thing to do — a drink was in order. He got to his feet and demanded that all retire to the bar.

The following day Robert was scheduled to leave on a long night patrol. That morning after breakfast he picked up his coat and hat, as if he were going for a walk. Antis was off his blanket in a flash, his master's leather gloves gripped in his jaws, in preparation for their stroll. Robert forced himself to snatch the gloves from his dog's jaws and order him harshly back to his bed. He did so in the voice that he reserved for when Antis had misbehaved.

Completely at a loss as to what he had done wrong, Antis slunk back to his blanket and flopped down disconsolately. He flicked his eyes up to Robert's face, but all he got in return was his master's back turned to him as he strode out and slammed the door. Robert tramped through the snow for three long hours, feeling sick at heart at what he

445

had just done. Never in his life had he so wanted to be able to speak to his dog in words that he understood, so that Antis might realize that he was trying to save him.

In all of Robert's very darkest moments — exiled from his homeland; with his fellow airmen and closest friends dying all around him; during the loneliness and fear that the next mission might be his last — he had always known that he had Antis beside him, a loyal and faithful friend upon whom he could unburden himself. While the animal may not have understood his every word, he felt his master's moods and caught the sentiment, and Robert had never once needed to worry about the shame of showing weakness, or tears, before his dog.

As Robert wandered across the snowy wilderness, Antis was staring at the closed door of their room and wondering what on earth he had done to displease his master. At first he'd wondered if it was all a joke; man and dog were forever playing tricks on each other. He'd waited for the first ten minutes for Robert to pop his head around the door again, declare it all an act, and with a big smile take his dog out to play. But of course, Robert hadn't returned.

Realizing it couldn't possibly be a joke, Antis was mortified. He lay on his blanket, trying to figure out what on earth he had done to warrant such treatment. All he had done was what he always did when his master was preparing to take him for a walk: he'd picked up his gloves and brought them to him. Yet his reward for doing so was to be shouted at and abandoned.

Several times while he was out on that walk Robert came close to faltering, and he almost turned back to embrace his dog and comfort him. But a voice inside his head kept telling him to be strong. The bond had to be broken, the betrayal seen as complete, for nothing else was likely to save his dog from a bitter death on the snowy wastes of the airfield.

When he got back to their room Robert had to force himself to go inside and face what he knew was coming. He turned the handle, opened the door, and there was his dog, gazing up at him anxiously for some sign of forgiveness and approval. He rose from his bed to greet his master, head down and tail wagging hopefully.

"Get back on your bed!" Robert snapped, turning his back to his dog.

Obedient as ever, Antis slunk back to his blanket, but his misery was clear to see. Robert had no doubt now that this process he had embarked upon was going to break his heart.

The following day he put stage two of the plan into action. He moved into a hut shared by his four co-conspirators — Vaverka, Adamek, Hering, and Rybar. His dog — who always slept on his blanket beside his master — was given a place in the center of the hut by the stove, as far from Robert's bed as possible. Uncertainly, Antis got hold of his blanket and went to drag it toward his master's end of the hut, but he got a sharp reprimand from Robert for doing so.

"That's your bed, now stay!"

The look of uncomprehending hurt in the dog's eyes was almost human, and it made Robert feel as if a sharp bayonet was being stabbed into his own heart.

Toward afternoon he began to make preparations for that evening's patrol. The preflight checks in the Liberator seemed to take an age, not to mention the briefings, and it was good to be ready early. Seeing his master getting ready for a mission, Antis grabbed his flight jacket — his sheepskin — and took a few uncertain steps toward the door. He gazed expectantly at his master, hoping for a gesture to signal that he could join him. Instead, Robert rounded upon him and sent him back to his blanket.

With Robert gone, Antis found himself besieged by the other airmen. They were acting very strangely, though not so out of character as his master. One tried to take his comb and brush Antis's coat — something only ever done by his master. Antis growled throatily — a warning to Flight Lieutenant Vaverka to put the comb down. Then Rybar tried to feed him. The food was left unlooked at and untouched.

Robert returned after a couple of hours. It would be well after midnight before he had to be airborne on the forthcoming patrol. He had with him the medicine that the vet had given him for Antis. Forcing himself not to relent on being cruel to be kind, he gave his dog the bitter-tasting pills with barely a word of encouragement, and no hint of any kindness.

The medicine swallowed, Robert pointed at Rybar, Vaverka, and the others. "Right, now you can go for a walk with one of your new friends."

Antis refused. Rybar, Vaverka, and Hering tried all they could think of to coax the dog outside, but he remained slumped on his blanket with his eyes fixed on the seemingly uncaring back of his master. Robert tried to catch some sleep in preparation for the long patrol.

At his new place by the stove Antis dozed fitfully, his sleep plagued by nightmares of abandonment and betrayal.

TWENTY-FIVE

Rescued from no-man's-land, wounded twice in action, shot by an irate farmer, impaled on iron railings, and frozen half to death — Antis proved himself a real survivor.

In the early hours of the morning Antis saw the shadowy form of the duty service policeman moving around the hut, quietly waking

Robert and the rest of his crew. Not knowing that the normal routine with the dog had been changed, he came over and roused Antis too.

"Come on, old boy," he whispered. "Up you get. It's flight duty time."

Antis didn't know what to do. He gazed from the kindly policeman to his master, trying to gauge his mood. Maybe he was back to his normal self? Maybe he wouldn't rebuff him anymore with harsh words and gestures? Haltingly, Antis rose from his rug and padded across toward his master's bed. He placed his big, powerful head on Robert's chest. Robert had yet to awaken fully, and he could feel Antis's eyes on him, pleading to be loved and cherished as had always been the way before.

Robert knew that this was crunch time. His instinctive desire was to take the dog's head in his hands and ruffle him behind the ears, just as he had done to the tiny little puppy he'd found in no-man's-land what seemed like a lifetime ago. But if he weakened now he knew that would be it: any attempt to break the unbreakable bond would be finished.

Instead, he forced himself to get up and take Antis back to his blanket. "Stay there. Be a good dog when I'm gone, and remember — you're with your new friends now."

Antis flopped onto his belly, looking as if his master had given him the worst thrashing of his life. In fact, he would have far preferred a beating. This inexplicable psychological torment was killing him. Robert dressed hurriedly, trying to avoid looking at his dog, and rushed out of the room without a word or gesture of goodbye.

That night the weather closed in again, and the Liberator was forced to divert to the Shetlands for a second time. It was fully forty-eight hours before Robert and crew were able to find a weather window to get safely in to RAF Tain. Once they were landed, Robert's first thoughts were for his dog. In truth, his worries over Antis had plagued him for the last two days, even during the hours they had been flying their patrol.

Rybar, Vaverka, and the others were waiting for him, and Robert could tell by their dark looks that it wasn't good news.

"Just like I said, it's impossible," Vaverka began. "It's no good. He won't eat or exercise without you. We tried everything we could think of but all to no avail. We were fools to imagine it might be otherwise."

"But surely he's eaten something?" Robert exclaimed. "It's been two whole days . . ."

"Not a damn thing!" Rybar cut in angrily. "And the only time he's been out is at night to pee, and then he had us scared half to death. The amount of blood he's passing is truly terrifying. You need to give it up, Robert. It's cruel and unfair. And I tell you something else: we can't stand it anymore, even if you can!"

Robert hurried to the hut. He discovered Antis lying on his blanket exactly where he had left him, his eyes open but with that glazed look in them once more. He showed few other signs of life, and if he recognized Robert he showed little evidence of doing so. Robert knelt and held his dog's head in his hands, gazing into his eyes. But for the first time ever Antis showed no sign of knowing who his master might be.

Tears rolled down Robert's cheeks as he tried to get some kind of reaction — anything — from his dog. "I'm back . . . I'm back . . ." he whispered in Antis's ear. "That bloody damn fool of a man who calls himself your master . . . Well, he's back. Wake up. Say something to me. I'm back, old boy, I'm back. Show me you know who I am . . ."

As Robert pleaded with his dog, something at last seemed to register. With what little strength remained, Antis raised one paw shakily. Hot tears pricking his eyes, Robert took the paw, held it gently for a second, then lowered it to the blanket again.

"That kind of loyalty and devotion — well, it's something that no one could ever break," Rybar remarked from behind them. "We should have known it all along."

"My poor old Antis," Robert whispered, ignoring Rybar's hard but fair words. "I know I've done you wrong, but forgive me. It was for your sake, boy, but I know now that you couldn't understand. And believe me, it's been torture for me, perhaps almost as much as it has been for you. But it's all over now. I promise you, whatever the future may hold, we will meet it together, you and I. Come on, get better. If I lose you now, Lord knows I won't be able to live with myself."

Antis managed to raise his head and place it on Robert's knee. He seemed to know now that his horrible, nightmarish trial was over. His master was back. They were together again. He settled himself, knowing in his heart of hearts that life was again worth fighting for. He drifted off to sleep, allowing nature to have her healing way.

A short while later Vaverka brought over a bowl of oatmeal. It was covered in thick cream, and though Antis's throat was as parched and dry as sandpaper, Robert managed to spoon a good deal of it down him. Once the bowl was empty, he allowed his dog to sleep again. He had a three-day flying break ahead of him, and he vowed to spend every waking minute concentrated on making his dog well.

For seventy-two hours he never left his dog's side. Each meal he fed to Antis by hand, and he made doubly sure he was taking his medicine. During the two days he had been away Antis had refused even that, and Robert had no doubt that his dog had been dying of a broken heart. On the third day a feeble winter sun broke through the clouds and Robert managed to get Antis out for a short walk. It seemed that the flying dog of war was on the road to recovery.

The weeks passed. Spring succeeded winter. Antis seemed to regain much of his former vigor and with time he stopped passing blood. In some strange and unfathomable way the days that Robert had spent trying to break the two of them apart didn't seem to have been wasted, after all. Now, when Robert flew missions Antis seemed to understand that something different was required of him. As if sensing the lesson that lay behind the recent torture, he'd go with

Robert to dispersal, watch for his takeoff, and once the Liberator had disappeared into the skies to the east, he would return to the warmth of their hut, and wait. It had been so very painful, but the lesson that was the key to Antis's survival seemed to have been learned.

Robert served out the remainder of the war flying missions in his sturdy Liberator over the North Atlantic. He carried out convoy escorts, which proved to be long periods of inactivity, interspersed with intense moments of action as they repulsed enemy attacks, from under or on the sea, or by air. They were ordered to search for enemy submarines and lone enemy ships trying to run the Royal Navy's blockade of Germany. On the rare occasion that they spotted a hated U-boat, the Liberator would pounce to attack with cannons, sixty-pound rocket projectiles, and depth charges.

But on none of those missions was Antis permitted, or even able, to fly. The flying dog of war had truly been grounded by those long periods of exposure waiting faithfully for his master's return. Antis continued to serve as 311 Squadron's mascot, of course, and by now his fame was redoubled. Not only was he the flying dog of war, he was a veteran of countless missions and injuries at the hands of the enemy and had many times come back from the very brink of death.

The dog's fame continued to spread, and it was in this way that he came to the attention of BBC reporters, who proceeded to file reports on the amazing veteran flying dog of war — one whom injury had finally confined to the ground.

In one of the last combat missions flown from RAF Tain, the crew of a patrolling Liberator spotted a U-boat with its conning tower clearly showing above the waves. Visibility was good, and from twenty miles out the aircraft began its attacking run. The Liberator dropped a series of depth charges that straddled the boat, its conning tower disappearing among the plumes of blasted seawater. The aircraft circled above the stricken submarine, seeing further explosions pierce the sea and oil spewing up to the surface. Finally, the upturned hull of the stricken U-boat was visible just below the waves.

By now momentous events were sweeping across mainland Europe. The Czech uprising had begun, one that aimed to expel the German occupiers, and calls were made for the Allies to come to the assistance of the Czech resistance. Robert was eager to go to the aid of his fellow countrymen. When the order came through for all Liberator crews to be on standby to fly missions into Czechoslovakia, Robert was ecstatic. With its range of three thousand miles, the Liberator was one of the few Allied aircraft with the ability to fly missions over distant Prague.

Many of the aircrew camped out in their aircraft, so eager were they to fly to their compatriots' aid. Robert took to sleeping in his Liberator, with Antis snuggled up to him for warmth. If they were suddenly ordered to go to the assistance of Robert's country-men, Adamek had strict instructions to take Antis from the aircraft and keep him safe until Robert's return. During those final days of the conflict in Europe, the last thing Robert could bear was to lose his veteran dog of war.

As matters transpired, the end of the war overtook the need for 311 Squadron to fly to their Czech brethren's aid. Even so, Germany's unconditional surrender didn't bring an immediate end to their flying duties. The aircrew of Coastal Command had to continue its relentless pursuit of the die-hard U-boat commanders who refused to accept the orders of German High Command to surrender and remained determined to pursue a futile war of their own.

The Liberators continued to fly out of Tain, attacking hostile vessels and rounding up those U-boats that were surfacing and looking for Allied forces to whom they could surrender. On May 10, 1945, four Liberators were out on patrol when they spotted two U-boats on the surface flying the black flag of surrender. They circled the vessels and took photographs so British surface ships could be vectored onto them. The U-boats were escorted into Stavanger, the nearest Allied base, or to the nearest British port.

On June 2, the Liberator that Robert was flying finally received its last recall to base. It had been searching for U-boats along the Norwegian coast, but all of a sudden the missions that had seemed as if they would never end were over.

On this most momentous of occasions, Antis was waiting faithfully as the graceful form of the four-engine Liberator came arrowing in from the clear summer skies. Long before it was audible to human hearing, Antis had pricked up his ears — though one remained semi-erect due to the old shrapnel injury.

He knew that his master was inbound, and that it would soon be time to do his very final war dance of joy.

EPILOGUE

On August 15, 1945, Robert Bozdech flew with Antis at his feet in one of a formation of Liberators as he and fellow surviving Czech airmen returned to their homeland. They passed over Germany, and there was no flak being fired at them anymore, nor any danger of being shot down. They received a heroes' welcome, and Robert set about rebuilding his life in his native land, along with his veteran friend and survivor, Antis, the now-famous dog.

But, sadly, less than three years later Robert would be forced to flee from Czechoslovakia for a second time, in a daring and death-defying escape. The country had fallen under the control of the Soviet Union, and the Communist purges targeted anyone with links to the West — of whom RAF airmen were seen to be among the foremost targets. By then Robert was married, and he and his Czech wife had a baby son, but

*Antis's Dickin Medal — the Animal Victoria Cross —
"For outstanding courage, devotion to duty, and life-
saving actions while serving with the Royal Air
Force . . ."*

he knew that if he stayed in the country his
life and maybe even theirs were in very real
danger.

Under threat of arrest by the dreaded
secret police, he was forced to leave without
breathing a word to his wife, for fear that
she would be punished once his absence

463

was discovered. The one being he refused to leave behind was his veteran war dog. During a knife-edge escape into the territory of the former enemy, Germany, Antis would save the life of Robert and his fellow escapees on more than one occasion, by warning them of approaching Communist patrols, and in one case by attacking and driving off the soldiers.

From Germany, man and dog made their way to the UK, and Robert rejoined the Royal Air Force. A year later Antis was formally recognized as a war hero, when he was awarded the Dickin Medal, more commonly known as the "Animal Victoria Cross." Field Marshal Wavell read out the citation at a ceremony attended by Antis, Robert, and many friends and fans of the famous flying dog of war: "It gives me great pleasure to make this presentation for outstanding courage, devotion to duty, and life-saving actions on several occasions while serving with the Royal Air Force and French Air Force from 1940 to '45, both in England and overseas . . ."

In 1951, Robert Bozdech was granted British nationality, and he formally changed his name to Robert V. Bozdech (V for Václav). In August 1953, after being ill for some months, Antis passed away and was buried at the Animal Cemetery in Ilford. The gravestone has a simple inscription: "Antis, D.M., Alsatian, died 11th August 1953, aged 14 years."

Below are two additions. The first, in English, reads:

There is an old belief
That on some solemn shore,
Beyond the sphere of grief,
Dear friends shall meet once more.

There follows an inscription in Czech, which translates as the simple truth: "Loyal unto death."

Shortly after Antis's death Robert Bozdech married Maureen, a British woman, and they settled in the West Country, bringing up a family. Robert continued to serve with the RAF — including a combat deployment to Suez — but he never got another dog. He refused to allow his children to get one either, for he had sworn that after Antis he would never own another.

REFERENCES AND SOURCES

In addition to the manuscript cited in the preface to this book, the following works proved enormously useful in clarifying Robert Bozdech and Antis's extraordinary story. The book *Freedom in the Air,* by Hamish Ross, is a detailed and well-researched biography of Bozdech, one that augments the story of the man and dog's wartime exploits. Any reader whose interest in their wider adventures has been piqued by reading this book would be well rewarded by getting a copy of Ross's work. It is especially good in relating the story of Robert and Antis's adventures after the war, which in their flight from Communist Czechoslovakia were almost as breathtaking as their wartime experiences. In addition, three short books written by Robert Bozdech in Czech — *Gentlemen of the Dusk (Gentlemeni soumraku), Enemy in Sight (Nepřítel v dohledu),* and *Bombers Attack (Bombardery utoei)* —

tell the story of his wartime exploits in the air. But they don't relate the story of his war dog, Antis.

ACKNOWLEDGMENTS

Special thanks to the following: my literary agent, Annabel Merullo, and her colleague, Rachel Mills, at PFS; my editor, Daniel Loedel, at Atria, and his fantastic team, including Judith Curr, Peter Borland, David Brown, Jackie Jou, and Mara Lurie. I am especially grateful to them for coming up with this book's wonderful title — *The Dog Who Could Fly.* My thanks also are extended to my film agent, Luke Speed, at Marjacq, for his redoubtable efforts as always.

Very, very special thanks are reserved for the family of Robert Bozdech: Robert Junior, Pip, and Nina, and their families, without whose generous and warm-spirited help this book would not have been written.

Finally, a heartfelt thank you to my wife and children, Eva, David, Damien Junior, and Sianna-Sarah, for putting up yet again with long spells of Dad's moodiness, while he was locked away in his study writing. Isn't it always thus, guys?

HERE'S HOW YOU CAN HELP A SPECIAL OPERATIONS K-9 TODAY

Damien Lewis supports Special Operations K-9s and military working dogs by donating a percentage of royalties from this book to the Warrior Dog Foundation.

The Warrior Dog Foundation was established by Mike Ritland, who fought as a Navy SEAL in Operation Iraqi Freedom and other deployments. Mike Ritland is the *New York Times* bestselling author of *Trident K9 Warriors* and *Navy SEAL Dogs* and is currently working on a third book. He is also the founder of Trikos International, a company that provides private protection dogs to companies and high-net-worth individuals. Mike Ritland created the Warrior Dog Foundation with the sole purpose of giving back to the Navy SEAL and special operations community.

The Warrior Dog Foundation is dedicated to serving the special operations community, their families, and Special Operation Forces (SOF) K-9s. The K-9s employed with these forces operate in the top tier of the working dog world. They are expected to work in the most austere of environments and face conditions that most human beings cannot survive. These are the environments in which these elite warriors operate. The K-9 units operate in all conditions and are vital to ensuring the success of every mission.

The Warrior Dog Foundation helps to transition dogs from an operational environment to their state-of-the-art kennel facility. This kennel facility is a K-9 sanctuary located on an expansive ranch in Texas. The ranch provides a peaceful transition space for SOF working K-9s as well as a forever home for those unsuitable to be rehomed. They strive to educate the public on the importance of SOF K-9s in the combat environment and showcase the level of sacrifice these dogs give in support of our troops. They care for each individual SOF K-9 with dignity and grace, including both mental and physical rehabilitation for the rest of their lives.

The support needed for these SOF K-9s cannot be understated. There are several ways in which you can make a difference: a monetary or in-kind donation, becoming an advocate for the cause at one of our signature events, and sharing the message with friends on our social outlets.

Without your voice, they have none, so get social and share the value that these K-9s have with everyone. Connect with us today, and on behalf of our SOF K-9s and their families, we thank you for your support.

Sincerely,
the Warrior Dog Foundation Team
info@warriordogfoundation.org
Twitter / @warriordogs
Facebook / warriordog

ABOUT THE AUTHOR

Damien Lewis is a lifelong dog lover and an award-winning writer who has spent twenty years reporting from war and conflict zones for the BBC, CNN, and many other news organizations. He is the author of more than twenty books, topping bestseller lists worldwide, and his books have been published in more than thirty languages. In addition to *The Dog Who Could Fly* — published in Britain as *War Dog* — he is also the coauthor of two acclaimed memoirs about military working dogs, *Sergeant Rex* with Mike Dowling and *It's All About Treo* with Dave Heyhoe, which is being developed as a TV drama series.